By the same author

IN THE FOOTSTEPS OF TIME
Geology and Landscape of Cuckmere Valley and Downs

SEVEN SISTERS
The History Behind The View

Monty Larkin
Cover and design by Gabrielle Vinyard

Monty Larkin

Ulmus Books

First published 2008 by
Ulmus Books
The Twin Oast, Chiddingly
Lewes, East Sussex.

ISBN 978-0-9553368-1-2

Printed and bound in England by CPI Antony Rowe Ltd, Bumper's Farm, Chippenham, Wiltshire, SN14 6LH

Dedicated to Valerie, Sonia and Dan
John Gascoigne
Airmen and women of RAF Friston

CONTENTS

ACKNOWLEDGMENTS

The author wishes to thank the numerous persons and organisations without whom, this book would not have been possible. Many are acknowledged in the text or in the sources at the end of each chapter; others are to be found in the following list. Firstly to John Wareing for helping to lay the foundations of my knowledge of history many years ago and for help relating to the shipwreck of the sailing ship Coonatto. To the late John Gascoigne, for inspiration and for laying the foundation for my knowledge of farming. Particular thanks are owed to Valerie Larkin and Ruth Sabey for providing life space for the research and writing of this work. Thanks are also due to Ingunn Ruffles who provided inspiration when motivation was lacking and for undertaking research of published works. Thanks are also due to Ann Murray for proof reading much of the manuscript. Lastly but most importantly, special thanks are due to Gabrielle Vinyard for design of the cover and book layout. I shall end, by adding an apology to all those many people who have offered time and information; help, advice and suggestions and are not mentioned.

Members of staff of the following:
East Sussex County Library Service
East Sussex County Records Office
The British Library
The National Maritime Museum
The Public Records Offices, Kew and London
Mr. D.A. Armstrong; Church Commissioners, London.
Joan Astell.
Pat Berry; Seaford Museum of Local History.
Peter Bailey; Newhaven Maritime Museum.
John S. Creasey, Institute of Agricultural History, University of Reading.
Brian Deeprose; Environment Agency.
Mr. C.H.H. Ellis.
the late Richard Gilbert.
Mr. G.M. Hoskins and Mrs. Dyson; former Eastbourne Waterworks Company.
the late George Jakens; formally of Seaford Museum of Local History.

Mavis Lister.
Michael Partridge; Eastbourne College.
David Paul, formerly farmer at Chyngton Farm.
M.A. Pearman, Trustees of the Chatsworth Settlement.
Christopher Robinson; Forestry Commission.
Andy Saunders.
Margaret Sharpe.
Richard Worsell.

ABBREVIATIONS

B.P. – Before Present
E.S.R.O. – East Sussex Records Office
P.R.O. – Public Records Office
S.A.C. – Sussex Archeological Collections
S.N.Q. – Sussex Notes and Queries
S.R.S. – Sussex Records Society

FOREWORD

by Lady Edna Healey

"Before you die," said the young man sternly to me, pointing to a patch of grass behind our house, *"make a clause in your will and have this grass protected. This is real old Sussex turf which is disappearing fast."*

It was my first meeting with Monty Larkin, one-time Senior Ranger for the Sussex Downs Conservation Board and the author of this book. Typically, he spotted some tiny wild flowers - ladies tresses - in the turf and felt deeply the importance of their preservation. The same combination of detailed observation and passion for the conservation of our countryside informs this book. Truly he is one who sees 'eternity in a grain of sand.'

At the moment Monty Larkin is a countryside contractor and wildlife habitat adviser concerned with Environmental Stewardship. He is also grazing co-ordinator for the Sussex Pony Grazing & Conservation Trust, responsible for most aspects of managing two herds of wild Exmoor ponies brought in to control the invasive tor grass on the chalk grassland. Having been Heritage Coast Ranger for Seven Sisters Country Park and Warden for Seaford Head local nature reserve he has a detailed knowledge of coastal chalkland and his experience of habitat management and extensive knowledge of grassland, scrub, hedgerow, wetland and woodland, have made him widely respected as an adviser to farmers and landowners. Between 1997 and 2004 the organised the control of East Sussex's Dutch Elm Disease Control programme protecting 54,000 trees across some 140 square miles.

Monty has a deep understanding of the importance of creating public awareness and has carried out a large number of popular educational walks and talks. This book is an invaluable study of a famous area of coast and downland by one who is passionately and professionally concerned in its conservation.

Lady Edna Healey

AUTHORS NOTES

After having set this volume down on paper, I thought I should complete the picture by giving a preface to its conception... I have known and savoured Exceat virtually the whole of my life. To us locals, it was pronounced 'Excet', where that silken artery, the Cuckmere River, is cradled within those soft chalk uplands. My earliest memories are of family picnics during high summer by cycle (pillion in my case) to Cuckmere Haven, where us children would dam the Cuckmere at low water with boulders of chalk and flint, before temporarily retiring for tea, with lettuce and Marmite sandwiches. Of accompanying father and neighbour David Comben to collect lengths of driftwood from the shore at Hope Gap and then climbing up through Hope Bottom with two heavily laden push-bikes, where once, we took shelter from an intense thunderstorm, I a very frightened, soaked small boy! Hope Bottom is the scene for another early memory from the mid 1950's; that of high summer, tinged with the putrid stench of rotting rabbit carcasses beneath the bushes, due to the decimation of the rabbit population from its post-war peak by the newly arrived disease, myxomatosis.

I count myself as being privileged at having secured a post of ranger on the then comparatively new Seven Sisters Country Park and becoming deeply involved with the stewardship of what is, one of England's finest pieces of landscape, the South Downs. Inherently intrigued by local history, I became increasingly absorbed by Exceat's history and of the surrounding area; of those many humble hard-working souls unrecorded by history, who had at one time or another when asked the question, 'where do you come from,' would have replied in a broad Sussex dialect, 'Excet.'

Having become somewhat preoccupied with the past, I started to delve into the annals of history; the catalyst came in the form of three people one of whom Will Holter, had by this time already passed away, thus introducing an element of urgency to the matter. The other two persons were John Gascoigne, the Country Park's head ranger who had carried out a limited amount of research and Will's sister Ester Miller, who had lived much of her life at Exceat.

John, a Yorkshireman with strong opinions, was an extrovert and an extremely knowledgeable man, who before the interjection of the Second World War, was studying at Nottingham to become a veterinary surgeon. Amongst his many talents could be listed: farmer, naturalist, artist, computer buff and after dinner speaker! I feel privileged to have worked with him, for he having been a farm manager much of his working life as well as being an acknowledged naturalist, was able to view conflicts in the countryside from 'both sides of the fence.' I believe this has and hope will continue, to colour my opinions and influence my professional decisions in the future.

To continue... A great deal of the early years of research concentrated on published work; at the same time I had begun to record by word of mouth, starting with dear old Ester. With experience I soon became adapt to charting the general course of events as I spoke to ever more former residents and workers of the Exceat and West Dean area. Soon, I was delving deeply into subjects that had always held a deep fascination for me, such as geology, agriculture and shipwrecks. Some of the subject areas have become my 'retreat' from the 21st century and its attendant consumerism and pollution. I still find it effortless to free fall, into a world of creamy-white Southdown sheep accompanied by their shepherd and rough-coated collie; docile red or black oxen ploughing on Downland slopes; scenes of storm-stressed sailing ships helplessly driven to their destruction beneath towering chalk cliffs; pack horses slipping quietly inland, burdened with smuggled shipments. By contrast, the scrambling of Spitfire fighter aircraft from Friston - shattering the downland music of larks, corn buntings and yellowhammers as their Rolls Royce Merlin engines cough, splutter and then roar into life.

After a number of years during which I spent time researching and giving talks, people began asking, was I contemplating writing a book upon my findings and if not, then I should! I invariably replied that it had not been the original intention and in any case I was no author! However, during the mid 1980's I finally capitulated and put pencil to paper and drew up an outline for such a book and gave the first chapter a try. Encouraged by this initial endeavour, writing continued apace, each succeeding winter saw more chapters evolve, the book virtually keeping to the original concept. Here I should apologise, for with the first draft almost finished, the manuscript then unfortunately languished 'on the shelf' for quite a number of years due to a number of unrelated circumstances! During the research I have often travelled widely afield, meeting many fascinating people; also I have communicated and met people from diverse corners of the globe. Research has also involved visiting organisations and receiving help from many depositories of archival material, many of whom I had not dreamt of until becoming engaged in this work.

The locality covered - the *"study area,"* comprises of Exceat, bounded by and including Chyngton and Dymock Farms to the west; north and eastwards taking in West Dean, Charleston Manor, Friston Forest and touching on Friston Place. The southern boundary along the coastline includes that from Seaford Head to Birling Gap including the famous Seven Sisters, and Crowlink.

I hope that what unfolds on the following pages will interest local people, visitors to the Cuckmere valley, ardent country lovers, but above all, serve as an accurate source of detailed knowledge, especially for students of history. To conclude, it is a record of life and times of what is without any shadow of doubt, a classic piece of English Landscape. I sincerely hope, that you will enjoy making discoveries on the following pages as much as I have in compiling them...

Monty Larkin
June 2008.

Map of the 'Study Area.'

MAP   15

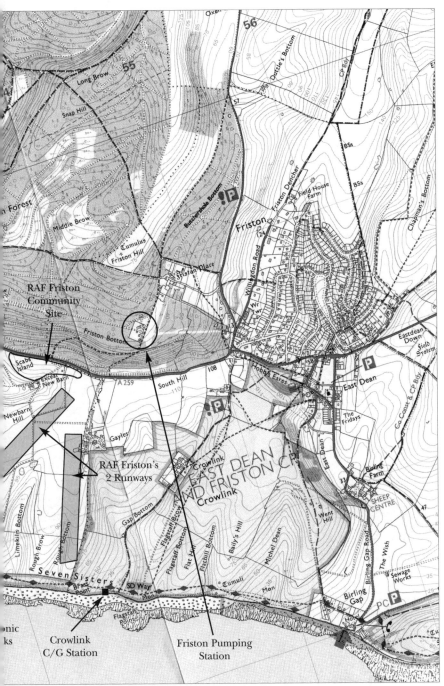

CHAPTER 1

EARLY SETTLEMENT AND LAND OWNERSHIP.

We shall begin our quest into the history of the 'study area' with the origins of today's settlements and villages, (and of those which failed and are now no more). We shall then take a look how land ownership has developed and how that ownership has sometimes influenced land use; how modern development in the twentieth century nearly came to obliterate today's stunning countryside of the study area. To take first, the development of settlements, this chapter proposes only to lightly sketch in the course of events prior to the first great ledger of England, namely the Domesday Book, compiled during the year 1086. Before this great milestone in English history, we have to speculate to some degree as to the likely course of settlement based in the main on the findings of archaeologists and researchers, aided by modern technologies, sometimes using evidence which has come to light due to accidental discovery during farming and construction operations. As we slip back further through the mists of pre-history however, so we have accept or discount the hypothesis put forward, often based on limited and scattered evidence. However, when dealing with the subject of land ownership, the evidence laid before us (at least since the medieval period), is far more tangible and readily traced. With the passage of time, the written word and legal dictate have between them recorded history in ever increasing detail, culminating in the vast abilities of today's computer.

The earliest tangible pieces of evidence to Man's presence in the study area, are the large numbers of humanly modified flints found. In the Hope Gap/South Hill area near Seaford, finds date from the Mesolithic period (14,000 to 5,000 B.P.), through to the Neolithic period (6,000 to 3,500 B.P.). An exception was the fine Palaeolithic period handaxe discovered in cliff deposits in 1975, by my colleague Richard Mash. It has been tentatively dated between 130-250,000 years of age. (1). Other flint tools or implements found in the study area, have included boring tools, scrapers, arrowheads and many flakes - the waste product resulting from production of flint tools.

The people of the Neolithic civilisation were the first to actually farm that is, to keep domesticated livestock and cultivate crops. Undoubtedly, they still supplemented their food with hunter-gatherer techniques. Although the Downs would have been covered in some form of woodland at that time, Man would have been attracted by the often light and easily worked soils to be found upon them. These early agriculturists would have begun by clearing the woodland cover using flint axes, aided only to a small degree by the agent of fire for, *"English native woods burn like wet asbestos."* (2). The clearings created would then have been cultivated until the soil had become exhausted. In the mean time, they would have proceeded to clear further areas, with the former clearings then probably being used for grazing livestock.

The next important period with regard to evidence in the study area, is centred on the Iron Age civilisation (700 B.C. to A.D. 43), which overlapped well into the Roman period, for life and technology evolved steadily, and flowed from one archeological period into the next. During this period, relatively large areas of the Downs were intensively cultivated after clearance of the tree cover, often leading to severe soil erosion problems with soil being washed downhill and into watercourses. (3). There are two areas within the study area where prehistoric, or 'Celtic' field systems exist. Under certain conditions such as drought, snow cover or grazing, the accompanying 'lynchets' (linear banks and depressions formed by soil movement due to

Field system revealed on Ewe Down after ploughing during the autumn of 1981.

cultivation), can be observed. One field system sprawls across Ewe Down at Chyngton stretching north towards the Hindover area. Another stretches across the hinterland of the western half of the Seven Sisters; in the vicinity of Short Brow, additional evidence in the form of pottery sherds, suggest a late Iron Age settlement here about. (4).

Other evidence of these prehistoric times can to be seen in the form of burial mounds, referred to as 'barrows' or 'tumuli'. The mystery of death and the treatment of the dead, has always occupied Man's thoughts and ingenuity; some civilisations devoted a great deal of social effort to it. At the centre of virtually all barrows, depressions show where Victorians have plundered these places of burial. A gentleman equipped with a group of labourers might excavate several in one day, hoping to unearth the centrally placed burial or urn chamber and perhaps its grave goods. Unfortunately, these excavations were largely carried out with no thought to recording their finds. The oldest of these locally, though strictly speaking not within the study area, is the remnants of a 'long barrow' dating from the Neolithic period, situated to the east of Litlington in Charlston Bottom at grid ref. TQ 535006. There are however, a number of 'round barrows' in the study area, with possibly three within the country park as follows: at grid ref. TQ 526983, to the east of Foxhole a listed ancient monument; another is situated at grid ref. TQ 520996, overlooking Exceat itself. A possible third barrow is located at grid ref. TQ 531985 and is an example of what has happened to thousands of other barrows across the English countryside, it having been virtually destroyed by ploughing.

During the fifth century, the Roman way of life gradually declined bringing the demise of both town and villa alike. From across the North Sea came the Saxons, who emanated from the region between the Weser and the Elbe estuaries in present day Germany, an area which being low-lying, suffered greatly during late Roman times from a rise in sea level subjecting it to marine incursion. The twin pressures of rising sea level and increasing population brought about a large-scale abandonment of settlements, with many communities migrating to the lightly populated lands of 'England.' The Anglo-Saxon Chronicle records that the first raid upon Sussex took place during the mid-fifth century. After these early raids, it is considered by some historians that the lightly inhabited block of Downland between the rivers Cuckmere and Ouse, was granted to the Saxons; this theory is substantiated by the existence of at least four cemeteries dating from the fifth century between the two rivers. (5).

During the period A.D. 700-1000, it appears that the Downland had achieved a high density of settlement, it being greatest in the river valleys with their diverse resources. Settlement also extended into the dry valleys whose agricultural potential was more limited, where occupation was necessary in order to achieve full exploitation of the Downs. As the population increased, an important new trading centre developed at Seaford, as did the establishment of settlements at Birling, East Dean, Friston, Exceat, West Dean and Sutton (now part of Seaford), with later additional expansion during the late-12th to 13th centuries. (5, 6). The second part of this chapter will take each of the settlements within the study area in turn, and delve into the derivation of their name, and outline the course of land ownership...

EXCEAT. Place name experts more often than not, can suggest the probable meaning and date of a names formulation, from their studies of the development of the Old English language. Having said that, the central thread of this book Exceat, has a name that cannot be easily explained. The name first appears in the Domesday Book in 1086 as 'Essete', which is suggested is a compound of the river name 'Exe' and the element 'saete', the whole name meaning 'settlers by the Exe', from which we must take to be the old British name for the River Cuckmere. The first element might alternatively be explained as the personal name 'Ecci'' and the whole name thus interpreted as 'Ecci's settlement.'' (7).

In the Domesday Book, three land holdings are cited for Exceat: firstly, the Manor of Exceat. This was one of the few cases of a native landowner retaining his lands after the Norman Conquest; Haiminc continued to hold Exceat together with land in three other local parishes. Exceat Manor was assessed in the survey at four and a half hides - a hide being in the region of 20-24 hectares (50 to 60 acres) in Sussex, which was the area a plough team of oxen could work in one year. (With the other land holdings in the parish this would have totalled ten hides, a multiple of the then common land division of five hides). During the Baron's War that took place during the 13th century, Haiminc's descendant William de Esshetes backed the losing side and forfeited his lands to the Lord of the Rape of Pevensey, Peter de Savoy. Some years elapsed, and after going to trial at the Kings Court regained most of his lands. In a contemporary grant, William granted Exceat to Thomas de Aldham; possibly this was by way of payment for his fine by the Kings Court? Thomas de Aldham's wife Isabella later re-married to Richard de Pevensey. (8).

During the 14th century, the manor passed to one John St. Clere, it then passing upon his death to his son John, who died in 1335.

Included in John's will, was *"the fishery of the whole river between Cookemere and Langebrigg worth 18d. per year."* (Langebrigg probably would equate with today's Long Bridge, the attractive red brick hump-backed road bridge situated between Lullington and Alfriston). His son, yet another John, inherited the manor when aged only three years of age. He was later to become Member of Parliament for the county of Sussex during four parliaments between 1370 and 1383. Eventually, during the 15th century, the manor passed to one of his great grand-daughters, Eleanor, aged eleven. She became married to Sir John Gage and so the Manor of Exceat became part of the Gage family's estates. (8).

The second Exceat land holding cited in Domesday was the Peverel Estate. 'Walter' held land assessed at two and a half hides; this probably refers to one Walter de Richerville who was Sheriff of the Rape of Pevensey in about the year 1095. The name Peverel later appears during the mid-14th century; Andrew Peverel is recorded as being Member of Parliament for Sussex 11 times. Upon his death in 1376, the Peverel holding was recorded as consisting of 32 hectares (80 acres) of cattle pasture and was inherited by the wife of Sir Reginald West, Joan la Warr. In 1536, Thomas, the ninth Lord de la Warr sold this land holding consisting of 24 hectares of arable, 16 of pasture, 12 of marsh, 8 of furze (gorse), a total of 61 hectares (150 acres) with common pasture for 300 sheep, to Sir John Gage whose grandfather had inherited the Manor of Exceat. (8).

Thirdly we come to the la Warr Estate. The Domesday holding was in the ownership of William de Cahaignes, and valued at three hides. This was later in the possession of the de Folkingtons, and then passed into the la Warr estates. During the mid-13th century, a John la Ware instituted Thomas la Ware as Rector of Exceat church, who held the post until his death in 1287. (6). A number of smaller land holdings originated on Exceat during the medieval period; the Abbey of Bayham was granted lands by William de Richerville and during 1329 the Abbey was given a grant of free warren. The abbey was suppressed during 1525 and their lands at Exceat eventually passed to Sir John Gage. During the 16th century, three smallholdings of ancient origin were still in existence; during the following century these were purchased by William Thomas of West Dean. (8).

Prosperity continued well into the 13th century. However, the latter part of the century and the early-14th century witnessed a retreat from marginal land, as in deed, much of Exceat was. The Nonarum Inquisitiones of 1341, (which was compiled in order to collect one ninth of the value of all agricultural production after deduction of the church's tithe which amounted to one tenth of total production), painted a picture of poverty and also destruction along the Sussex coast caused by French raids, as happened at Friston and Seaford. It can be assumed that Exceat did not escape the attentions of the French either. Other setbacks faced during the 14th century, were that the growing seasons suffered from a sustained increase of inclement climatic conditions, rising sea levels and possibly impoverishment of the inherently poor soils. (9).

Matters came to a head in 1348 when the Black Death reached the shores of England and went on to rapidly decimate the population. At about the same time, the great wooded interior of Sussex was being opened up, creating new opportunities for people and attracting a substantial proportion of the Downland population. By the year 1460, there was only one recorded householder recorded as living in Exceat, one Henrius Chesman. Eventually, a decree was signed on March 3 1528 by the Bishop of Chichester, whereby the parish of Exceat was absorbed into the neighbouring parish of West Dean; this named a Roger Blyth as *"parishioner or inhabitant of Excet."* (10).

Exceat remained in the ownership of the Gage family until 1823, when under a private Act of Parliament an exchange was made between the Gage estate and the Dean and Chapter of Chichester. The West Dean and Friston Estate (Exceat and Friston), was exchanged for the Parsonage of Firle. Included within the Exceat holding were 1.6 hectares (4 acres) of land immediately south-east of Exceat Bridge, on the south bank of the old river. A map of Chyngton Farm dated 1764 stated that a rent of 12 shillings was paid annually for it to the tenant of Exceat Farm, although by the late 19th century no person could recall the rent having been paid. (11). The area in question would have been reduced in area during 1846-47 by the construction of the new river channel.

Concurrently with the exchange of 1823, the West Dean and Friston Estate was then leased back to the Gage family until 1895, when the then Lord Gage surrendered the lease. The two farms then became administered by the Ecclesiastical Commissioners (the Church Commissioners as from 1948), through their land agent, Cluttons. In 1956, Exceat Farm was sold to a group of businessmen headed by Oliver Stutchbury who lived at The Gayles near Friston for the sum of £20,000. The life tenancy of Arthur Pattenden was to continue until his death in 1970. (11). During 1971, overtures were made by Stutchbury to East Sussex County Council regarding the possible sale of Exceat for use as a public open space; the sale went ahead and was completed in April of that year.

THE GAYLES. Situated between the former Exceat and Crowlink Farms is the several hundred acres of Gayles Farm. The early development of this property happened when John Wycliffe-Taylor acquired a two acre plot of land from John Maitland of Friston Place during June 1901, for the purpose of building a modest holiday residence sited overlooking a chalk pit, with superb views towards Crowlink and the Seven Sisters. This acquisition was not made without a certain amount of arm-twisting. John Maitland was at first not prepared to sell the land, until Wycliffe-Taylor purchased a plot near Friston Pond and threatened to build a tall house which would have marred the view from Friston Place. Eventually, an exchange of ownership was agreed to by Maitland involving the two plots. A further piece of land amounting to 4 hectares (11 acres) to the east of the driveway leading to the new house was purchased during 1910. (12).

During the late 1920's, the property passed to his daughter Rosamond and her husband Mervyn Stutchbury, who then proceeded to develop the house extensively. During 1935, Colonel Alexander Watson who then tenanted Exceat Farm, allowed the RAF Territorial Squadron to hold a summer camp on land immediately to the west of Gayles. Stutchbury was so outraged by the disruption to their tranquillity, that in 1937 he bought the neighbouring 47 hectares (116

Hawker Audax aircraft of the RAF Territorial Squadron parked in close proximity to The Gayles.

acres) of Exceat Farm from the Ecclesiastical Commissioners. (12). As part of the sale agreement of Exceat in 1971 to the East Sussex County Council, approximately 81 hectares (200 acres) of land laying to the north of the Seven Sisters were transferred to Gayles Farm in exchange for the above parcel of land.

WEST DEAN. Probably the first record of West Dean occurs in the year A.D. 885 when it was simply known as Dene. During that year Asser, Bishop of St. David's in Wales, travelled to meet King Alfred at his royal residence situated in the village of West Dean. As the bishop required Saxons to guide him on the last stage of his journey, it is considered to be here rather than the village of the same name near Chichester. (13).

By the late 12th century, Ralph de Dene (born c.1109) held the lordship of the manor, the family taking their name from the village. A later descendant was Sybil de Icklesham who married Nicholas Heringod sometime before 1210; (incidentally, her son Ralph, became Sheriff of Hampshire and was the only man of rank to be killed in Simon de Montfort's forces at the Battle of Lewes in 1264). Nicholas was succeeded by his son Sir John who between 1302 and 1313 was elected Knight of the Shire; he died in 1329. (8). A notable date in the history of the village was June 25 1305, when during the morning Sir John welcomed King Edward I to the village, the King staying in Lewes at the time. (13). The manor through the 15th century had connections with Thomas, Archbishop of Canterbury, and the Earls of Oxford from whom the manor gained its alternative name of 'Earlscorte.' The manor was owned by a succession of families through the 16th century culminating with the sale of the manor in 1596 to Thomas Bray. (10).

This leads to the sale of the West Dean manor by Bray during January 1611 to William Thomas, gentleman of Lewes for the sum of £4,000. His father Thomas Thomas, was a merchant tailor in London and owned land in the capital, Sussex and elsewhere. The residence where his father died in 1602 was named The Key and stood at the north-west end of London Bridge, where his mother continued to live until her death in 1628. (10). An ambitious newcomer to the county, William Thomas went on to hold one of the most influential positions within Sussex, that of Clerk of the Peace. This position which he held from 1615 to 1640, involved management of the whole of the counties judicial system: arranging court agendas, collecting fees, helping poorer persons to word petitions and producing a final record of all court proceedings. The position provided excellent opportunities for social and economic advancement; his town house in Lewes, School

Hill House was situated in the very prestigious High Street. He invested his wealth in acquiring and expanding his estate within the parish of West Dean. (14, 15, 16).

In December 1631, the manor of West Dean was mentioned as part of the marriage arrangements of Williams's son, William jnr; marriage customs in those days could be very formal. In consideration of his future daughter-in-law Katherine's marriage portion of £2,000 being received he would grant to his son and Katherine the following: a rent of £80 from the manors of West Dean and West Dean alias Earles Court (a separate manor by the early 17th century), the manor of Clapham in Litlington and a portion of the tithes from Charleston in West Dean, in addition to other lands worth a total of £240 yearly. (10).

In another settlement of July 1676, the two West Dean manors were again included in a marriage settlement involving in excess of 607 hectares (1,500 acres) in this area of Sussex. This was by Sir William Thomas (the third successive person to carry that name), and his widowed mother Katherine of Lewes, when he arranged to marry Barbarah Springett, youngest daughter of Sir Herbert Springett deceased, of Broyle Place, Ringmer. It included the land and tithes mentioned in his own marriage settlement and including amongst others, land in Exceat involving approximately 32 hectares (80 acres); Friston and Sutton in Seaford. Upon his death in 1702, the lands in West Dean and Exceat were left to his two widowed sisters and upon their deaths, passed to William Dobell and then to his wife who died in 1764, West Dean Farm being recorded as containing 900 acres. The estate was inherited by the Harrison family of Seaford who eventually sold it to a J.H. Durrant. (10). After a period of some 15 years Durrant sold the estate to the Cavendish family, it then descending via the Earl of Burlington to the Dukes of Devonshire in 1862. During the 20th century, the bulk of the estate was then sold to the Eastbourne Waterworks Company; for further details of this refer to Chapter 9. (16, 17, 18).

Through the remainder of the twentieth century, various properties and parcels of land within the parish have been sold to private individuals, leading to a population which today, is entirely divorced from the land. During the 1920's the meadow land adjacent to the river, West Dean Brooks, was sold to E.C. Arnold, headmaster of Eastbourne College as a bird and shooting reserve. (19).

He described it as *"90 acres of pasture with an invaluable strip of bog running through it."* On a number of occasions over the years he tried with little success to introduce various trees, bushes and flowers to his reserve. The only attempt that succeeded was the willow copse to be seen today at Gypsy Corner; he considered the problem to be that the area had *"been soaked so often by salt water."* One of his favourite areas was the then salting area adjacent to the two former loops of the river which resembled, *"A replica in miniature of a Norfolk salting..."* This was sadly destroyed by river embanking and pasture creation for grazing in the late 1950's. (19).

The following are taken from the many observations he had made whilst bird watching or wild fowling. November 1928. *"Went to see how the brothers Winchester, of West Dene, were getting on with the digging of the pond. Despite our bursar's confident prediction of suicide, I found them going strong, with half the pond completed."* He had asked two local men to dig a pond some 45 metres x 18 metres x 1 metre deep (50 yards by 20 yards and 3 feet); *"I had toyed for a moment with the suggestion of a sapper friend that the pond should be dug by exploding guncotton, but eventually we fell back on less heroic methods, viz., human toil with the spade. The men evidently found the job bigger than they expected, but they stuck to it without whining, and at the finish I felt constrained to add a tip to the covenanted sum."* This pond may have been in what has today become the area known as Charlston Reedbed?

November 18 1929. While out wild fowling one day he could not leave the river bank, *"I was half-afraid of getting marooned as the water was coming over in places."*

April 28 1930. *"I at last found a lapwing's nest with eggs on the Oval Marsh. I believe others breeding on the Brooklands, having been driven from off the down by the advent of the tractor. If so, there is some use in the modern contraptions after all."* This is probably referring to ploughing on what is now Friston Forest; (see Chapter 8). (19). (Incidentally, the lower Cuckmere valley was in 1982, the last location in Sussex where Cirl Bunting were proven to still be breeding; they're decline coincided with the disappearance of winter stubbles due to the shift from spring-sown to autumn-sown cereal crops).

CHARLSTON. Taken from the Saxon 'Ceorl' meaning peasant and 'tun' meaning a farm or settlement, the modern spelling with the inclusion of the letter 's' is an falsity. (7). Though only a small hamlet, it is recorded in the Domesday Book compiled in 1086 when it was owned by Ralph, Count of Mortain. During the 15th to early-16th century the Halle family owned it and through much of the 17th century it was owned by the Draper/Wood family. In 1833 the manor was purchased by the Rev. Thomas Scutt, clerk of Brighton and owner of the Clapham Estate in Litlington, it remaining with that family for fifty years until it was acquired by Sir John and Dame Mary Godfrey. In 1922, Dame Mary by now widowed, sold the manor to farmer Richard

Canning Brown who resided at Clapham House and so the manor briefly passed back into the Clapham Estate. (15, 16, 17). Through much of history, this farm flanked the northern boundary of West Dean Farm, the boundary forming the edge of today's Friston Forest along the top of an escarpment. (Incidentally though just outside of the study area, during the early nineteenth century Mrs. Maria Fitzherbert who was mistress to the Prince Regent, George IV and bore him several children, lived at Clapham House; he reputedly would ride over from Brighton to visit her).

During the 1930's, the buildings and adjacent land were sold to Sir Oswald Birley who proceeded to spend a great deal of money renovating the old buildings and the laying out of formal gardens, which are still today noted for their great variety of roses. This beautiful house and grounds were described by Nikolaus Pevsner in the Sussex volume of the authoritative series *'The Buildings of England'* published in 1965, as *"a perfect house in a perfect setting."* A fashionable painter Sir Oswald was a favourite of the Royal Family and is well-known for his portraits of royalty. He painted several highly regarded portraits of his friend Sir Winston Churchill and Prime Ministers Baldwin, Chamberlain and Atlee. His portraits of war leaders include those of General Eisenhower, Montgomery and Lord Mountbatten. (20).

Sir Oswald Birley was born in New Zealand on the 31st March 1880. In 1921 he married the Irish beauty, Rhoda Pike who was twenty years his junior. The Birley's took an enormous interest in theatre and the ballet, their London studio and gardens at Charlston were the background for many concerts and entertainments involving the Russian ballet on their various visits to the United Kingdom. This again resulted in commissions from the leading dancers of the day and Danilova, Leon Woizikiovski and Kyra Nijinski are all represented in his work. Sir Oswald served as a Major in the Sussex Home Guard from June 1940 until 1943. He was knighted in 1949 just three years before his death on the May 6 1952. Lady Birley continued her interests in the theatre, the arts and in her gardens after her husband's death. The house and gardens at Charleston were almost continuously open to the public sometimes for special occasions such as the Charleston Festival. Lady Rhoda died in 1980 she being buried next to her husband in West Dean churchyard. (20).

CHYNGTON. The name is possibly derived from '-ingas' meaning either followers, dependants or descendants of, and 'tun' referring to a farm or settlement. (7). The first mention of 'Chintinges' occurs in records dated 1180. The first person recorded in connection with the

manor was Richard de Luci who amongst others, was granted
Chyngton by King Stephen's surviving son Count William. Later it
passed to Gilbert de Aquila, Lord of the Rape of Pevensey and founder
of Michelham Priory in 1229. (21). A successor of his, Gilbert of Laigle
gave the manor to the priory later in the 13th century. (22). During
1349, Robert Longe of Seaford who was vicar of Cuckfield in mid
Sussex, stood down in order to make way for a nominee of Pope
Clement VI, a certain William of Chinting. (23). During the late
medieval period the settlement suffered greatly, presumably for
similar reasons as for Exceat. The site of the actual village judging
from finds and field-marks, lays to the south-east of the present day
farm and is referred to as 'Poynings Town,' the Poynings being lords
of the manor at one time during the medieval period. After the
dissolution of Michelham Priory the lordship of the manor is rather
chequered; names associated with the manor include Henry, Earl of
Northumberland; Sir Edward Seymour and the Duke of Dorset (it
forming part of the manor of Bexhill). By 1715 Chyngton Farm as it
had become, belonged to Thomas Holles, Earl of Clare and heir to
Lord Thomas Pelham, the ownership staying within the Pelham family
until the 20th century. (24).

During the early 1920's, Hugh H. Northcote who came from
Fritham, near Stoney Cross, in Hampshire purchased the Chyngton
Estate. He was a wealthy, enlightened landowner and proceeded to
spend a great deal of money on the estate. During November 1927 the
National Trust wrote to the Ecclesiastical Commissioners, owners of
Exceat, stating that they had been offered a covenant upon a
substantial area of the Chyngton estate by Northcote on the condition,
that if the Commissioners were to sell Exceat, it would be offered first
to the National Trust. By May 1928, a mutual covenant had been
agreed between Northcote and the Commissioners, not to build on
the greater part of Exceat. This opened the way for the National Trust
to secure the cliffs and most of the eastward facing slopes of Chyngton.
The Trust's efforts were however thwarted in 1929, by Hugh
Northcote's untimely death before the agreement could be clinched.
(11).

On what could have become a very depressing day, Monday, July
25 1932, the Trustees of Northcote's estate sold Chyngton by auction.
Several of the auction lots were subdivided into individual building
plots which had they been developed, would have been a catastrophic
intrusion into the tranquil, rural setting of the Cuckmere valley. The
plan which accompanied the sale brochure, shows building plots
fringing the whole of the A 259 road descending Chyngton Hill from

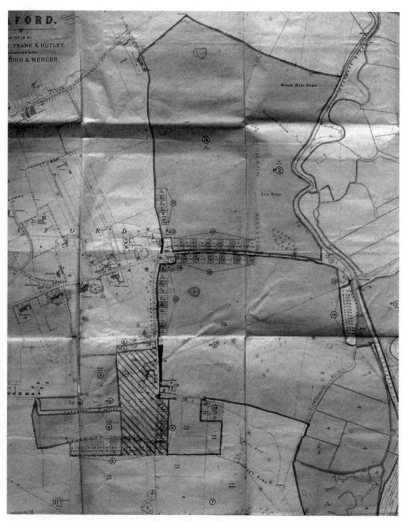

Part of the plan from sales brochure for the Chyngton Estate, 1932, showing proposed building plots down Chyngton Hill and adjacent to Exceat Bridge.

Seaford; between what is now the Golden Galleon and Exceat Saltings was laid out *"a unique miniature building estate"* for 16 houses. On February 2 1936 the Sussex Express announced that a party to the purchase, a Nathan Duncan Maidman, had applied for a provisional full 'on' licence for a proposed road house to be built 200 metres from Exceat Bridge, which was going to be known as The Cuckmere Hotel. The Seaford Down Estate Company (formed by Maidman the previous September) and the Peel Estate jointly owned the land. These two companies were jointly proposing to construct 2,300 houses upon the 364 hectares (900 acres) of open Downland across Chyngton up to the Seaford to Alfriston road.

The local planning authority Seaford Urban District Council, four breweries and the Esplanade Hotel in Seaford, opposed the hotel licence. Fred Morgan, Clerk to the Council stated that *"the land on which it was proposed to build the hotel had been scheduled as agricultural land after protracted negotiations with the owners of the land on the other side of the river, and on behalf of the Seaford Urban Council, he wished to say that they would strenuously object to any building on that site."* Oddly, Colonel Watson the tenant of Exceat Farm, made it known that he was in favour of the licence being granted and thought the proposed road house would be of great benefit to the neighbourhood, despite the fact that the 'neighbourhood' had not yet been built! Despite opposition from the district councils to this extensive sprawling development, the chairman of the licensing bench Mr. J.I. Blencowe announced after private deliberations, that a provisional licence would be granted for an initial five-year period.

Several months later, an article appeared in The Times of April 16 1936, stating that Seaford Head and several hundred acres of Downland bordering the seaward end of the valley, had been bought for nearly £20,000 by the Seaford Urban District Council. The two development companies followed this by offering a carrot to the council. If 6 hectares of land near Exceat Bridge were re-zoned, they would not build on the adjoining 125 hectares (310 acres) declaring this a 'private open space' under the 1932 Town and Country Planning Act. The council stood steadfast and still refused an interim development order, full marks to the councillors of Seaford! Later the same year, a local development company approached the same council for a tenancy agreement concerning the beach area at Cuckmere Haven for the creation of a 'pleasure beach.' Fortunately neither this development saw the light of day, for had it been allowed it would have carved a gaping wound in the preserved coastline between Seaford and Eastbourne. (24).

CROWLINK. Mention of this picturesque hamlet situated within the parish of Friston, is first recorded in 1267 as Crawelinke, probably taken from 'crawe' and 'hlinc,' meaning Crow-hill. (7). On June 24 1544 the property then recorded as 'Crowlynke,' was sold by a John Crypps of East Grinstead to Sir John Gage. (25). Crowlink Farm remained part of the Gage family estates until 1823 when like Exceat, it was exchanged for the Parsonage of Firle. (11).

During 1896 Mr. J.E.A. Gwynne of Folkington Manor, entered into negotiations with the Ecclesiastical Commissioners to purchase both Exceat and Crowlink Farms, amounting to 605 hectares (1496 acres) for the sum of £15,000 but he eventually withdrew his offer. The following year Frederick de Costabadie, the sitting tenant offered to purchase the farm for £3,500; the Commissioners land agents Cluttons refused to consider any offer below £5,000, which he then later offered. This was however refused as there had arisen, the prospect of a railway being built directly between Eastbourne and Seaford; this would have substantially increased the value of the land in view of its potential development value. (11).

Eventually on October 31 1922 the Ecclesiastical Commissioners sold Crowlink to Mr. G.O. Howship of London for the sum of £5,000; probably due to failure of the proposed railway and Crowlink's poor soil fertility their land agents viewed the farm as something of a liability. (11). Four years later in 1926, the Sunday Observer published an article which stated that a syndicate had acquired Crowlink for building development. This signalled the start of a determined campaign to safeguard this stretch of Downland and coastline. A group known as the Seven Sisters Committee, quickly raised £20,000 and successfully purchased Crowlink, subsequently donating the property to The National Trust.

FRISTON PLACE. The early name for this one time farm was Bechington, perhaps meaning 'farm of Becci' or 'of his people,' and according to the Domesday Book, was held by the Saxon, Azaline. The earliest known occupier of the existing house was one William Potman in 1428. Ownership descended by way of the Adam family until sometime during the latter part of the 15th century when Margery Adam married Thomas Selwyn of Sherrington in the parish of Selmeston; Selwyn proceeded to enlarge the house considerably. (24). The property was to stay in the ownership of the Selwyn family until 1704 when Judith Medlecott (neé Selwyn) inherited the property and almost immediately sold it to Thomas Medley of Buxted Place near Uckfield. In July of 1810, Julia Evelyn Medley married Charles Cecil Cope Jenkinson, who in 1828 succeeded to becoming the third Earl of

Liverpool. Prior to succeeding the baronetcy, he was for ten years M.P. for East Grinstead and had also held separately, two under-secretary posts in government. Indeed, the then Princess Victoria together with her mother, the Princess of Kent, used to stay with Jenkinson at Buxted Place. (26). After the earl's death in 1851 the property was purchased by the Lees family who owned it until 1869, when it became part of the estates of the Dukes of Devonshire. In 1897 the property was sold to John Andrew Maitland, the family residing there until Second World War. (17). The accompanying farmland however, was sold back to the Devonshire Estate during October 1912, in order to consolidate the Eastbourne Waterworks Company's water catchment area for their Friston pumping station. (18).

When the property was de-requisitioned after the Second World War, it was purchased by Hartley William Shawcross, one of this countries leading lawyers, politician and businessman, who had spent his childhood in Sussex. (In 1939 the same year that he was appointed a Bencher of Gray's Inn, he took silk, some seven years earlier than was usual in those days. A man of some style, with wavy dark hair, Shawcross would appear in chambers on a Saturday morning wearing tweeds, a canary-coloured pullover and for that time and in the provinces especially, socially daring suede shoes. In tow would be a vast St Bernard dog). (27).

After the Second World War, Shawcross was appointed Attorney General in the historic post-war Labour government. A lawyer of multiple talents, and chairman later of many commissions, companies and committees, he was offered the highest offices in the judiciary and was once mooted as a leader of the Labour Party. But he consistently rejected the *"glittering prizes"* proffered him. He acted as Chief Prosecutor for the United Kingdom before the International Military Tribunal at Nuremberg, following which he always maintained a sneaking regard for Hermann Goering. The majority praised his intellectual mastery and the way in which *"with his slight nasal drawl he scathingly trounced the Nazi warlords."* He also prosecuted the Irishman William Joyce known as Lord Haw-Haw, hanged for treason following his wartime Nazi propaganda broadcasts. (27).

By now, Shawcross was regarded as one of the high-flyers of both the Bar and politics. He did not endear himself to his colleagues when he explained, *"As my political expenses considerably exceed my parliamentary salary I am compelled to earn a living outside politics."* Nor were his Lancashire constituents too happy with their absentee member who had made his home in Sussex. In 1959 he was created Baron Shawcross of Friston, one of the Britain's first life peers, sitting apart from a flirtation with the SDP, as a cross-bencher; he was also closely connected with Sussex University being Pro-Chancellor, 1960-65 and Chairman, 1965-85. When asked the object of life he agreed with the observation of the doctor at the end of David Lean's film 'The Bridge on the River Kwai:' *"Madness. Bloody madness."* After the suicide in 1943 of his first wife, he married Joan Mather, who was a niece of Sir Malcolm Campbell and had been Shawcross' driver during the war. She was killed in a riding accident in 1974 on the Downs near the family house at Friston. He died at Cowbeech on July 10 2003. (27).

SOURCES

1) S.A.C. vol. 117, p. 224.
2) Rackham, Oliver, 'Woodlands' (New Naturalist Library). Collins. 2006.
3) Larkin, Monty, 'In The Footsteps Of Time.' Ulmus Books. 2006.
4) S.N.Q. vol. 10. 1964.
5) Brandon, ed. Peter, 'The South Saxons.' Philimore & Co. 1978.
6) S.A.S. Monograph No.1. 1982.
7) 'The Place Names Of Sussex,' (2 volumes). Cambridge University Press. 1929-30.
8) S.A.C. vol. 58.
9) S.A.C. vol. 114.
10) S.R.S. vol. XXIX, 'Sussex Deeds and Documents,' p.113. 1924.
11) Chichester Chapter Estates of West Dean and Friston management files.
Church Commissioner's archives.
12) Stutchbury, Wycliffe; verbal comm.
13) S.A.C. vol. 3, p.13.
14) Fletcher, Anthony, 'Sussex 1600–1660 - A County Community In Peace
And War.' Philimore & Co. 1980.
15) S.A.C. vol. 93, p.5.
16) S.A.S. 'Cuckmere Valley Project,' Volume Building Surveys. 1995.
17) E.S.R.O. Land Tax Assessments.
18) Eastbourne Waterworks Company, minutes of Board meetings.
19) Arnold, E.C. 'Bird Reserves.' H.F. & G. Witherby Ltd. 1940.
20) Charlston Manor website.
21) S.A.C. vol. 32, p. 181.
22) Victoria County History, vol. 2.
23) S.A.C. vol. 43. p. 52.

24) Sussex County Magazine. vol. 10. 1936.
25) E.S.R.O. Firle Place MSS. part 2.
26) Dictionary of National Biography.
27) The Independent. Obituary article. July 11 2003.

CHAPTER 2

LOCAL ARCHITECTURE.

TRADITIONAL BUILDING MATERIALS. When considering traditional building materials in relation to the South Downs, one's mind begins to conjure up Sussex flint barns, lichen-encrusted farm and cottage walls. England has probably made greater use of flint than other countries where this material occurs. It has been a source of inspiration for generations of artists, writers and in more recent times, photographers and film directors. Most flint structures are built of field or land-picked flint, material which has been collected from off the arable fields of the Downs. This practice had several benefits: it made for the betterment of the land, for crops do not thrive with large stones beneath their roots! Once collected, flint provided a useful building material within the district and a durable road stone for use locally and also further afield.

When standing and considering a large flint building such as may be seen at Exceat, one cannot but startled by the amount of flint which has been laboriously collected by hand for such a building. Flint structures are bonded together not with cement but lime mortar; examine for example, a ruined or broken section of flint wall and it will be noticed that a large amount of mortar has been used, even though the maximum bulk of flint has been utilised. Considerable skill is required in constructing good quality flint work: to keep an even 'batter' or vertically taper, in keeping individual courses level and the arranging of individual flints with the same rake or tilt. Often, the flints are 'knapped' that is, having one surface struck off so as to expose the blue-grey interior of the material.

It may be noticed, that where a section of flint work has been recently added to, re-built or re-pointed, the colour and texture of the modern lime mortar does not match the original older work. This is due firstly to the aggregate used; in the past it was partly composed of fine shingle from the coast. Secondly, the lime formally used would have been lump lime, known as quick lime; hydrated lime as used today gives a much greyer colour to the mortar as does the incorporation of modern portland cement. Finally, exposure to the sun, wind and rain will have sculptured the mortar leaving the aggregate slightly raised. It is fair to say that most flint work undertaken today with exceptions, is less agreeable to the eye. Some of the faults observed are: too few flints used; finishing off of the mortar with a broom, rather than by trowel as the courses are laid and finally, too much cement in relation to lime in the mortar, which creates the 'wrong colour,' though it must be said a stronger structure.

The construction of a flint wall is a time consuming, laborious job requiring considerable skill. The flints forming the two exposed outer surfaces of the wall are laid first, followed by the hearting or interior of the wall, composed of material unable to be used in the outer surfaces and mortar. The process is repeated for each course. Owing to the inherent small size of the material, flint walls are liable to be deficient in longitudinal and transverse strength. To overcome this problem and to obtain regularity around doors, windows etc., quoins of brick produced from wealden clay (e.g. as were once produced at Berwick), are incorporated which give a satisfying mellow texture and colour contrast. Within the study area, little use has been made of cobbles; these are flint boulders collected from the shoreline, which have been rounded by the ceaseless action of the sea and are usually grey in colour. Being far more uniform in shape, these give a pleasing symmetrical appearance to the eye. The only example of cobble walling is on Exceat House, where the lower level of the front elevation has utilised this material. Several good examples of flint barns are readily accessible to the public when visiting Exceat.

Within some of these older buildings, a substantial amount of timber framing was used, in addition to the large amount within the roof itself. Oak was the timber generally used, there being a plentiful supply on the heavy clays just to the north of the Downs. Over the years, particularly during the 19th and 20th centuries, sometimes part of, or the entire roof timbers were replaced with softwood. Finally, complementing the rustic flint walls and mellow brick quoins, is the roof cladding itself. Until the early years of the twentieth century many of the barns, cattle lodges and cottages would have supported a thatched roof, often laid by the farms own thatcher using wheat straw grown on the farm. Straw thatch lasted for a period of some ten to twenty years. Thatch though has been succeeded by clay peg tiles, so called because they are held in position by small wooden pegs (or metal today), placed through two holes, as they are laid. In time, clay tiles mellow and become encrusted with lichens or on elevations with a less sunny aspect, studded with numerous buttons of green moss. Slate was also later sometimes used.

Flint as a road making material was used up until the 1930's, farmers then receiving one shilling (5 pence) for each cubic yard. During the 1930's this practice was superseded with the arrival of tarmac by rail; sometimes this would arrive in such a solid state, that steam from a steam roller would be directed into the railway trucks in order to soften up the material! Having explained something of the traditional building materials, we will now look at a selection of the more notable buildings in the study area, from humble barns through to idyllic country manor houses, ranging from the medieval period through to the 20th century.

EXCEAT. The oldest remaining building structure at Exceat is the foundation of the former parish church, situated near the summit of Exceat Hill and clearly marked by a large piece of engraved stone. These foundations which were excavated in 1913, date from the Early Norman period and have been dated to c.1050-80. The outline of the porch is visible upon the south-west corner. Although this was built during the same period, it is not bonded to the main structure being presumably built at a slightly later stage. The church was built mainly of flint, but other buildings materials were also unearthed: French caen stone, greensand stone, pieces of moulded or carved chalk and some coloured window glass dating from the period 1275-90. In places

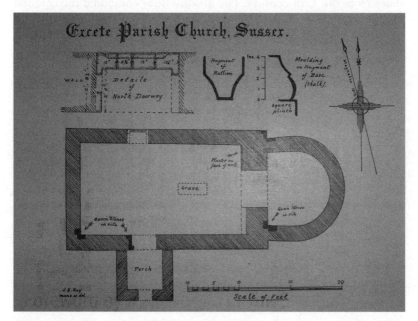

Ground plan of Exceat parish church on Exceat Hill, drawn when excavated in 1913.

there were signs of a plaster floor beneath which in the nave, was a slab of Sussex marble concealing a well-made grave. The overall dimensions of the church were 14.78metres (48ft. 6ins.) including a nave of 9.45metres (31 feet); the width of the church was 4.95metres (16ft. 3ins.). The best occasion to view this site is during, or immediately after a prolonged dry spell during the summer, when the grass turns brown above the foundations, so forming a clear outline of the church. (1).

Exceat House, situated amongst the cluster of buildings which formed the nucleus of Exceat Farm, is an example of an old building of moderate proportions, which has evolved over many years and is Grade II listed. The south facing elevation is considered to date from c.1820; up to the level of the first floor the walls are faced with flint cobbles, above which is timber studding faced with mellow clay tile. This main elevation is almost symmetrical with a generously sized, centrally placed door, creating a sense of dignity befitting a farmer of some means. The rear of the house consists of three older gabled sections at right angles to the south-facing principle elevation. (2).

The western-most section, has the ground floor built of flint and the first floor partly of timber framed construction clad with tile hanging. This section is the oldest part of the house and probably dates from the 17th century. The ground floor contained the original kitchen (and nowadays forms a seating area for a tearoom) and still boasts a generous inglenook fireplace; to its left was situated the

Farmer Percy Gorringe and his wife Eleanor, about to depart from Exceat House.

boiling copper, where water could be heated or large items of food boiled. To the right, is situated a beautifully constructed bread oven; access was gained through a door-opening of 48cms x 30cms (18 inches by 12 inches), into the oval shaped interior measuring approximately 1.52 metres x 0.91metres (5ft. x 3ft.). The sides are 23cms (9 inches) high, consisting of bricks placed upon their ends supporting a domed ceiling rising in the centre to 48cms (18 inches), built of circular courses of bricks. The first floor until extensive renovation during the 1980's contained a number of small rooms without windows, with the interior walls consisting of timber studding in-filled with plaster and lathe. These rooms probably formed accommodation for living-in servants and farm labourers. The central gabled section is built of flint and is probably of 18th century construction, containing the present day kitchen area with a ceiling of ancient re-used timbers carrying the first floor.

The large eastern section extends away from the main body of the house to form a barn. Within this, there are several typical wooden-framed bays supporting the roof (re-built in the 1980's) and possibly, originally an aisle along either side, although the western wall appears to have been rebuilt and now incorporates the wooden uprights. This wooden post and truss framing appears 'wrong' and would seem to have belonged to an older building. (2). In the section between the barn and the house, the floor level is substantially lower than that of the adjacent brick-paved courtyard, creating a cool shaded area. Built into the wall farthest from the small doorway, is a small alcove measuring one metre across. Would this have been constructed in which to keep milk vessels cool so as to reduce the risk of milk turning sour?

At the front of the house, where a flight of brick steps lead up to the front elevation, large blocks of greensand can be observed forming quoin or corner stones of the house. These may well have been removed from the ruins of Exceat church about a mile to the south, and originate from the greensand outcrop at Meads in Eastbourne. The first mention of a substantial house at Exceat is in a lease dated December 16 1577, which refers to *"Thomas Markwick of Excett, yeoman, of the Manor house with barns closes etc. belonging, called Excett."* In another lease dated September 30 1614, Jeffrey Widdgyer had to employ within two years 20,000 tiles upon the mansion house at Exceat. An insight into the domestic life within the house is given in a lease of 1722 that mentions the use of *"two lodging chambers over the Milkhouse* [probably the later old kitchen in the western gable section] *and conveniency to dress and eat their meat in the house."* (3).

The *Country Park Information Centre* is housed in a fine example of a Sussex flint barn. It was probably built when Exceat Farm was taken in hand that is, farmed by the landlord, Lord Gage during the period 1766-79. The interior gives one the chance to admire the massive wooden post and truss framing, which was probably assembled on the ground and erected with help of oxen or horses; these large timbers support the weight of the mighty roof rather than the walls. Note the following features; high up on the interior of the gable end wall, chalk boulders have been used, chalk making a reasonable building material provided that it is not exposed to the weather. Within the southern elevation a large wagon entrance is incorporated to accommodate entry of wagons laden with the harvest and opposite, a much lower exit doorway for leaving when empty. Being located on a slope the barn has a two-level floor, very unusual in the south of the England. Livestock could be housed on the lower floor level with fodder or straw on the upper level; alternatively the whole building could have been used to storage of un-thrashed corn, the area between the two doors then being used as a thrashing floor. Externally, there are no brick quoins to the corners of this barn. This together with the other large flint barn is Grade II listed.

Close to where the brick pathway leading away from the Park Information Centre meets the A 259 coast road, stands an example of a combined granary and wagon lodge, a combination that was commonly built during the 18th century. At ground level, the building would have been open at both ends to allow the storage of wagons while above, was the granary providing storage of that proportion of the farms crops that had been thrashed and were awaiting sale or use. Until the advent of the combine harvester, corn would have been carried up a flight of wooden steps (now removed) on the southern side of the building, thence through a dormer door at eaves level, using large hessian sacks which weighed up to 114.3kgs (252 pounds) each. The storage area was until conversion during the 1990's, divided into a number of large storage bins constructed of timber which were 1.22metres (4 feet) deep. There would have been until the mid twentieth century, a range of cattle lodges between the farmyard and the A259 between the two bends.

The hamlet of Foxhole is situated on a site which is considered by archaeologists to have been in occupation for many centuries. Behind the cottages, there are remains of a medieval bank and ditch that originally is likely to have been topped by a fence or palisade, so forming a compound. Until the late medieval period, by which time the valley had silted up and the river largely embanked, this site may well have been a fishing community. Artefacts found here include pottery sherds (pieces) from a nearby rabbit burrow and dated from between the Bronze Age and late Saxon times. Within the cottage gardens there have been found 13-14th century pottery, tudor redware, 17th century German stoneware (possibly from wine bottles) and an abundance of 18-19th century pottery, glass bottles and broken clay tobacco pipes. All these artefacts were examined and dated by the Sussex Archeological Society.

During the medieval period salt may have been produced at Foxhole. During extensive works carried

Exceat Farm 1916, looking towards the building from the southeast. Note the pond near to where today's phone box stands and the narrow road.

out to improve the pond at Foxhole during autumn 1989, it was deepened by approximately 0.75metres at its centre. Before a new clay lining was puddle in, the machine employed made an exploratory hole in the centre of the pond revealing in excess of one metre down, a 15cm layer of jet-black material containing a mass of heat-fractured flint, possibly indicating the existence of a former saltern, where sea water was reduced to produce salt?

Foxhole Cottages comprises of three cottages: No. 1 (the eastern most), is of unknown age built probably as a barn for within its walls are brick-lined air vents, a common feature of barns; these now blocked-up. The brick chimney flues also appear to be of later construction. On the 1840 tithe map, the building is shown as being 'L' shaped, with a wing extending from the western end towards the pond. During 1937 the present shaped building was converted from being two cottages to just one. It was at this time that the thatched roof was replaced with clay tiles, (re-tiled again during the 1990's). The pair of semi-detached cottages standing next to the above are of later construction; they were erected sometime between 1840 and 1860, for they are not shown on the tithe map but do appear on an estate map dated 1860. Major improvements were carried out to these during 1938 when wash houses (today's kitchens) were added to either end; floors, staircases, most windows, ranges and coppers were replaced. The two single sliding sash bedroom windows on the north elevation are the only remaining original windows. They were also completely re-roofed, this being when they lost their thatched roof; also drainage was provided together with new privys (outside toilets). Cluttons, the Ecclesiastical Commissioners agents stated that the estimate for the works would be £550, minus a grant from the County Council of £200 under the Housing (Rural Workers) Act. (4).

The flint barn sited within Foxhole Bottom referred to as *Foxhole Barn*, again lacks any brick quoin work upon its corners and so probably also dates from the 18th century as with the barn described earlier at Exceat. The clay tiled roof is finished at either end of the building with small, what is termed as 'half-hipped' roofs (these are something of a Sussex feature); virtually all the timbers of the roof structure are of softwood, so almost certainly not the original timbers. Formally in the stockyard on the southern side of the barn there stood an 'L'-shaped open cattle lodge or shed, of timber construction standing on/mortised into greensand blocks; this was demolished during the 1980's due to its unsafe condition. During the following decade the character and use of the building changed when it was converted for

Foxhole Cottages taken when the Eastbourne Boys Brigade camped there in 1905.

use as a camping barn. Nearby, is a delightful example of a chalk ashlar (block) lined well; these blocks having mitred ends, which when butted together, form a robust well lining. The original depth of the well is in the order of some 21 metres (70 feet), but is now partially filled with former farm debris.

The modern concrete framed, asbestos cement clad barn (or covered yard) at Foxhole was erected during the late 1960's, together with a milking parlour of concrete block construction attached to one corner. At the same time the concrete road from the A 259 was constructed, to facilitate the then trend towards the collection of milk by bulk tanker as opposed to collection in milk churns. Until then milking had taken place at Exceat. It was also at this time that Foxhole was serviced with electric power and telephone.

Situated over a mile to the east of Exceat itself and situated at the head of Newbarn Bottom, stands the third group of buildings on Exceat. The dominating building here is *Exceat New Barn*, a large flint barn built on a north south axis. It has four large wagon entrances with a largely softwood roof dating from the 1890's to 1900's. Sadly today this is clad with completely out of character modern concrete pantiles, which replaced the clay tiles; this was part of £40,000 worth of dilapidation works carried out on the of buildings and fixtures when the former farm tenancy ceased in 1971. Internally the barn reveals the fact that the present structure is a combination of works carried out at differing periods. Within the walls, are remains of large hardwood uprights and the wooden plates capping the walls are of reused timber. Probably it was originally of 'post and truss' construction as with the Park Centre barn, but is now of 'box' construction as at Foxhole.

By 1896, sections of the barn's walls were suffering from substantial bulging, causing concern and leading to extensive rebuilding works being carried out. Adjoining the barn on either side are two large livestock yards. Situated along the northern side of the western yard is an open lodge or shed with a somewhat chequered history. The original structure carried a roof of thatch; during a cold spell in January of 1929, a carter was attempting to thaw the water pipe that ran along the eaves of the building with a blowlamp, which by misfortune ignited the thatch and so destroyed the building! This was rebuilt the same year, but was destroyed a second time by the forces of nature, namely timber rot and the storm of January 1990. The adjoining stable dates from 1897, built on the site of a building partially destroyed by a March gale. As the existing stable was by then in poor condition it was decided to re-build the stable in this same position as it offered shelter to the western stock yard from the prevailing winds. It also enabled the tenant to keep one team of horses as well as a team of oxen at this end of the farm. (4). Standing a little way down the valley stands *Exceat Newbarn Cottage* which until 1951 formed two cottages. This was extensively renovated in the early 1990's.

THE GAYLES. Sandwiched in a secluded position between Crowlink and Exceat Farms stands the imposing country house, *The Gayles*. Originally built as a small holiday home by John Wycliffe Taylor in 1901, it was designed by the architect Stewart-Taylor in the classical Edwardian style. With his wife Freda, Taylor shared a mania for economy - walls were of breeze block with a pebble dash finish and rainwater was stored in a large underground cistern. In or about 1910 the house was enlarged.

After the death of her husband in 1925, Freda could not endure living on at The Gayles and so the property passed to their daughter Rosamond and her husband, Mervyn Stutchbury. Rosamond's parents may have been obsessed with economy but not so her husband Mervyn. He commissioned his brother-in-law, Sir Edward Maufe who was responsible for designing Guildford cathedral, to transform The Gayles into the perfect country house with no expense spared. It was extensively enlarged, connected to mains water and had an expensive drainage system installed. All gutters and downpipes were constructed of copper and one of the first domestic oil-fired heating systems in the country installed. A little to the west a gatehouse was erected which spanned the driveway, in which the gardeners were accommodated; this also contained an engine room for the diesel-powered generating set and stables. The cost after lengthy arbitration of this extravagant upgrading of The Gayles was finally settled with the builders at £20,000. During the Christmas period of 1961 the entire gatehouse complex which then contained the farm manager's accommodation, was gutted by fire one icy evening; fire fighters were hampered by a lack of water pressure. Ownership of the house was separated from the remainder of land holding in 1986 when Stutchbury's sold the house. (5).

WEST DEAN. *"The hamlet consists of very few houses, all so compactly grouped about the old church that from this distance* [Exceat Hill] *it seemed as if the hand could cover them. The roofs were overgrown with lichen, yellow on slate, red on tiles. In the farmyards were haystacks with yellow conical coverings of thatch. And around all closed dense masses of chestnut foliage, the green just touched with gold. The little group of houses had mellowed with age; their guarded peacefulness was soothing to the eye and the spirit. Along the stretch of the hollow the land was parcelled into meadows with a tilth of varied hue. Here was a great patch of warm grey soil, where horses were drawing the harrow; yonder the same work was being done by sleek black oxen."* So wrote the now forgotten Victorian novelist George Gissing, an author of high distinction, in his novel *"Thyrza."* (6, 7). Still dominating the architectural setting of the village today is the parish church.

The church, dedicated to *All Saints*, dates from the Norman period and is predominantly of Norman and 14th century construction and notable for its short gabled spire, clad with shingles. Internally, at the west end of the nave a large Norman archway leads into the base of the tower. A number of other features in the church including the font, the east and south facing windows, date from the Early English period (early 14th century). The two ancient tombs in the chancel are probably associated with Sir John Heringod and his wife. By contrast, the large, ostentatious mural monument was erected in memory of William Thomas who died in 1639; this would have been one of the last of this style to be erected, the Puritan movement coming to power shortly afterwards. During 1878, the interior of the church was 'improved' in the Victorian manner including the laying of the black and white floor tiles; earlier during the 1840's, the wooden screen and rood-loft which separated the chancel from the nave was removed. (8, 9, 10, 11).

The impressive residence adjacent to the church is *The Old*

Looking northward from today's South Downs Way towards an 'un-forested' West Dean village.

Parsonage, of which there are two theories as to whom was responsible for its construction. One is that it was erected by the Benedictine monks from Wilmington Priory which was suppressed in 1413 during the reign of Henry VI; if correct, construction of the eastern portion of this building would predate that year. The second theory is that it was built on the orders of Sir John Heringod, lord of the manor. Internally, the windows on both floors are surrounded by attractive, perfectly bevelled chalk masonry. Projecting from the north-eastern corner of the building is a small spiral stone staircase leading up to the hall or main living area on the first floor. Facing on to the road from this room, is a projection forming a garderobe or wardrobe and which has now been converted to form another stone staircase. Beneath this ancient building there is a small cellar. The western section of the building is far younger having been erected in 1891. (8, 9).

In the centre of the village once stood the Manor House; this was probably of medieval construction and was demolished due to decay in or about 1825. Close by stands the Grade II listed remains of the manor house dovecot. Circular in construction, this dovecot varied from the other eight examples in the neighbourhood due to the fact that the nesting holes lining the building and built of chalk, are arranged in double rows, with 44 'L'-shaped nesting boxes in each tier. The dovecot was very imposing before its demise, for a watercolour painting by George de Paris and dated 1885, shows the building with a tiled roof capped with an elaborate lantern through which the birds could enter and leave. The nest boxes were reached when required by a revolving ladder attached to a potence (central wooden upright). (12). At the western end of the property facing *West Dean Cottages* built in 1948 for forestry workers, are the remains of two ancient stone-mullioned windows within a section of an old, high flint wall.

The imposing *Westdean Manor*, a Grade II listed building dates from the early nineteenth century. Designed with a hipped and slated roof; stuccoed with an eaves cornice, its large windows flanked by Venetian-style shutters. (11). Through the twentieth century several famous people have been connected with Westdean Manor. During the early 1920's Kit Williams, wife of the farm bailiff Maurice Williams, would let rooms to people wishing to holiday in the area. One couple was the distinguished children's illustrator Mabel Lucie Attwell who together with her husband painter and illustrator Harold 'Pat' Earnshaw, fell in love with the Cuckmere valley. When Westdean Manor came on the market in 1932 they decided to sell their London home and move into the village. During 1934 her daughter Peggy Wickham gave birth to one of her sons while staying there. However, husband Pat's health was deteriorating fast and during 1935 they decided to moved back to London. Her most notable works were for the publisher Raphael Tuck and include *'Alice's Adventures In Wonderland; The Water-Babies'* and the illustrations for J.M. Barrie's *'Peter Pan And Wendy.'* Her *"endless pictures of chubby, dimpled babies and infants"* were also to appear on all manner of merchandising and in the *'Lucy Attwell Annual's.'* (13, 14).

Between 1948-51, Westdean Manor was owned and lived in by Major Bruce Shand MC, his wife Rosalind whom he married in January of 1946 and young family. He was born in 1917 and possessed a calmly philosophical approach to life and 'was perfectly content with his station in life.' The Honourable Rosalind neé Cubitt born in 1921 was the daughter of the 3rd Baron Ashcombe; her maternal grandmother was Alice Keppel, a courtesan of Edward VII. It was during this early period of their marriage and the year before they moved to West Dean, that their daughter Camilla was born in London, she destined later to become the Duchess of Cornwall. (15, 16).

Commissioned into the 12th Royal Lancers from the Royal Military College Sandhurst in 1937 he showed marked military ability and personal gallantry in the early years of the war, he being awarded the Military Cross for his gallantry during the BEF withdrawal from Belgium during 1940. At the end of the battle of El Alamein in North Africa in October 1942 Shand's squadron was ordered to the coast to ensure it was clear of enemy. The area was approachable only by descending a steep track down from the desert escarpment. While negotiating this, a large group of enemy came into view on the escarpment. Shand's lightly armoured car was set ablaze in the ensuing firefight, his two crew members killed and he was wounded by a bullet passing through his cheeks, a knee wound and was taken prisoner. (16).

After the end of hostilities he eventually spent many years with the prestigious West End wine merchants Block, Grey and Block. The family after leaving West Dean continued to have a long association with Sussex. But it was in riding and the hunt that his real passion lay, a passion that is inherited by Camilla. He was variously joint and acting Master of the Southdown Fox Hounds during the period 1956-75 and was also Deputy Lieutenant for Sussex. The constant media attention and stress on his family arising from the relationship between the Prince of Wales and his daughter Camilla, tried his patience. He possessed an aversion to being pushed around or seeing anyone he held dear being treated in a likewise manner. Major Shand died on June 11 2006 aged 89, twelve years after his wife Rosalind passed away.

West Dean Manor; a spacious Victorian house once the country home of Major Shand and his family.

During the 1950's, Westdean Manor was the residence of John Anderson later knighted as Viscount Waverley. Anderson is considered possibly to be the greatest administrator this country has ever had. Cabinet posts which he held included Lord Privy Seal in 1938; then in September 1939, Home Secretary (air raid shelters, 'Anderson shelters,' were named after him; (see Chapter 9) and in 1943, Chancellor of the Exchequer. (13).

Other buildings of note are *The Long House* was formally two cottages and is of 18th century or earlier construction. *Pond Cottage* also probably dates from the 18th century and is now of two storeys but the end wall clearly shows that it was originally a single storey cottage. The elevation containing the garage is of modern construction. *Forge Cottage, The School House* and *Old Coach House* are also Grade II listed. (11). *The Glebe* a dignified, tile hung house in the Tudor style is of early 20th century vintage. Many of the flint-built farm buildings within the village date from the 18th century and were converted during the 1980's into very desirable properties with large double-glazed windows and oil-fired central heating, far removed from their original function of providing storage for crops, equipment and housing of livestock.

CHARLSTON. Situated in the north of West Dean parish is

Charlston Manor, a beautiful house in an idyllic setting. The house consists of a north-south wing with two later east-west wings of 17th and 18th century construction. However, it is the north-south wing which is of the greatest antiquity, dating to c.1200. The first floor would have housed the principal rooms as was customary with other Norman houses, of which there are over 40 surviving in England. The principal feature of the house is the two-lighted French caen stone Norman window, situated along the northern wall of this wing. The structure consists of three circular stone shafts supporting two semi-circular arches over the lights. Within the southern gable survives a similar but less ornate window constructed from local greensand, with a much weathered internally hung hinged shutter. This wing also accommodates a 13th or early 14th chimney and fragments of a first floor fireplace. (11).

Until the mid or late 19th century, the Manor site formed the principle building accommodation of a farm stretching along the northern flank of the parish. After purchasing the property minus its farmland during the early 1930's, Sir Oswald Birley engaged the eminent architect and architectural historian W.H. Godfrey, to firstly survey the house and then transform it and the former farm buildings. The laying out of the extensive formal gardens and its noted rose collection also date from this period. (11).

Close by the manor house, is a circular probably medieval, dovecot with a roof of clay tiles; it measures some 4.30 metres (14 feet) in diameter, with the floor level some 91cms. (3 feet) below the surrounding ground level. (11). There are eleven tiers of chalk nesting boxes numbering some 300 in total, each with a projecting chalk ledge for birds to alight upon. In the past this would have provided fresh meat to the house especially during the winter period. By 1804, the eminent agricultural commentator the Rev. Arthur Young noted of the keeping of pigeons that *"they are not propagated to any extent."* (17). Adjacent to where the long gravel drive from the manor house strikes the Exceat to Litlington road, stand a pair of fine flint cottages which initially bring to mind Georgian architecture; in fact these were commissioned by Sir Oswald.

CHYNGTON. The principal building of this former hamlet, the dignified *Chyngton House* situated to the west of the farm building complex, was originally of six bedrooms together with accommodation for servants. Until the 1970's, this hamlet stood isolated from the encroaching sprawl of modern Seaford. Nowadays this fine flint built residence, has been converted into two separate dwellings; modern housing development is now just across the gravel driveway.

To the south-east of Chyngton House is situated a superb example of a dovecot (or columbarium), probably dating back to at least the 17th century. This dovecot is constructed of flint, brick and with a limited amount of greensand, capped with a tiled roof. Entry was gained by way of a 1.52metre (5 foot) high doorway upon its southern side. Inside, the walls are lined with row upon row of nest boxes, constructed from chalk blocks approximately 10 centimetre (4 inches) in thickness; incised into this chalk are hundreds of deep gouges some eight inches in length, formed by generations of pigeons cleaning their beaks. These nest boxes create a pleasingly symmetrical effect to the eye, rising tier upon tier to the roof in cloistral fashion. As the total number of nest boxes numbered some 600, the dovecot had the potential to supply a substantial amount of fresh meat. The disadvantages of this form of livestock were that a flock of at least a thousand pigeons would have made considerable inroads into the corn and fodder crops of the farm. They would also have also caused damage to the thatched roofs then existing as they foraged for food and nesting material. (17). Today the building has been incorporated into a modern residence, the dovecot forming the master bedroom.

Situated in a prominent position upon the crest of South Hill a

Looking across the former large pond at Chyngton Farm towards dovecot and granary, early twentieth century.

half mile south of the farm itself, stands *South Barn* locally known as *Begger's Barn,* and reached via a concrete road constructed during the Second World War to access a tank firing range in the vicinity of the cliffs. During an outbreak of smallpox in or about 1880, it was allegedly pressed into use as an 'isolation hospital' for Seaford. The public house *The Golden Galleon* started life as a shepherds cottage known as *Exceat Bridge Cottage* for Chyngton Farm, the adjacent land to the south formally being known as Shepherds Green. When the Chyngton Estate was auctioned during July 1932, Lot 12 was listed in the sale catalogue as a cottage together with a teahouse. During the post war years until the 1970's it was one of the exclusive seafood restaurants belonging to Wheelers of London. Since, it has been developed into an extremely popular pub providing good food in agreeable surroundings with fine views across the Cuckmere valley. *Dymock Farm* located on the brow of Chyngton Hill, north of the A 259 coast road, was built in 1965 by farmer Jack Wynniatt, to replace the original farm *Suttonfields,* the farmhouse of which is now incorporated amongst bungalows forming Stirling Avenue in Seaford. The name is taken from the family's ancestral home Dymock Grange, in Gloucestershire.

CROWLINK. Nestling within the broad, sweeping valley descending south from Friston towards the Seven Sisters, lays the hamlet of Crowlink. This remote cluster of mellow flint buildings which formed the nucleus of Crowlink Farm until the late 1920's, are now residential dwellings. The first residence to be reached on approaching from Friston is *The Granary,* which as the name implies, was the farms grain store; the building is now much altered and marred by red masonry paint. The most notable building within the hamlet is the former farmhouse, *Crowlink House.* Being a house of heightened proportions, this attractive building has suffered unforgivingly at the hands of the prevailing wind and rain. (4). The front elevation of the house presents an agreeable facade of mellow flint and brick. The house is nowadays divided into several separate dwellings.

The buildings on the farm were described in a lease dated April 1850 as thus: *"House (Brick flint & tile) contain of Kitchen, Back kitchen, 2 sitting rooms with 6 bedrooms & attic over – The Farm buildings comprise detached Granary (flint & tile) with small stable adjoining, Wood & fowl houses, well house, Barn with oak floor (flint and tile) Building used as fatling stalls (flint & thatch) with open shed adjoining Small stable (flint & thatch) & open shed adjoining - Another Barn (flint & tile & thatch) with oak floor & small stable adjoining - New shed tiled & 4 enclosed yards. Four cottages*

(Brick flint & tile) each containing 2 rooms on Ground floor & 2 rooms over." (4). The term 'fatling' used in the extract means 'young farm animal fattened for killing.'

In 1913, overheating hay was to cause considerable expense and disruption to both the landowner and Gorringes the farmers as the following account relates: *"We beg to report that on the 22nd. August last, a hay rick fired at Crowlink, owing to combustion. The fire spread to two other ricks, and to a thatched cowhouse adjoining which was totally destroyed, and to the barn and other adjoining buildings which were damaged - portion of the tiled roof of the barn being destroyed. Mr. Gorringe, on the outbreak of the fire, telephoned both to the Eastbourne and the Hailsham Fire Brigades for assistance. The Eastbourne Brigade would not come and the Hailsham Brigade could not, being at the time engaged with another fire. The latter Brigade came 24 hours after the outbreak, and rendered assistance in putting out the remains of the fire, and minimised the risk of further damage, which might have occurred in event of the wind shifting its quarter. We have prepared a plan and obtained an estimate for rebuilding the cowhouse and making good the damage to the other buildings, and find the cost will be £290..."* (4).

FRISTON PLACE. Hidden from view in a secluded valley just to the north of Friston, is the magnificent *Friston Place* together with its attendant buildings. Veiled now by the expanse of Friston Forest, this ancient manor house has seen many changes occur over the surrounding countryside, not least the establishment the forest. The present structure has been greatly enlarged over the centuries, the oldest sections being the medieval residence of the Potman family, who resided here during the 15th century. The house is a feast of flint, greensand and mellow Sussex brick, including much exposed timber. Internally, the grandest feature is the Great Hall, part of an extensive building programme carried out during the reign of Henry VIII by its then owners, the Selwyn family. They were also responsible for the superb wall painting adorning one of the first floor bedrooms, consisting of soft blues and greens with traces of gold, depicting flowers and hunting scenes. Completing this beautifully artistic room are some faded portraits upon the stone quoins of the windows, depicting some of the early members of this noble family. Nearby stands the small square well house which contains a wooden donkey wheel, which provided power for lifting water from the 136-foot (41m.) well. (18).

SOURCES.

1) S.A.C. vol. 58.
2) pers. comm. Norman Hutchings, ESCC Historical Buildings Inspector.
3) Firle Place MSS. E.S.R.O. SAS/G.
4) Chichester Chapter Estates of West Dean & Friston management files. Church Commissioners archives.
5) pers comm. Wycliffe Stutchbury, snr.
6) Gissing, George. 'Thyrza.' Eveleigh Nash & Grayson Ltd.
7) Ward, A.C. 'Longman Companion To Twentieth Century Literature.' Longman Group Ltd.
8) A History of West Dean Church & Parish. 1977.
9) S.A.C. vol. 3.
10) S.A.C. vol. 70; p. 144.
11) S.A.S. 'Cuckmere Valley Project, Volume 2, Building Surveys.' 1995.
12) S.C.M. vol. 6; p. 635.
13) Dictionary of National Biography, 1951-1960.
14) Beetles, Chris. 'Mabel Lucie Attwell.' Pavillian Books Ltd. 1988.
15) pers. comm. Assistant Private Secretary to HRH Duchess of Cornwall.
16) The Times. Obituary article. June 12 2006.
17) Young, Rev. Arthur. 'General View of the Agriculture of the County of Sussex (1813).' David & Charles Reprints. 1970.
18) S.C.M. vol. 10; p. 294.

CHAPTER 3.

RIVER AND HIGHWAY.

"The country through which the Cuckmere flowed had a melancholy picturesqueness. It was a great reach of level meadows, very marshy, with red-brown rushes growing in every ditch, and low trees in places, their trunks wrapped in bright yellow lichen; nor only their trunks, but the very smallest of their twigs was so clad. All over the flats were cows pasturing, black cows, contrasting with flocks of white sheep, which were gathered together, bleating." So wrote George Gissing in the late 19th century, describing a scene which in many respects, has changed little to this day. (1). The subject matter of this chapter deals with the historical aspects of roads, bridges and that key element of the local landscape, the Cuckmere River itself.

THE A 259 COAST ROAD. Let us enquire of the road first. As the many motorists and their passengers speed along on their journeys, how many ever contemplate the course of the road? Many probably admire the scenery or disapprove of eye-sores that they pass, admittedly only a transient glance for the driver. Let us for example follow an imaginary motorist who is travelling in an easterly direction along the A 259 coast road. On reaching the eastern outskirts of Seaford near the brow of Chyngton Hill, a magnificent vista greets the traveller. Away to the left, the distant grey-green downland turf and scrub of Windover Hill towers above the upper reaches of the valley. Scanning slowly right in a southerly direction, the vastness of Friston Forest, wearing its various seasonal coats of colour: grey-brown, with the occasional clump of green pine in the winter; this transforms during the spring with an infusion of purple from swelling beech buds, before emergence of their delicate, bright green leaves and finally the golden and russet tints of autumn. Nestling at the foot of the Downs just above the valley floor in the central field of view, stand the mellow, ancient buildings of the former Exceat Farm, with the open downland rolling across to the heights of Haven Brow, the tallest of the Seven Sisters. To the extreme right, the sea stretches distantly beyond Cuckmere Haven, this watched over by the cottages of the former coastguard station. In the low foreground, lies the silvered, meandering river snaking sinuously across lush green meadows. On having descended Chyngton Hill our traveller is faced with the tight left-hand turn on to:

EXCEAT BRIDGE. A bridge has existed upon this site for many centuries. In 1654 at the County quarter sessions, a jury found against the Rapes of Lewes, Pevensey and Hastings, who were jointly ordered to pay for repairs to Exceat Bridge. (2). The present bridge was constructed in 1866, it consisting of brick abutments carrying two plated main girders, with cross girders carrying a domed plated floor, all of wrought iron construction; the bridge has a clear span of 17.68metres (58 feet). During the period 1941-42, strengthening of the bridge was carried out for military purposes, when four timber trestles were constructed, two upstream and two downstream. Spanning each pair of trestles was a large steel girder which gave added support to the main span. By the 1970's, the condition of the bridge was giving cause for concern; the floor or decking had becoming severely corroded and the wooden trestles were probably no longer carrying any load due to decay at the base of the wooden piles. The situation was not helped by the opening of a new swing bridge at

Exceat Bridge before major re-construction in 1975. Note WW2 wooden trestles and the original railings.

Newhaven which removed the weight restriction there on heavy lorries travelling between Brighton and Eastbourne. To rectify this situation, major reconstruction commenced during October 1975, this being completed during the following July. Considerable traffic delays were experienced during summer rush-hours and weekends, due to traffic lights on the bailey bridge temporarily installed alongside to the south, while the work lasted. Part of the works included the addition of a footbridge to the northern side of the main bridge. (3).

As the two following newspaper extracts show, Exceat Bridge also proved useful to the military authorities on at least two occasions. The Sussex Weekly Advertiser of August 17 1859 contained an article concerning the summer camp at Seaford of the Honourable Artillery Company of London. One of the day's manoeuvres was as follows: *"...they proceeded to storm Exceat-bridge, affording a great treat to a large number of spectators, much amusement being created by an assault on one of the labourers cottages near the bridge, and it might well have been imagined the enemy had really arrived and taken possession of our coast. At Westdean the large party was kindly received by Mr. Charles Waters."* Almost a century later, The Sussex Daily of September 29 1952 ran the following story. On September 29, some 650 Territorial soldiers, paratroopers and frogmen took part in Operation Golden Martlet involving Exceat Bridge. Firefly aircraft from RAF Ford started the operation at 5-45pm when they took part in 'softening-up' operations, ready for an assault to commence with landings at Cuckmere Haven from landing craft, leading to the capture of the bridge. Later on, the aircraft 'changed sides' from the forces of 'Belgonia,' who by now held strong positions around Seaford and South Hill. Men taking part included those from the 4/5th Battalions Royal Sussex Regiment, 10th Battalion Paratroop Regiment, 257th Field Regiment Royal Artillery and Royal Navy ratings.

EXCEAT CAUSEWAY. On leaving the bridge, the road continues across the valley floor at its narrowest point, upon a causeway or embankment largely built of chalk boulders, its origins being of great antiquity. A Royal Commission reported in 1369 that the *"dyke across Cokemareshaven erected in ancient times had been obstructed by incursions of the King's enemies."* Until modern times, landlord or tenants of Exceat were placed under an obligation to keep the causeway in good repair; until 1846 the causeway acted as the valleys main sea defence. (4). As there was no embanking alongside the river meanders, the valley floor within their vicinity consisted of saltmarsh, and during spring tides would have flooded to a depth of some 1.2 to 1.8 metres (4 to 6 feet). Travellers in those days crossing the causeway would have to of contended with sea spray if high tide was accompanied by gale force winds, making it a somewhat alarming journey!

The original height of the causeway was the same as the present day footpath which runs along south side the carriageway, but its average width was only 4.27 metres (14 feet). As there were no railings or verges, accidents were frequent, culminating in a cart careering off the embankment resulting in the death of the driver's wife. This brought about serious discussion aimed at improving safety along the causeway. Eventually, a scheme was put forward by local farmer Charles Ade of Milton Court Farm near Alfriston, which involved reducing the height of the carriageway and increasing its width, but leaving a section along the southern side at the original height, presumably as a defence against the sea, today's footpath. Ade supervised this work which was costed at approximately £135, he receiving the last instalment for the cost of the works on December 13 1842; for his services he received a silver cup (now in the care of the Sussex Archeological Society). Subscribers to the improvement were Viscount Gage, lessee of lands along the eastern river bank, the Earl of Chichester, owner of the west bank, the Earl of Liverpool, of Friston Place, the Earl of Burlington, owner of the manor of West Dean; Earl Amhurst, the Rev. Thomas Scutt of Charlston and Rector of Litlington, and John Davies-Gilbert, a prominent landowner from Eastbourne. (4). The causeway remained a narrow carriageway by modern standards until at least the 1930's, for then in the event of two lorries wishing to cross the causeway, one lorry would have to wait till the passage of the other. (5).

Our 'motorist' on leaving the causeway at its eastern end negotiates the sharp double bend passing the former Exceat Farm. These bends have caused the demise of many motorists, sometimes due to wet or icy road conditions but frequently to driver error. Two of the more notable incidents in recent years have been the following. During the 1970's, a six-wheeler lorry loaded with soft drinks ran out of control on its descent of Exceat Hill; as it left the road on reaching the first bend, it clipped the rear of the loaded scaffold lorry in front flipping that over. It then ploughing on, narrowly missing the large corrugated iron granary which then stood next to the car park entrance, finally coming to rest just into the river meanders. The second involved a large articulated vehicle with a canvas clad TIR trailer, carrying a large number of heavy, used aircraft tyres. Upon reaching the first corner having just crossed the causeway in an easterly direction, it was presumably travelling too fast. The front of the trailer clipped one of the farm buildings and at the same time, the

The old stable block at Exceat Farm severely damaged by a lorry in 1979.

weight of the tyres against the framework beneath the canvas caused the whole side of the trailer to give out, disgorging the tyres and virtually demolishing the whole of the old stables. The driver had loaded the tyres at Gatwick and was making for London, so I leave it to the reader to ponder as did the insurance companies, why he was at Exceat on a cold February evening!

Returning to our imaginary motorist, who on ascending Exceat Hill is rewarded with the finest view of a meandering river to be found anywhere in this country. Encompassed within a magnificent stretch of unspoilt country, this view creates a lasting, evocative memory for visitors to this corner of Sussex. From the summit of the hill the road once formed the parish boundary between Exceat and West Dean, and was shown on an early 16th century map as the 'Whapullway,' meaning a bridleway along which horses can pass but not carts. Here, we will leave our imaginary motorist to continue upon their journey.

Two road schemes were drawn up during the 20th century, which would have drastically altered the appearance of the Cuckmere valley. During 1933-34, the East Sussex County Council proposed to build a new carriageway, leaving the existing A 259 just north-west of the present-day Golden Galleon pub. It involved a new road, bridge and embankment, taking an almost straight course to a point on the existing road a short distance up Exceat Hill from Exceat Cottages, dissecting both the old causeway and the river meanders. (6).

The second scheme prepared during the 1970's, proposed building a new bridge approximately 100-150 metres to the north of the present bridge together with a new road crossing the valley meadows and the Litlington road. From here, it was to have skirted around to the north of the Exceat buildings rejoining the existing road towards the summit of Exceat Hill. To enable this scheme to progress a small area of Friston Forest was purchased. When the scheme was abandoned due to local authority spending cuts, this wooded area was used to create additional car parking for the then new Seven Sisters Country Park. Fortunately neither scheme came to fruition for they would have drastically altered the valley and have left several sections of abandoned highway within the landscape. We shall now move on from the subject of the coast road and delve into the Cuckmere River and Man's manipulation of its course and uses of, including the adjacent meadows.

THE RIVER. The earliest detailed document relating to the Cuckmere is an extract from the Water Court of the Cuckmere dated July 27 1618 and reproduced here together with explanations to assist the reader. *"It ys ordered and decreed that the common sewer* [river] *betweene Brokehole* [Brock Hole Bottom] *and Cessingham bridge* [Sessingham near Arlington] *shallbe made 20 foote wyde in all places wher now it is narrower and that for the doing thereof a scott* [charge] *of 3s.* [15 pence] *the acre ys granted of all the lands lying betweene Excete bridge and Cessingham bridge and of all the freshe* [fresh water] *marshe betweene the said bridge and the sea. Item yt is ordered that a scott of iid.* [almost one pence] *the acre shallbe yerely made for ye cuttinge ye weeds in ye haven* [estuary] *and this to be done betweene maie day and midsomer.*

Item yt is ordered that ye levell [meadows] *shall be measured by Mr. John Deward and a plotte* [map] *thereof drawne and for doinge thereof a scott of iid. the acre is granted."* (7).

This document gives us a close insight of the river in the early 17th century together with some of the issues which landowners and farmers then faced. There are four particular references made which are of interest. In paragraph one, the Court ordered that the width of the river the river shall be increased to a width of 20 feet (6.1metres) where it was narrower between Brock Hole Bottom and Sessingham bridge. This shows that much of this section of the river has been widened by Man over the years, for southward of Longbridge near Alfriston, no section of the river narrows to near twenty feet.

In the same paragraph mention is made of all the freshwater marsh between Exceat Bridge and the sea. The inning, that is the building of floodbanks to enclose a given area of saltmarsh from regular tidal flooding, appears to have taken place in four distinct phases south of Exceat Bridge. These are as follows. On the west side of the river, the northern half of Chyngton Brooks; these would have been protected by a floodbank which still forms part of the present west river bank. Along its southern side protection was afforded by Shepherds Bank, a large bank and ditch running east-west across the meadows, a popular roosting area for herons; these constructions are sometimes referred to as borrow banks as a ditch was excavated to create material for the bank. The second phase of inning would have extended seawards of the above on to what is nowadays the low foreshore. Both phases are of medieval origin, as is the third area of inning; on the east bank and lying between the southern end of the meanders and the sea. The fourth phase we shall discuss later, belonging as it does to a later age.

The second paragraph refers to weed growing in the haven. This almost certainly refers to Eel Grass (*Zostera marina*) which was recorded as growing at Cuckmere as late as the 1930's (8). This was presumably eliminated by a disease which swept through the British population of this plant in the 1930's; (the disease occurred again during the 1960-70's). The third paragraph is of the greatest interest, as this brought about the surveying and drawing of the first detailed map of the Cuckmere valley, carried out the same year, 1618. The original map is kept in the archives at Chatsworth House in Derbyshire, seat of the Dukes of Devonshire; the map in colour shows that the layout of meadows and their intersecting ditches has scarcely changed through 400 years.

During times of heavy rainfall or fast thaws, flooding has been of a regular natural occurrence within the Cuckmere valley and the rivers catchment area immediately to the north of the Downs, where the heavy impermeable wealden clays rely on the Cuckmere for drainage. These occurrences were encouraged by the tortuous natural course taken by the river, which reduced its rate of discharge seaward considerably, especially when the additional effects of tide are factored into the equation. (9). During the agricultural revolution of the 18th and 19th centuries, the Commissioners for the levels decided to improve drainage by realigning sections of the rivers channel. The first improvement was carried out just to the north of Brock Hole Bottom where there existed two short, tight loops in the rivers course; a channel some 450 metres (500 yards) in length was constructed. As to the date of this work, the 1813 ordnance survey map shows the cut in existence as where Gardener and Gream's map of 1795 shows the river

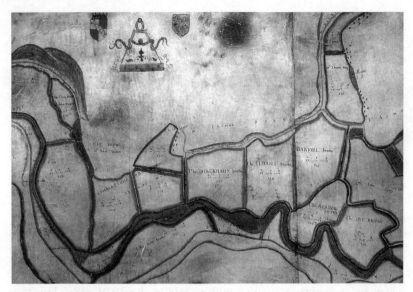

Part of John Deward's map of the Cuckmere levels, showing section between Charlston and West Dean.

still flowing through the two natural loops. After this work had been carried out the former loops became bays which only flooded during spring tides, supporting areas rich in saltmarsh vegetation; (see Chapter 1). During reconstruction of the river bank during 1958, these bays were finally isolated from the course of the river, levelled, and now form pasture.

The second and final piece of river channel alignment was by far a more ambitious piece of engineering, involving the bypassing of the extensive meanders south of Exceat Bridge. The natural course of the Cuckmere involved it travelling a distance of 1.7 miles (2.75kms.) from the bridge to the sea; the more direct, realignment resulted in this distance being reduced to just over one mile. It was also hoped that the improved flow of the river would reduce the build up of shingle within the river mouth. The decision to embark on this work was taken at a General Session of the Commissioners of Sewers for the Levels of Cuckmere on May 21 1846, held at The Lamb Inn, Eastbourne. Firstly the nine commissioners agreed to consolidate the existing three divisions of the Level into just one management unit, and to charge one general scott, or charge per acre for the whole Level.

The scheme agreed upon for the realignment of this section of the river called for the following: an agreement was to be entered into between the Commissioners and the Earl of Chichester owner of the west bank and Lord Viscount Gage, the lessee of lands on the east bank. They were jointly to pay for construction of a new eastern riverbank alongside the new watercourse or river channel, so preventing the entry of the tide into the existing meandering river channel and adjacent lands. They were also to pay for the installation of a sluice at the point where the meanders were to be dammed off from the new watercourse near Exceat Bridge. The works were to be carried out under the supervision of Mr. M. Vidler, who would receive a year's salary of ten pounds. That the existing meandering river channel should become part of the two land holders above named, and that land so inned from the tide by these works should be charged the general sewer rate or waterscot commencing from the next Water Court held one year after completion of the works. To pay for this scheme, a scot of eight shillings (40 pence) per acre was ordered to be paid on all lands on the said levels between Sessingham bridge and the sea. This scot had to be found by the various tenants *"but to be wholly allowed to them by their respective Landlords and to be paid on or before the 24th. day of August next to."*

The final account for the new watercourse dated April 16 1847 was for a total cost of £751-16s-11?d (£751.85). The major item of expenditure listed in the account was for the payments to nine persons (and presumably their labourers), totalling £478 for *"digging and wheeling out"* of 24,809 cubic yards (18,969 cubic metres) of material. The final account went before the Water Court for approval on May 20 1847. (10).

SHINGLE EXTRACTION. A problem which successive generations have wrestled with is the accumulation of shingle within the river mouth or estuary, caused by the continual eastward movement of shingle along the south coast due to the Longshore Drift process. For example, as far back as 1582 when a presentment was made on March 24 by *"Waterbayley"* John Browyn and others stating that *"the haven mought ther dyrun tymes in wynter ys stopped with preble stones by reson wherof the hole levell ys drowned and that we cannot be suffered to cut the same haven up."* (7). Until the construction of a groyne to retain the shingle to the west of the river mouth, possibly sometime between the two world wars, the river would periodically change the point at which it entered the sea. The known extremes of this cycle were 1874 when the river mouth lay half way along the present east beach and 1908 when it lay half way between the present position and the coastguard cottages to the west of the Haven. The river mouth was finally stabilised during the early 1970's with the construction of a second retaining groyne, along its eastern side; (though I suspect Nature will be having other thoughts!). Until the advent of modern machinery, contractors or farmers from within the valley would periodically take action to clear the river mouth using two horses in traces, that is, the horses harnessed in line one behind the other. Their traces were hitched on to a wooden 'box', which was an implement with an open front measuring some 1.22metres (4 feet) across with only one end, and with a metal blade running across the front edge of the floor. At the rear were a pair of shafts which the teamster or carter heaved down upon, so causing the blade to dig into the shingle; the operation was carried out at right angles to the river channel. Towards the closing stages of the operation, care had to be exercised for when nearing the point at which the river was impeded, there was the hazard of the trapped water suddenly breaking through. (11).

During 1932, Cluttons the land agents who managed the Ecclesiastical Commissioners properties, entered into discussions with the Cuckmere Catchment Board who were then charged with responsibility for land drainage within the valley. The Board wished to construct a light railway between a small loading gantry adjacent to the river mouth and an area opposite the farm buildings at Exceat where another gantry and wharf were to be built. The purpose of this scheme was to extract shingle from the river estuary so as to reduce the incidence of shingle impeding the rivers flow, thereby improving the drainage of the whole river system. The plan proposed that once the shingle had been transported to Exceat, it would be sold and collected by lorries for use as aggregate by the building trade. The licence, for a period of seven years was signed on November 17 1932 and involved the payment of a ground rent plus a royalty of a halfpenny (0.21 pence) for every tonne carried by the railway, estimated at between 30-40,000 tonnes per year. During 1936, a new lease was drawn up but never signed which would have allowed for the erection of a washing and crushing plant together with storage bins, to be situated behind the grass floodbank where the present day trackway passes across the bird lagoon. It was proposed that this exposed site would be successfully screened with trees! The operation of the lease was sub-let to A.F. Smith Limited of Hailsham, later known as Sussex Sand & Gravel Limited. The railway was presumably taken up with the outbreak of the war and reinstated again during the late 1940's. (12). Due to a lack of river maintenance during the war years, large shoals of shingle built up within the river mouth, extending for a short distance upstream. These were dealt with by the use of explosives which hurled large plumes of water and shingle high into the air. (13). Tony Hastings, son of the proprietor recalled going to the beach with his father shortly after the cessation of hostilities; the route was clearly defined with stakes as this was the only area cleared of mines at that time. (14).

April 1950 saw the signing of a new seven year lease to a new operator, the East Sussex Transport & Trading Company Limited; this allowed for the working of shingle along the whole beach stretching eastwards from the river. October of that same year saw the Cuckmere Catchment Board incorporated into the East Sussex River Board. The small 'locomotive' used for hauling the trucks along the light railway was powered by a two-cylinder Dorman diesel engine, the trucks often providing transport for the campers staying at Exceat during the summer months! The operation was managed in those post-war years by a Mr. Green with John Clark as foreman. The course of the railway is still discernable in places; it takes a mainly straight course between the river mouth and the present-day main car park - the former shingle wharf. The old metal railway sleepers still show in places, together with the concrete culvert that once carried the railway across a ditch some 450 metres (500 yards) south-east of the car park. On the original plans, it is shown as tightly following the course of the river meanders, but there is no evidence that this route was ever followed. (6, 12).

Ironically by the late 1950's, concern was growing at the reduction in the amount of shingle east of the river, leading to the cessation of shingle extraction. Cliff End itself was now being eroded rapidly by the sea; waves were often topping the remaining shingle ridge during winter gales. The new Sussex River Authority decided that action must be taken to remedy this problem and so alleviate the possibility of flooding and to improve the river mouth. Early in 1959, work commenced upon the construction of a wooden groyne running out from Cliff End in order to reduce the eastward movement of shingle, essential for the next phase of their scheme. The following winter, saw the former light railway re-laid from near the river mouth eastwards along the remaining shingle ridge. This was to enable shingle to be dredged from the river mouth and taken eastwards to replenish the ridge; on at least one occasion the sea strove to wash away the rails! The trucks were loaded by a dragline; the transported shingle was then pushed up into a high ridge by bulldozer. This explains the steep north facing backdrop of the shingle ridge today. These works have led to further shingle accumulating naturally, forming a far more substantial shingle beach than has probably ever existed at Cuckmere. (13).

PAST BRIDGES. Apart from the existing river crossing at Exceat

Bridge, there were possibly up to three other locations where bridges formerly provided a means of crossing the Cuckmere. Certainly during the First World War, a footbridge was constructed opposite the eastern end of Shepherds Bank so affording access by troops garrisoned on the South Camp at Chyngton to their rifle butts or firing range, located on the meadows north of the beach on the Exceat side of the river. The other two possible sites are both situated upstream of Exceat Bridge. One site is at the southern end of the more northerly river loop where the river was first aligned. Judging from old wooden piles which existed until 1958, it was approximately 1.22 to 1.52metres (4 - 5 feet) wide. From this point, a raised causeway still runs eastwards to near Gypsy Corner on the Exceat to Litlington road. The second possible site is situated at a point where another causeway known as Dickermans Walk, meets with the river bank after crossing the meadows from a point along the Litlington road just south-west of Charlston. Here on the lower levels of the riverbank are remains of brickwork which may have been associated with this crossing; alternatively it may have been simply a facing to lessen erosion? (15, 4). These causeways may well have been originally built at earlier stages of inning or reclamation of the valley from the sea.

USAGE OF THE CUCKMERE. Apart from the obvious purpose of being a means of enhancing land drainage, what other uses has the river been put to? The earliest recorded reference to the river in this respect was when John St.Clere, lord of the manor of Exceat died in 1335. Included in his will was *"the fishery of the whole river between Cookemere and Langebrigg worth 18p. per year."* Langebrigg presumably refers to Longbridge situated a little to the north of Alfriston. (16).

During the reign of Charles I, a lease dated June 14 1626 was signed *"by Sir John Gage of Firle, bart., to John Hopkins of Exceate, millar, - in consideration of the building and erecting of certain Water Cornemilles upon his River of Cookmare neere unto Exceat bridge. Also a piece of salt marsh lying to the said mills, containing 2ac."* The lease went on to state that the *"Lessee to defend and keep that parcel of Salt marsh on that side where he had new caste or made the new ditch or watercourse, and so much of the Causey [Exceat causeway] as lieth adjoining to the said new ditch or watercourse."* So it would appear that John Hopkins viewed the area laying just to the east of Exceat Bridge as a favourable site for building and operating a water or tide mill. (17). However, in the Firle estate accounts for the following year 1627 the following short reference is recorded. *"The water milne was pull'd doune."* There is no explanation as to why the scheme failed. (18).

The Cuckmere has been used in a limited manner for the

transportation of several commodities. From at least the late 18th century, coal was brought up the river certainly as far as Alfriston by barges loaded at Newhaven. Listed in the invasion returns for Alfriston in July 1803 are two sailing vessels, *'The Adventurer'* of 14 tons and *'The Good Wife'* of 7 tons, both open decked vessels. These returns listed the population, livestock and equipment such as bread ovens and wagons within each parish likely to be of use to an invading Napoleonic army. (19). During the first half of the 19th century it is recorded that shingle was taken up upstream of Alfriston to Sherman Bridge, (today's A 27 roadbridge). (20).

During the 1920's and 1930's, barges operated by Wilson's of Newhaven were loaded at the beach with blue boulders (rounded flint boulders), which were then punted upstream to a wharf situated near Exceat Bridge; this continued well into the 1930's. There are no records, or vestiges of towpaths having ever existed alongside the Cuckmere. Due to its torturous course and the intimate size of the valley, it is unlikely that the river itself was ever used for the purposes of smuggling contraband as in the case of the larger, swifter flowing Ouse at Newhaven.

At the height of the railway building era, serious consideration was being given to continuing the London, Brighton and South Coast Railway eastwards towards Chatham and Dover. One possibility had been to route it from Seaford via the Cuckmere valley. During the early twentieth century, the Cuckmere Light Railway Company was formed, once again bringing the possibility of a railway running along the valley. (6, 21).

Increasingly during the 20th century the river has taken on another use, that of recreation. On at least two occasions during extremely cold weather local people could recall skating taking place on the meanders; on one occasion in the winter of 1936-37, approximately one hundred people were observed skating on the river between the bridge and Exceat. During the 1920's, Eastbourne College an independent school for boys leased land at Exceat and had built, the large boat house adjacent to the meanders from where they taught sculling, together with holding regattas on the main river. (22). Today this building is occupied by the Cuckmere Valley Canoe Club. The river is also popular with many walkers and bird watching enthusiasts.

SOURCES.

1) Gissing, George. 'Thyrza.' Eveleigh Nash & Grayson Ltd.
2) S.A.C. vol. XCI. p. 164 -172.
3) Highways & Transportation Dept., East Sussex County Council.
4) S.N.Q. vol. 16.
5) pers. comm. Frederick Larkin.
6) Chichester Chapter Estates of West Dean & Friston, management files. Church Commissioners.
7) E.S.R.O. Firle Place MSS. G5/48.
8) Wolley-Dodd ed. 'The Flora of Sussex.' Reprinted, The Chatford Press. 1970.
9) Larkin, Monty. 'In The Footsteps Of Time.' Ulmus Books. 2006.
10) E.S.R.O. RAF 9/6.
11) pers. comm. Albert Reed.
12) pers. comm. John Clark.
13) photographs. Environment Agency, Pevensey office.
14) per. comm. Tony Hastings.
15) E.S.R.O. AMS 5764.
16) S.A.C. vol. 58.
17) E.S.R.O. SAS G Box 13.
18) E.S.R.O. SAS G Box 11.
19) E.S.R.O. Lieutenancy Papers.
20) Ellman, Edward Boys, 'Recollections Of A Sussex Parson.' Reprinted by St. Michael and All Angels, Berwick. 2006.
21) Minutes of Board Meetings. The Eastbourne Waterworks Company.
22) pers. comm. Arthur Haynes.

CHAPTER 4.

THE COAST AND ITS BOUNTY, PART ONE.

INTRODUCTION. The striking coastline between Eastbourne and
Seaford has remained largely unchanged through time
immemorial. In previous times, this stretch of coast with its
sparsely populated hinterland, has provided an ideal isolated location
for smugglers to ply their trade in contraband. However, during times
of storm or poor visibility, the cliffs stood as silent witness to many a
ship driven by storm or steered on a fateful course due to imprecise
navigation, into the shallow waters above the rugged wave-cut
platform. Today there are many more people walking the cliff tops,
once walked by the patrolling 'preventative men' and the occasional
shepherd tending his flock. Smugglers no longer frequent the coast,
though today's Customs officers are ever vigilant for possible drugs or
people smuggling. Modern ships with their vastly superior
seaworthiness and sophisticated navigational aids have meant no
shipping casualties for over sixty years. The sea floor immediately
offshore forms a valuable fishing ground for pot boats working for
crab or lobster and is also a marine wildlife conservation area.

DEFENCE. During times of hostility, the authorities had always
been mindful of the four access points in the otherwise sheer cliffs,
namely Hope Gap, Cuckmere Haven, Crowlink Gap and Birling Gap.
Indeed Friston is recorded as having been raided by the French during
the 14th century; Exceat probably also suffered attention as did
Seaford. From time to time the gaps have had cannon batteries
stationed to protect them. For example, according to a report entitled
"General Defence of the Southern District, February 1798" a battery was in
existence at Cuckmere Haven. (1). During 1806, Henry, Viscount
Gage wrote to the Quarter-Master General Robert Brownrigg, asking
for the associated barracks to be removed as among other things, dogs
belonging to the soldiers chased the sheep of his tenant John Ellis.
Brownrigg replied enclosing a letter from the Barrack-Master General,
Lieutenant-General Hewett turning down Lord Gage's request stating
that Sir James Pulteney had the barracks placed there. Pulteney did
not take command of the defence of this part of Sussex until the

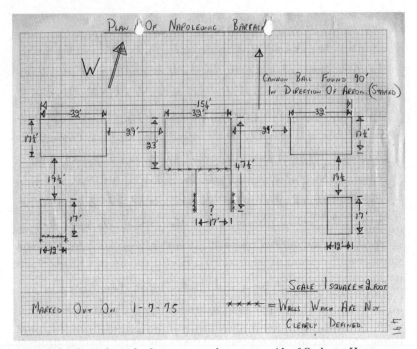

Plan of Napoleonic barracks that were erected on eastern side of Cuckmere Haven; surveyed 1975.

autumn of 1803, making it most probable that the barracks were not built before 1804. Hewett also stated in relation to this particular complaint, the existence of barracks to the west of the Cuckmere and that here, compensation had been paid out under similar circumstances. (2).

In the issue of the Sussex Weekly Advertiser dated September 5 1814, the government was commended for having reduced defence expenditure by dismantling and selling the barracks at Cuckmere and elsewhere. In the issue dated September 19, there appeared an advertisement announcing the sale by auction of the materials by Verrall & Son of Lewes on September 23. Today, particularly during dry spells the site of the barracks can easily be made out some 450 metres (500 yards) northwards from Cliff End at grid. ref. TQ 520979.

BACKGROUND TO SMUGGLING. Smuggling is one of those subjects where most people conjure up a colourful picture of a cottage industry which harmed nobody. This notion has been fostered over many years by books, guides and films giving a false or inaccurate picture; in truth it was highly organised, sometimes sinister and brutal. Another contributing factor to these commonly held beliefs is the fact that most smuggling exploits for obvious reasons, were not recorded. Detailed accounts are in a vast majority of cases, only of occasions where the authorities were successful in thwarting the smugglers or retrieving their contraband. The first part of this section deals with the background to smuggling, followed by a closer look at the practice within the study area. The author is indebted to *"Smuggling In Kent & Sussex 1700 – 1840,"* by Mary Waugh, published by Countryside Books in 1985 for information contained in the following section.

Smuggling arose many centuries ago when the monarchy needing to raise extra revenue, imposed a duty or tax on particular commodities either being exported or imported; the task of collecting these duties fell to the officers of the port Custom Houses. During the 18th century an increasing number of commodities became liable for duty, often doubling or even trebling their eventual retail value. In some instances restrictions were imposed to either protect the security of the nation or one of its major industries; two examples of particular concern for Sussex were iron cannon and wool exports.

EXPORT SMUGGLING. With regard to wool, by the reign of Edward I (1272-1307), the government was far more anxious about the well-being of wool than any other English commodity. Wool was the main source of government revenue and when exported brought in foreign income; needless to say, the government was very concerned about the loss of revenue by the illegal export of wool, known as 'owling.' From 1337, the smuggling of wool out of England became an offence punishable by death but still the trade continued. During 1353, Chichester became one of ten centres within England appointed as 'staples' where wool could be weighed for duty; ten years later a declaration was made whereby wool could be shipped out of Lewes. By the early 15th century the duty on wool had become very heavy. By 1454 wool growers were greatly alarmed by the fall in value of wool, it fetching just over two-thirds of its value 110 years earlier; to rectify this situation prices were then fixed by law. By the Tudor period, a considerable woollen weaving industry had developed in Kent and to a lesser extent in Sussex. After the Restoration in 1660 an act was passed entirely prohibiting the export of wool; two years later the offence once again carried the death sentence. During 1698 the death sentence was yet again repealed, but an enactment was made banning the buying of wool within 15 miles of the coast of Kent and Sussex without a bond. Producers of wool within ten miles of the coast within these counties were obliged within three days of shearing, to account for the number of fleeces held and where they were stored. The owling trade only ceased with the outbreak of the Napoleonic wars.

IMPORT SMUGGLING. Much of the 18th century was marred by warfare between England and France. This had the effect of isolating England from the sources of a number of commodities which affected all levels of English society, particularly the wealthier classes. 'Free-trading' as the importation of smuggled goods was termed, was basically an opportunist trade. During lulls in hostilities, rates of duty would fall due in part to government not having to finance a war; smuggling activity would tail off as commodities become available again. The trade was important to the local economy; during the second quarter of the 18th century the economy of Kent and Sussex was in a depressed state. With farm labourers unable to earn no more than seven or eight shillings (35-40 pence) for a six day week, the prospect of earning up to ten shillings (50 pence) for a nights work smuggling, must have been extremely tempting! Members of society higher up the rigid social scale could also be involved with the trade, they often providing the financial backing and organisation, albeit in a clandestine manner.

The mainstays of the trade were tea, tobacco and spirits; other regular items included chocolate, coffee, jewellery, spices and French fugitives. During hostilities, luxury items such as high fashion, lace, silk, china, glassware and wine were also handled. By 1740 the English had become a nation of tea drinkers, with tea carrying duty at a rate of four shillings (20 pence) per pound. However, it could also be bought for as little as two shillings per pound in Holland and resold in England for a handsome profit. This compared with five shillings (25 pence) for the cheapest legal tea available in the country. During 1784 in a bid to reduce the huge consumption of contraband tea, probably amounting to one third of national consumption, the government slashed the duty on tea from 129% to only 12%. Towards the latter part of the 18th century, tobacco replaced tea as the main commodity being worked by smugglers. At the height of trade in this commodity a profit margin of some ten fold could be expected between the price paid in Holland and its eventual resale price in England. Gin or geneva was also smuggled in from Holland; well over half of all smuggled gin arriving in this country arrived along the coasts of Kent and Sussex. The Board of Customs calculated the amount of contraband gin smuggled into the country during the three years around 1780 to have been in the region of some two million gallons. Some gin was labelled as *"Genuine Crowlink"* and reputedly fetched a higher resale price. Brandy was also worked, often smuggled in at 70% to 180% above proof and then later watered down; although this cut down on handling, it posed the additional problem of requiring a large number of empty tubs in readiness for its resale.

PREVENTIVE ORGANISATION. By the end of the 17th century the Board of Customs had a small fleet of Revenue Cruisers together with a small force of men along the coast. After lengthy discussions between the Board of Customs and the Treasury, a force of Riding Officers was formed. Their function was to prevent the movement inland of smuggled goods which had eluded the Revenue Cruisers at sea and the port Customs officials. Initially 299 Riding Officers were appointed covering 19 counties; of these, 50 officers were posted along the coasts most frequented by smugglers, those from the Isle of Sheppey in Kent around to Emsworth in Hampshire, a distance of more than 200 miles. They were paid £60 per annum plus an extra £30 towards their horse and a servant. On occasions they were assisted by Dragoons assigned from the army.

To tackle smugglers who had evaded the revenue cruisers further out to sea and to check their effectiveness, the government in 1809 formed a Preventive Water Guard to patrol inshore waters. This also had responsibility to giving assistance whenever a ship was wrecked. This new force worked closely with the Customs for the local Collector of Customs would become involved in their cases as he was responsible for receiving and auctioning of seized goods, payment of rewards and conducting the crown's case in court. Attracted by the large rewards Customs officers were not immune to carrying out preventive work themselves; these rewards could create considerable rivalry between the various forces involved in prevention.

The year 1816 saw the establishment of a new shore-based preventative service the Coast Blockade, composed of naval seamen freed-up by the cessation of hostilities. Administered by the Admiralty, initially this new force operated along the coast between North Foreland and Dungeness, but was soon extended westwards as far as Chichester. The existence of so many services resulted in much duplication of effort and function. In 1822, with the exception of the Coast Blockade, the Preventive Water Guard, Revenue Cruisers and Riding Officers were merged to form the Coastguard. Nine years later the Coastguard absorbed the Coast Blockade.

SEAMAMSHIP AND METHODS. Smugglers were regarded as being some of the best seaman in the land. Much smuggling was carried out during the winter months when weather conditions could suddenly deteriorate. Added to this were the dangers of locating the correct landing point often in near darkness and at the same time endeavouring to avoid the preventive forces and possible attack from French privateers. Press gangs were an ever present danger to be avoided when ashore between operations.

The Revenue Cutters which patrolled offshore were of clinker construction, that is, overlapped boards for strength; smuggling craft were sometimes of carvel construction, boards butted edge to edge for speed. Boat builders at Rye and Hastings specialised in building vessels for the smuggling trade until outlawed, the trade then passing to France. Due to an often short working life, caused by the frequent seizures by the preventative forces, some vessels were built of softwood for economy. Some of these vessels could have a tonnage of up to 200 tonnes, armed with swivel cannon and often carrying a large crew. These were formidable craft, especially when taking into consideration that the Waterguard patrolled the coast in small open boats. These large smuggling cutters often took out Letters of Marque so as to operate as privateers thus making their cannon legal.

Crop Sowing. The tubs or 'half-ankers,' in which spirits were transported, had a capacity of 16 to 18 litres (3? to 4 gallons); as the preventative forces became more numerous greater care had to be exercised in their concealment. 'Crop sowing' was practised by anchoring a line of lashed together tubs with a grappling hook and weighting the tubs so that only the last tub floated on or close to the surface. Another method was to lash the tubs so as to form a pyramid sometimes painted green, which would then float low in the water, secured to a grappling hook. These methods relied upon small local smuggling craft retrieving the tubs; tubs were sometimes towed beneath the keel of a vessel to avoid detection if challenged.

Landing Procedure. Smuggling gangs were organised at the landing beach into two groups. Half the gang were posted around the scene of activity to act as sentries and defenders should the preventative forces surprise the operation. Often armed with staves or 'bats' they were referred to as 'batmen,' and were sometimes accompanied by more seasoned criminals armed with cutlasses and pistols. The remainder of the gang would be employed in the actual landing, either from a beached vessel or more likely from several small open boats. The men would form human chains to ferry the goods ashore and on to the waiting pack horses or wagons. Speed was essential to the success of the operation, for the quicker goods were packed and away from the vicinity of the coast, so the risk lessened of being intercepted by the preventative forces. The most probable routes taken from this locality would have been towards Hailsham and thence towards Ashdown Forest. Eventually most contraband arrived in the then sparsely populated countryside south of the Thames, before being sold to dealers from London. Much of it was carried on pack horses each of which could manage in excess of 102 kilos (two hundredweight); these were sometimes clandestinely 'borrowed' from local farmers.

Although a punishable offence, many of the middle classes would not accept that smuggling was an illegal trade. Indeed most of the labouring classes thought the only evil involved, were the efforts by the authorities to prevent the trade. Many of the gentry and therefore the magistrates, considered the penalties more than sufficient. This often led to instances of endeavouring to save the accused on legal technicalities in court, therefore encouraging smugglers to ply their trade in the knowledge that if caught, they stood a reasonable chance of being freed. There was a widespread belief by the labouring classes that the food they would receive in prison, was of a better standard than that offered by the parish workhouse. They would prefer the risk of helping with smuggling rather than applying for relief to the guardians of the workhouse.

SMUGGLING WITHIN THE STUDY AREA. Having provided an insight to the general history and nature of smuggling, we shall now look at the recorded incidents within the study area ; the following incidents have been gleaned from a number of sources and publications. Those incidents dating from 1822 are taken almost entirely from an excellent set of articles dealing with smuggling between the years 1820 to 1840, published in the Sussex County Magazine in 1930. Entitled *"Smuggling In Sussex 100 Years Ago,"* they were compiled and written from Board of Customs papers by Customs Officer Bertram Richards and is a must for any student of smuggling along the south-eastern coastline.

1714. The earliest recorded case of smuggling within the study area was after a French vessel had landed a consignment of brandy at Cooden near Bexhill. Having successfully discharged her cargo, she set sail for Cuckmere Haven where she was due to load wool for the return passage to the continent, but was captured before embarking. The five crew including one Englishman, were fined £60 each but unable to pay their fines, were incarcerated in Horsham prison.

1733. Thirty armed men with ten pack horses laden with tea were surprised at Cuckmere Haven. They held captive the preventive officers from Newhaven, so as to make good the escape of their contraband.

1776, December. The Sussex Weekly Advertiser contained the following item of news: *"Early on Tuesday last some Revenue Officers assisted by a party of dragoons, seized near Friston Mill in this County, upwards of 17cwt. [864 kilos] of tea, nine casks of Gineva."* This mill formally stood approximately 183metres (200 yards) south-east of where today the drive to The Gayles meets the A 259 coast road.

1777, July. The readers of the above mentioned newspaper were once again informed that Excise Officers from Lewes, assisted by a party of dragoons, *"seized near Friston Mill, about 18 cwt. [914 kilos] of tea and four horses."*

1788. Again the Sussex Weekly Advertiser informed readers of yet another smuggling run. *"Early in the morning, Seaford officers made a considerable seizure of tea and tobacco hearing a large body of smugglers laden on Exceat Causeway who were in consequence thrown into such confusion that they rode over one another, and, the better to escape with their horses, cut the girths of their saddles and galloped off without them, leaving the officers in possession of a wagon load of goods which they afterwards conveyed to the Customs house."*

1817. The Coast Blockade was extended westwards, with *HMS Hyperion* moored at Newhaven with her two attendant cutters *High Flyer* and *Viper*, under the command of Captain Mingaye.

1822. During an attempted run at Crowlink, 300 smugglers were disturbed by a preventive man. The gang departed and four nights later the run took place at Splash Point, that is where the cliffs rise at the eastern end of Seaford. Three hundred half ankers were successfully landed with the loss of 63 tubs and a horse. During the same year 100 tubs were landed at Cuckmere Haven, but with the seizure of the boat. Not all the Riding Officers were as energetic as the Seaford officers, Prior, Rippington and Taylor for the following report cast suspicion on the East Dean Riding Officers: *"13-12-1822. - In estimating the extent and value of these officers' services during the last 3 years we have to observe that the only seizure delivered into our charge by John West was made by information (a labourer having found 8 tubs at Birling Gap and reported them to him), and of these taken to Eastbourne three are so insignificant as to make us believe their detention to be mainly attributable to accident. James Woolgar appears to have made no seizures except in conjunction with Mr. Marsh (his supervisor), and the only one brought here was made by information."*

1823. The following is taken from the Sussex Weekly Advertiser: *"Custom House, London, 13-2-1823. Whereas it has been represented to the Commissioners of his Majesty's Customs that between the hours of six and seven in the evening of Wednesday the 22nd ultimo, William Taylor, a Riding Officer, in the service of the Customs stationed at Seaford within the Port of Newhaven, in the County of Sussex, was out on duty and fell in with a smuggler in the parish of Friston, carrying a small cask of foreign spirits, which the officer seized for being run, and detained the said smuggler for upwards of an hour, when three men came up to him and attempted a rescue of the smuggler which the said William Taylor prevented by firing his pistol at them, upon which other smugglers came up and succeeded in getting the first smuggler away having first struck the said William Taylor with bludgeons and otherwise ill-treated him."* A reward of £100 was offered, but was withdrawn a month later without success.

1824. Occasionally, a smuggler at great risk to his own life, would inform upon his fellow smuggling companions to the authorities; the following sworn statement was probably made out of spite: *"James Gibson of Ninfield states that on Sunday, the 1st August, 1824, at about 2 o'clock in the morning, he assisted in illegally importing and landing at Cuckmere, sixty-four casks of spirits or thereabouts, containing about three gallons and a half each of spirits of brandy and spirits of Geneva, that he was one of the seamen employed in navigating the boat that imported said spirits which were taken on board at Boulogne in a boat called the 'Vine,' of Hastings, and by the crew of which sunk in Pevensey Bay, that the goods were taken up by himself and others and put on board the 'Ann' of Ninfield and by her conveyed to Cuckmere Haven where they were landed and part seized by the Coast Blockade, that the principal party on shore that gave directions and assisted in landing the goods were Thomas Freeman of Hoe [Hooe], Sussex, carrier; James Carey of Hoe, Navigator ['navvy' or labourer]; Thomas Maynard of Ninfield, also in Sussex, carpenter, and that the said parties were present when a seaman of the Coast Blockade was obstructed in the execution of his duty, and this deponent [witness who makes deposition or statement] further states that he has frequently heard the above named Freeman, Carey and Maynard boast of having treated the seaman in the manner they did and that the said Freeman, Carey and Maynard were the principles concerned in and belonging to said goods."* Nothing came of this affair, as the injured seaman, a quartermaster, had left the service and could not be traced. Gibson was obliged to leave his home for fear of assault or worse, and applied to be employed in the customs at Newhaven or 'kept in pay as a ten shilling man.' The request was turned down and Gibson drifted to Hastings and continued in smuggling.

1824, September 28. The Coast Blockade boat stationed at Crowlink captured a punt called the *'Try'* of Hastings, in the act of discharging tubs near Cuckmere Haven. The crew of the punt escaped on board the *'Robert'* of Bexhill which was assisting. Two of the smugglers turned informers and it transpired that the two boats were attempting to land 24 half-ankers containing foreign spirit.

1824, September 29. The Customs were in action yet again, as is related in the following short report by the Collector of Customs: *"29-9-1824.-A run of smuggled goods was effected this morning near Seaford, but from the enquiries we have every reason to believe the quantity is small, the goods having been previously sunk. Richard Prior, the Riding Officer at Seaford, having heard firing on the coast about 3 o'clock, immediately proceeded inland, taking with him two of the 12th Lancers, and at 5am. in the parish of Jevington, succeeded in securing six casks of spirits with a horse and cart. The driver observing the officers approach, made his escape across the hedges, etc., so as to prevent his being captured. The name on the cart was 'James Sharwell, Herstmonceux, Sussex.'"*

1825, September. The following statement was made by one Cornelius Mahoney, a seaman from HMS Hyperion, who was stationed at the Crowlink Watch House as part of the Coast Blockade, and gives a detailed example of smugglers attempting to bribe a member of the preventative services in order to secure a safe passage for their contraband. *"On the fourth of September, 1825, I was posted as sentinel on duty at the point near the mouth of Cuckmere Haven when two men came up to me. One of them, who has since called himself John Clare, laid money on the bench desiring me to pick it up. I told him I did not want it. The two men then sat down for some little time underneath the cliff when John Clare put on a lump of chalk £20 and pointing to it said there should be twenty pounds for me, a horse and cart in readiness to carry me to what part of the country I pleased admitting I allowed them to work tubs, asking me at the same time which was the most convenient spot for that purpose. I replied I could not give them an answer but would endeavour to be there on the following afternoon. John Clare put his hand to his breast declared he would be as good as his word if I proved jonnick [staunch]. When on the point of leaving me his companion, David Dennis, took a yellow purse from his pocket and shaking it at me exclaimed, 'Here it is.' On being relieved I immediately reported what had occurred to my officer, Lieut. Pratt, who reprimanded me for not securing their persons and bringing them to him. By order of the lieutenant I took my station on the following day nearly at the same place where I had before been met by the men in question, my petty officer, James Long, keeping himself some little distance from me. I had not been long there when I saw the before-mentioned John Clare accompanied by a young woman, but on seeing me the latter drew back. John Clare and myself entered into conversation when he repeated what I have before asserted. I was upon the point of arresting him, agreeable to the orders I had received, when my petty officer, James Long, came forward and obliged him reluctantly to go with us to the lieutenant. On our way thither we met the man who was with him the day before, David Dennis, and I acquainted James Long of it, who compelled him to go also. John Clare, by the way, called me a rogue."*

The following is a statement made by Lieutenant Pratt of HMS Hyperion, who was superintending the Crowlink station: *"On the two men John Clare and David Dennis being brought to me the former made the following representation. He was on the beach when Cornelius Mahoney first spoke to him by asking if he could give him a chew of tobacco. He said he had none, but threw him down some coppers, which Mahoney refused saying that was not what he wished for, his object was to leave the service as he did not like his employment. He (Clare) then said he would not mind giving him twenty pounds if that would do him any good. As I considered this representation of John Clare's to be almost a direct corroboration of the statement made by Mahoney I detained them at the Watch House."*

Two other seamen continued the story, the first stating: *"While I was on duty as sentinel over John Clare and David Dennis I heard the former say to the latter, 'We must stick to one story when the governor comes, and mind we say I was out for a little pleasure with my daughter when you joined us; if we started when my daughter waved we should have been alright.'"* The daughter was presumably trying to warn her father of the presence of James Long. The second seaman related the following conversation: *"Being on duty as sentinel over Jno. Clare and David Dennis the former asked me what was the punishment for attempting to bribe. I made answer I thought the penalty was three or four hundred pounds or transportation for five years, on hearing which, the said John Clare shrugged up his shoulders."* Upon further questioning, it emerged that John Clare was landlord of The George Inn at Hailsham; David Dennis's widowed mother kept The Grenadier also in Hailsham. Incidently, The George Inn was a hostelry where conveyances could be hired, and where the local Petty Sessions were held in two rooms upstairs!

Later in the same month, September, the Coast Blockade stationed at both Crowlink and Cuckmere were again reporting action against smugglers: *"Cuckmere, 26 Sept., 1825.- I have to acquaint, for the information of the Honourable Board of Customs, that yesterday morning about nine a.m. a hog boat was seen close in shore near Crowlink in the act of picking up tubs, when Lieut. Pratt, there stationed, proceeded to the spot and conceiving that the said boat intended to carry away the tubs for illicit purposes he caused some muskets to be fired over her upon which she desisted and stood out to sea, and Lieut. Pratt found 29 half ankers of foreign spirits floating in the surf, which he accordingly seized. Observing her afterwards make another tack towards the land I launched my galley and succeeded in getting near her as I believe before the crew were aware of my boat having been launched, there being considerable surf at the time. The vessel proved to be the 'John', of Shoreham, commanded by Thomas Vincent, a notorious smuggler, who has lately had a vessel seized from him for smuggling at Shoreham. I found on board of her 17 half ankers of spirits, the greater part with slings and evidently newly cut from a raft rope. I thought the circumstances warranted me in detaining the said 'John' and her crew consisting of three persons until I had laid the case before my commanding officer, Lieut. Edwd. Chappell. As upon mature consideration he is of opinion that there is not sufficient evidence of the smuggling intent to procure a conviction against these men he has directed me to liberate them and to restore the vessel. I have accordingly done so. But we are of the opinion that the 'John' never intended to deliver up the 17 tubs if they could have conveniently escaped with them, and therefore trust that the Board will resist any application for reward which may be made by Thomas Vincent or any other person on behalf of the 'John.' I am fully persuaded that this boat is connected with the tub boat that was frustrated in endeavouring to land the tubs, an attempt to that effect having been made three nights previously near the same part of the coast. -C.W. Poynter, Lieut."*

Later that same year, Thomas Vincent did apply for the reward on behalf of himself and two fellow crewmen: *"Shoreham, 19 Dec., 1825. On the morning of 24th September last, about a mile from the shore and a little to the eastward of Cuckmere Haven, I fell in with some casks of spirits. In getting one on board I immediately hoisted it to the masthead as a signal to the officers of Customs and Blockade on shore and then proceeded to pick up the remainder floating near the boat. The Lieutenant of the station at Cuckmere with his boat's crew then put to sea. I bore towards them, and on his boat coming alongside, stated that I had picked up 17 tubs including the one at the masthead, upon which he took charge. I was informed that between 30 and 40 more casks were picked up at the same time by the blockade in consequence of the signal I had given..."* The Board of Customs after considering their application for salvage duly turned it down.

1826. For the second time within a year, we read of a Coast Blockade seaman within the vicinity of Cuckmere Haven having been approached with the intention of bribing him. It involved one Patrick Brien of Bantry, County Cork, Ireland, a seaman from HMS Hyperion. His statement is as follows: *"That on the morning of Sunday 9 July, 1826, he was doing duty as a patrol, at a place called Hope Gap, near Cuckmere Watch House in the Parish of Seaford, in the County of Sussex, and between the hours of six and seven o'clock, he observed a man on the rocks, apparently employed in collecting shell fish; that after the lapse of about half an hour, the same man came towards the place where deponent was stationed, and after bidding good morning requested a bit of tobacco, to which deponent replied that 'he had none and did not use it.' The man then remained looking down the Gap Way and observed, 'That is a good place for working a boat,' and deponent answered 'Yes!' The man then said, 'Damn me, I should like to make a bargain with one of you for working a boat.' Deponent then said, 'Suppose I make a bargain with you, what will be your cargo?' He answered 'It will be all spirits.' Deponent next enquired, 'How much will you give me if I let you work a cargo?' He said, 'I will give you forty or fifty pounds.' Deponent observed, 'You do not appear able to give me forty or fifty pounds,' to which the man replied, 'Never you mind that, you shall have the money directly the boat beaches. There will be a horse and cart in readiness to take you away, and a suit of our clothes for you to put on. We'll put you on the London road and there will be no suspicion of you being a Blockade man,' and requested to know when he could see deponent again on the business. Deponent informed him that he would meet him at any time he would mention, at the same place; to which the man replied, 'It can only be on a Sunday, for if I leave my work any other day I may be turned out of employment,' and added, 'If I come down near the Watch House, could not I speak to you, and I could then tell you when I could meet you?' Deponent observed 'that would be a bad place as it would create suspicion, a Blockade man being seen speaking to one of the inhabitants.' The man then said, 'I often come down here fishing; not so much for that, as to get an opportunity of speaking to one of you. My name is Verrall. I live on Exceat Farm, and if you will give me your name I can write to you.' Deponent enquired by whom he could send a letter, and Verrall replied, he did not know; but required deponent to say what would be the best plan to send it. Deponent observed that 'the safest way would be through the Post Office at Seaford.' Verrall then said, 'You had better tell me your name and I'll write to you,' and deponent replied, 'As I find you are in earnest in the business, my name is John Sullivan,' and Verrall assured deponent that he might depend upon having a letter from him before the end of the week; and enquired if deponent could write; which being answered in the affirmative he replied, 'That will be alright, and no one will know anything about it but ourselves.' Verrall then continued to say, 'You know the people at the watering place at Foxes Hole; they know me, and if you leave word with them when you will be on guard I'll come to you.'"*

"And after some other conversation not to the purpose shook hands with deponent and went away. Deponent further saith, that he neither heard, or saw, any more of Verrall for several days, and that in consequence thereof he took the opportunity of being sent to Foxes Hole for water, on the nineteenth of July following, to speak to a young man whose name (as deponent believes) is Shields, and requested him to tell Verrall to have word with him what time he could appoint to meet deponent, and that deponent would then meet him, which Shields promised to do. Deponent further saith that he was again sent to Foxes Hole for water, on Friday the twenty-first July following, and saw Shields who acquainted him that Verrall would see deponent on the Sunday morning between the hours of six and nine o'clock, if it would be deponent's look-out at that time, to which deponent replied, that it would; and Shields said, 'Well, then, if that's the case, he'll meet you Sunday morning at seven o'clock, let it rain, blow, hail, or sunshine.'"

On the morning of the named day, Verrall arrived at the said location and started to go over the agreed arrangements, being unwittingly drawn towards a spot where Lieut. Finemore was concealing himself. Verrall was subsequently arrested and escorted to the Cuckmere Watch House. Whether Verrall was prosecuted is not recorded; in a similar case at Lewes the defendant was acquitted. The defence was that the seaman should not be believed because he had probably fabricated the charge in order to get relieved from land duty, it being usual to send seamen back to their ship under such circumstances to avoid further temptation; seamen preferred ship board duty.

1827. Another run of smuggled goods took place at Cuckmere Haven; this involved about 100 tubs, and although the gang were well armed, the Blockade seamen managed to seize 18 tubs and a boat.

1832. A similar incident again happened in January: *"We have to report that a run of smuggled goods was effected on the night of the 26th ult. at Cuckmere Gap with the loss on the part of the smugglers of a boat and 10 casks of spirits, which were seized by the officers of the Coast Guard stationed there. This run was not made by people belonging to this neighbourhood. We have therefore not been able to obtain authentic information of the quantity of goods landed, about which many different accounts have been in circulation, but the seized boat will easily convey three hundred casks."* This is the first known account from within the locality to record action by the newly formed Coast Guard.

Although several cases of attempted bribery of Coast Blockade seamen have been mentioned in this chapter, no doubt the 'free traders' were rewarded occasionally with runs which 'escaped the eyes' of the Coast Blockade men. In 1839, after the operation had been taken over by the Coast Guard, the local Collector of Customs was obliged to report that: *"Smuggling has increased during the last three years owing to bribery and collusion at Crowlink."* At about this period, duties on many of the items which were the backbone of the trade were greatly reduced, thus making smuggling unnecessary. By the end of the 1840's smuggling was virtually a memory. However, from time to time smuggling has once again arisen due to shortages e.g. wrist watches following World War Two, illegal immigrants or banned substances such as drugs.

SOURCES.

1) P.R.O. WO 30, piece 68.
2) S.N.Q. vol. 17. (1970).

CHAPTER 5.

COASTGUARD - SENTINELS OF THE COAST.

CHANGING CIRCUMSTANCES. In 1856 following the Crimean War during which the Coastguard Service primarily functioned as a reserve for the Royal Navy, its control was transferred to the Admiralty. During the following 66 years the service acquired a variety of different responsibilities laid down in the Coastguard Service Act of 1856. These provided for the defence of the coasts of the Realm, the rapid manning of the Royal Navy in the event of war or emergency, and the protection of revenue (smuggling). Other duties were to include assisting vessels in distress, operating life saving apparatus, assisting the lifeboat service, taking charge of wrecks, searching for mines and torpedoes lost at sea and various duties in relation to signals, telegraphs, wild birds and beached rare 'fish.' During the 20th century, the service was substantially reduced following the First World War and for the 1923 to 1939 period came under the auspices of the Board of Trade.

CROWLINK STATION. This was situated midway along the Seven Sisters cliffs on the western slope of Gap Bottom east of Brass Point, with Flagstaff Brow rising to its east on which was situated a flagstaff used for hoisting of signals. The site of this station formed a rectangle running back from the cliff, positioned just to the west of the 'gap' that provided access to the foreshore until the first years of the 20th century. It was subject to two leases dated June 1 1822 and December 1 1832, which allowed access to and use of the site for as long as was required by the Coastguard service; this lease was surrendered in 1921. (1, 2, 3, 4).

The buildings consisted of a cottage near the cliff top for the supervising Chief Boatman (a rank not necessarily implying the existence of a boat, as was the case during the latter part of this station's life from about 1880), with an adjoining watch-room and living quarters for a man. At least in its latter years, it appears to have been painted black and was bounded on the seaward side by a low white-washed wall until about 1890. At the beginning of the 20th century, cliff falls took away part of the building and the remainder was demolished, the materials being re-used in East Dean. This ceaseless encroachment by the sea has been a constant threat to all three coastguard stations along this stretch of coast, Birling Gap having to be rebuilt in 1875 and now its buildings disappearing for the second time. Through the Crowlink station ran the clifftop footpath, which was waymarked along its entire length from Beachy Head to Seaford by the placing of small heaps of chalk at regular interval, thus enabling the coastguards to follow the path during the hours of darkness. Where the clifftop footpath passed through the station it was flanked on either side by tamarisk hedges. (4).

To the north of the footpath and facing eastwards, was a white-washed block consisting of three double cottages containing quarters for six men, (originally a detachment of Cuckmere coastguards). These were subsequently converted into separate quarters for four men; in 1911 they were again converted, this time into three dwellings. They had long gardens running down almost to the floor of the valley. Large tanks which collected rainwater from off the roofs seem to have been the stations only means of water until the early 20th century when a little further up Gap Bottom, a wooden staging was built on which was mounted a wheel and chain pump above a well. (4).

Two occurrences involving the Crowlink coastguards at a personal level are as follows; Boatman John Higgins who served at Crowlink

The former Crowlink coastguard station viewed from the sea; early twentieth century. (Courtesy of Newhaven Maritime Museum)

between 1843 and 1850, was transferred to another station because of his *"wife's misconduct."* The archives do not elaborate on what Mrs. Higgins was so guilty of as to demand their removal to another station! (1). The other occurrence was when the stations senior coastguard, Chief Boatman John Best died; he was buried with full military honours as the following newspaper article (Sussex Weekly Advertiser) recalls. *"On Saturday [June 17 1899] the funeral of the late Mr. John Best, chief boatman in charge of the Crowlink Coastguard Station, took place at Eastdean. The funeral was of an impressive character, naval honours being accorded the deceased. The cortege left the Crowlink Station about two o'clock, the naval escort consisting of twenty blue jackets drawn from the neighbouring stations and under the command of Mr. John Porter, chief officer of Blatchington. The coffin was covered with the Union Jack, and eight men of the Crowlink and Cuckmere Coastguard Stations acted as pall bearers. The mourners were Mrs. Best (widow) and family; there was a large number of friends at the church and by the graveside, and among the many floral tributes was a beautiful wreath from Capt. Somerset, inspecting officer of coastguards, Brighton. At the close of the service three volleys were fired over the grave. Deceased, who had been at the Crowlink Station, was on the eve of promotion and was much esteemed."* (5).

CUCKMERE STATION. The agreement for the use of land upon Short Cliff just to the west of Cuckmere Haven was signed on May 22 1822. (3). The men's quarters or cottages appear to be of a similar design to those at Crowlink, though the Station Officer's house and equipment store are of mainly timber construction. There appears to be no remaining record as to the date of their construction whether from about 1822 or later; the station was closed down in 1921. The remainder of this chapter deals with life at the Cuckmere Station and is taken directly from accounts and interviews given by children of serving Cuckmere coastguards, depicting life during the latter years of the station.

From August 27 1832, Lieutenant Frederick Phillips, R.N. commanded the station until his leaving the service on January 23 1856, a period of almost 24 years service. (1). As befitting a man of his position the 1851 census records show that living with him and his wife Eliza, was their servant 18 year old Alice Pratt. Possibly he left the service on the grounds of ill health for on the following July 1 he passed away. He was laid to rest in the church yard of Seaford parish church, his grave lying close to the organ room on the south-east extremity of the church.

Eddie Ransom came to live at Cuckmere when just six years of age, during the 1890's. His earliest recollection was when on arrival, he and his brother aged seven were told not to play on the narrow strip of land separating the cottage garden wall from the cliff edge. They promptly did so and received the wroth of their father! They did not receive any formal schooling while at Cuckmere but were set work by their mother. One Christmas, he and his brother went carol singing with the aid of a glass lantern down at the bungalow that stood at the top of the beach, in which lived a fisherman by the name of Johnny Hicks. He recalled that after the horses had been used to clear the shingle from the river mouth, the increased river flow often made it difficult for the coastguards to ford the river in their small boat. This was pulled across hand over hand along a fixed overhead rope, this being particularly precarious at night. He also recalled the heaps of chalk, which he thought were placed every 1.5 metres along the cliff top path? When the stations whole company were called out during a stormy night in 1899 to assist in the rescue of the crew of the stranded sailing ship Peruvian at Seaford, the piles of chalk were barely visible in the gloom and the whole crew nearly plummeted from off the cliff!

When the water tanks which collected the rainwater were exhausted, water had to be drawn from Chyngton Farm using a 232 litre (52 gallon) bowser on wheels with ropes for assisting its movement. On one occasion, a dispute arose involving a newly arrived Station Officer named Lamburgh and Eddie's father who was the Senior Commissioned Boatman. The officer was insisting that all routine duties were to be completed before the bowser was taken to be filled. At this, his father insisted on wishing to report the matter to the Area Commander; consequently the officer withdrew his order. (6).

For supplying the following two accounts involving the Jeffery family, I am deeply indebted to Mrs. Margaret Sharpe, grand-daughter of James Jeffery who was stationed at Cuckmere between July 1 1910 and April 3 1918. (1). The first account is by Coastguard Jeffery's son Len who was a keen artist and talented writer; here is his unabridged account of life at Cuckmere during the early years of the 20th century.

"In the early years of this century it was common to find families living on a Coastguard Station. These were generally situated in lonely places, and although the motor car had been invented, there were very few of them about, so you had to live close to your job then, which is how I came to be born at Shoreham Coastguard Station in Sussex, to spend my boyhood in a very small community, rather cut-off from other people. Sociologists would probably describe ours as a "deprived" childhood, but actually we were far better off than a lot of people at that time.

At Shoreham we were closer to civilisation than we were to be at Cuckmere Haven, to which station we had just been transferred when war was declared on Germany in 1914. At Shoreham I can just remember being lifted on to the parapet of the road bridge spanning the railway sidings, to watch the big railway horses that hauled the wagons in shunting operations. We also watched the cargoes of timber being unloaded from sailing ships that came from the Baltic: there was plenty going on all the time.

By comparison, Cuckmere was a remote station, three miles from anywhere and bounded by towering chalk cliffs. Food was scarce in those war years and I think the coastguards were the first to "Dig for Victory" from dire necessity. Ships were being sunk daily, and eventually their cargoes came ashore - cases of New Zealand butter, Chicago pork, dried fruits, etc. Unfortunately the sea water had generally ruined it, but coal and peanuts were among the cargoes which survived in a usable form. One stormy day the beach was littered with bodies of cattle from a sunken ship, and the coastguards had a hectic time hauling their smelly carcasses above high-water mark and burying them in the shingle. Sometimes we found horses and mules as well. One day the tideline was strewn with thousands of bunches of grapes, but all were putrid - a great blow to us children. And there were always piles of bottle corks, which were used for lighting the kitchen range at home: we missed nothing that could be put to use. Todays rubbish dumps would have amazed us, when so much is thrown away needlessly.

As I grew older I had to walk with my two older sisters to Seaford School, being excused for lateness in inclement weather. There were only a footpath, often ploughed-up, and a track across the golf links. Our school-days were governed by the weather. High winds or sea fogs were a danger on our cliff path, and winter evenings entailed either of our parents coming to meet us carrying a storm lantern: The approaching glimmer of this lamp would gladden our hearts as we trudged through rain and snow. Our dog, Caesar, a fox terrier, always came with us to school. He was left with us while his master, an Army major, served in France, but he never returned.

By to-days standards the Coastguard Station was rather primitive. Rain water was piped from gutters to large storage tanks. There were oil lamps and candles and outside earth closets, but at that time and in that remote spot nothing better could be expected. Being a Naval station everything was neat and orderly: hedges trimmed, cobblestones weeded, paintwork and brasswork gleaming. Many people in cities and in country districts as well, lived under far worse conditions than us.

The actual Lookout was a mile and a half up on Seaford Head with a view from Beachy to Brighton and beyond. Many thousands of troops were living in a large transit camp at Seaford, and were shipped to France from Newhaven. Sometimes during ploughing we had to pass through the camp to school, and I remember how we felt scared of the Canadian Indians, Gurkhas, Sikhs and coloured Colonials, having never seen such people before. But they were very *good to us and we often came home with a bit of sugar, then very scarce, or some scraps of meat for the dog. One day I met a Scotsman marching up and down squeezing what I took to be a piglet under one arm, but he was only practising on his bagpipes - another thing I had never seen or heard before. The First World War caused many men to travel out of their own area for the first time in their lives, and even us children were affected to a certain extent, seeing things and people that we would normally not have done in peace time, when life was far more static in the country.*

The estuary of the Cuckmere was a wild, lonely place, frequented by vast flocks of wildfowl and sea birds. We thrived on plover, partridge and gulls eggs in season, blackberries, sloes and crab-apples for jam. Dad would set fish lines and also caught prawns and shrimps. We children scoured the rocks for shellfish, rabbits were snared, and sometimes a hare. It was a survival economy that brought out all our ingenuity. Mum baked delicious scones and bread (I can smell it yet!) and milk was collected in a can from a farm two miles away - not so nice in a howling blizzard! We also gathered piles of driftwood which burnt with a wonderful blue flame in our fireplace. In fact we had much in common with the "Swiss Family Robinson," that classic of life on a dessert island, only the island was England during the First World War.

As the war progressed many ships fell victim to mine and torpedo. Some were salved by tugs before foundering, and beached on sandy parts of the coast, but one I recall, the Oushla, of the Union SS Co., was less fortunate, although not due to enemy action. It was a typical January day, a blustering south west gale, driving rain and poor visibility - often reduced to half-a-mile. The seas were crowding in to the bay, intent on destruction. We children, being confined to the house in such weather, were gazing through the rain-lashed window and saw, between squalls, a large steamer riding light in ballast. She was making heavy-weather of it, and seemed dangerously close inshore for a course down Channel. I cannot recall if the crew were taken off by lifeboat then or later, but it appeared that the Arab firemen were unable to keep a full head of steam to her boilers due to the excessive rolling of the ship, and she lost way and drove on to a ledge of rocks running out from Crowlink. Later, tugs attempted to tow her off, but she was so damaged underwater that she was abandoned and drove slowly up, tide by tide, until eventually she lay under the towering cliffs. I understand that she was bound for Barry, South Wales, to load coal for Malta.

I remember a Sea Scout, Frank Lever, who acted as an auxiliary Coastguard, carrying me on his shoulders out on to the slippery rocks and helping me climb the pilot ladder, seemingly reaching to heaven. She had been armed, and I remember her stern gun being salved: it was unshipped, lowered, hauled along the beach on rollers by soldiers and then up on the cliff top by means of a temporary derrick. She was, of course, stripped of almost anything movable, and was soon broken-up by the sea though for years her engine casings and boilers defied its ceaseless battering. I still have a plane, chisels, a teak binocular box and a tenon saw, retrieved from the Chinese carpenters shop aboard the Oushla.

Although we had long sunny days in the summer when we used to swim out to the mainmast of a sunken schooner projecting some 10 feet above the surface, it is the winters that remain most vivid in my memory. When the snow was deep and we had our home-made sledges out. Once, when the sea breached the shingle bank and flooded the valley right up to Exceat, the waves rolled along behind us, made worse by the fact that they were from an unexpected quarter. The buildings were white with flying foam, telephone cables and wire shrouds shrieking in different keys, smoke blowing down the chimneys, and having to shout above the roar and crash of the breakers as they hurled themselves at the shuddering cliffs. You may wonder at the reference to telephone cables in view of the isolation of the site, but Coastguard Stations were among the first places to have telephones installed, so that messages could be quickly transmitted inland.

Summer was always welcome when it came. Sometimes, if dad was off duty and the weather was fine, he would row us up the Cuckmere River under Exceat Bridge and on to Alfriston, where we would go to the ancient Star Inn and we children would have a glass of lemonade and a lovely big arrowroot biscuit while sitting outside in the garden. This was a treat in deed - not one that often came our way.

One sunny morning I was hopping from rock to rock to get round the Point and climb the steps to Hope Gap to visit a partridge nest containing 20 eggs due to hatch. On rounding the point I came face to face with a fierce looking bullock, its head jammed between rocks and looking most lifelike. I think my dog and I beat all records to leap from rock to rock in the opposite direction. Another time it was a drowned ship's engineer, recognisable by his oily overalls, spread eagled on a flat topped rock, but we got used to such sights as the war progressed and more ships fell victims to the lurking U-boats.

Amusements were few. We read a lot, and had a phonograph. As I grew older I began to take an interest in studying the passing shipping and later to draw the craft on a slate, helped by my dad, who was sail-trained in the Pentland brigs and who had served on H.M.S. Raleigh, a steam frigate. I still have an old oil painting of H.M.S. Terrible, done by a Chinese artist while he was serving on the China Station. Dad was a stern critic of my drawing: no incorrect detail escaping his eye. Christmas, as with all youngsters, was the highlight of our year. We took turns in shouting up the chimney to let Father Christmas know our needs, although they were seldom granted. Our grandfather always came at this time, bringing a bag full of silver threepenny bits to share out. One year he wrote to say he was arriving on Christmas Eve. Dad walked to meet him as usual, but he never appeared, so he came home about 10p.m., thinking that he would come the following day. About 2a.m. our phone rang: it was from Seaford Camp, asking Dad to identify a suspect spy. On proceeding there, he met his father in the guardroom. It turned out that he had come on the last train, lost himself on the way to Cuckmere, and had come across two field telephonists, who promptly arrested him when he asked the way to the Coastguard Station. He never forgot that Christmas, and neither did we.

I only remember leaving Cuckmere Haven once during those war years, when my mother took us to Seaford and thence by train to Brighton. What a day that was, but, oh, the weary walk home in the dusk from Seaford...

What a lot of has changed since those days. The whole pattern of coastal shipping has altered; the Coastguard is now under the DTI instead of the Admiralty and many of the old stations are closed down, while others are manned only in bad weather. I suppose our generation is the last to remember the Coastguard Service as it was, when the men patrolled on foot, meeting their opposite number from the next station. When radio was a new invention and radar wasn't even thought of. Before the motor lorry took over a lot of freights that had previously gone by sea. But not quite before the Flood, although it may sound like it, because all these changes have happened within my lifetime."

The second account is taken from a letter recalling life at the Cuckmere station by Len Jeffery's sister Ethel, and once again paints an evocative picture of life during the First World War for the Jeffery

Coastguard James Jefferys pictured at Cuckmere coastguard station.

children at Cuckmere.

"I believe the top four houses were there first, and the Officers bungalow was built later. It originally was built for a big shed to house the Life Saving apparatus, and then a bungalow was added, to house the Station Officer, and the life saving house (L.S.A.) went on the beach. We lived in the 2nd. house from the top end. A Mr.Russell lived in the first one, with his wife, and two boys, the same ages as Auntie Cis and I. We went to school with them. There was a Mrs. Churcher in the 3rd. house, and Mrs. Fields on the end.

When the houses were first inhabited a donkey cart was used to take the women into Seafood shopping. But we never had one. The Station Officer was a Mr. Curtis when I remember, and his wife was a big Irish woman. There were boys in the family, but their names I do not know.

The only thing I do remember, was when the son, Alec, a Sea Scout, who lived with the other sea scouts in an army hut at the bottom of the path, accidentally shot himself. One scout had to stand watch with the Coastguards, and act as messenger for them in the lookout hut on Seafood Head. This night, the Coastguard slipped home for some reason, leaving the boy alone. He picked up the revolver, (which the man should have had with him), and when looking down the barrel, it went off and shot him in the forehead, and killed him.

I remember his funeral, and the other scouts walking behind the coffin, to Seaford, I suppose!! The Coastguard was sent to another station. An old lady (to us!!) lived in a wooden bungalow, on the top of the beach. She always dressed in black and wore mittens. She sold teas in summer, and minerals, sweats and chocolate. Les and I used to search for the choc wrappers, and smell them, and enjoyed that as though we were eating them!! She had a donkey cart, to go to Seafood for her supplies, and we used to tease the donkey. I believe her name was Funnell.

The houses were originally built with two families to each house. The stairs went up, side by side, with a dividing wall, to the top rooms, from the porch. There were three roms up, and three down, and Mum said when we went there first, the back bedroom had a sink in it!!

The toilets were in a long line, at the top of the garden, and it was a bit eerie at night to go there, so we had a bucket in the back porch. All rubbish and sewerage went over the cliffs and there were rubbish heaps at the end of each garden, which were divided by fences.

At first there were several children, the two Russell boys, May Curtis, and her brother Alec, and Cis, Les and I. We used to have our dinner in school, and when it was winter, went over the road to a bakers shop [bombed during World War Two and now where the post office is situated], where a Mrs. Funnell sold us cups of soup or cocoa! Our dog "Caesar," used to come to school, and lay on the mat in the hall, and share our lunch!! He was a good watch dog, and guardian!! The soldiers in Seaford camp used to give us chocolate over the fence, where we had to walk past, on our way home.

In the end it was decided that no children would live at the Station, so we were moved back to Kingston-by-Sea, Shoreham, where the eighth child was born, John.

There was a long rowing boat, used by the Sea Scouts, moored on the river, at the end of the long bank. We had a small one, also, and Dad used to row us up the river to Exceat Bridge, the nearest shop!! Sometimes he took us out to sea, on calm days.

When babies were born, a nurse had to be fetched from Seaford, and you can imagine, most of them were delivered by a neighbour, before she arrived!! The vicar from Litlington used to come out to christen them, in the Watch Room; he also held a Sunday afternoon service there, once a month. Mrs. Curtis played the organ! Another outstanding event was when an airship sailed up the Valley enroute to Cardington base..."

On one occasion Coastguard Jeffery and his colleagues had to put to sea in their open boat, it being a very dark night with no stars or coastal features to navigate by. After some considerable time his wife became concerned by the length of their absence; despite there being a wartime blackout in operation she decided to light a fire to act as a beacon in case they were experiencing difficulties. This action was to arouse a lot of concern from the authorities, she having broken the blackout regulations, but the men insisted that but for her action they would never have found their way back.

In connection to the references to Sea Scouts, the following facts were related to the author by Sidney Page, who was born in 1898. During the Christmas period of 1914 he spent time attached to the coastguards at the Cuckmere Station and the following Christmas at the Blatchington Station at Seaford; these periods of duty lasted for a month. He was a Patrol Leader in the Senior Scout Troop of Tottenham County High School in London. Their duties included patrolling the cliffs from Cuckmere to Seaford Head and logging shipping movements, sometimes at night; during one night patrol he was fired upon by a sentry!

The last sketch of life at the Cuckmere Station comes from an interview with Bill Gerrard. During 1919, his father was transferred from Christchurch, Hampshire and served at Cuckmere for some 18 months, probably until the station was closed down in 1921. There were four coastguards in addition to the Chief Officer Mr. Ayres, who later retired to Seaford. Just prior to the Gerrard's arrival at Cuckmere, the wooden bungalow on the beach was wrecked by the sea. During their time there items of value washed ashore, known as flotsam, included tallow and candles. Through the winter period, Bill

Sea Scouts from Tottenham County High School at Blatchington coastguard station, Christmas 1914-5.

and his sister might pick up as much as 400 - 450 kilos (eight to nine hundredweight) of sea coal for use at home.

Bill walked to school in Steyne Road, Seaford a distance of some 1? miles. On one occasion he arrived at school thoroughly soaked, upon which he was told he must return home and get dried out! After this incident his father said that he need not set off for school in future if it were raining heavily. Sometimes he would play truant from school and relied upon soldiers who were still billeted at the Seaford Camp until the 1920's, to inform him of the correct time. This worked well until one day he was given the incorrect time; his father who was on duty that particular afternoon and saw him arrive home too early!

SOURCES.

1) P.R.O. ADM 175.
2) Church Commissioners Chichester Chapter Estates of West Dean & Friston management files.
3) P.R.O. CUST 42 piece 66.
4) E.S.R.O. AMS 5764/13. Notes by Richard Gilbert.
5) E.S.R.O. PAR 345 1/5/1.
6) Newhaven Historical Society, vol. 134.

CHAPTER 6.

THE COAST AND ITS BOUNTY, PART TWO.

The precipitous chalk cliffs between Seaford and Eastbourne, which lie diagonally across the path of the prevailing south-west winds, have posed particularly for sailing ships, a navigational hazard often of woeful consequence. These cliffs have stood silent witness to the demise of many a ship due to storm, fog, navigational error, un-seaworthiness, enemy action or a combination of several of these reasons. The remnants of the former extent of the cliffs, consisting of a gullied, sombre-coloured chalk wave-cut platform which extends seaward from the present-day cliff-line has, aided by its accomplice the sea, often made rapid work of dashing to pieces the once proud wooden hulls.

Many seafarers have perished often in dark, cold, wet and terrifying circumstances; others were sometimes more fortunate, having been helped by the local inhabitants as is borne out in many of the following accounts. There appears to be no evidence of the practice of 'wrecking' in the sense of the deliberate luring to destruction by the placing of lights as was sometimes practiced elsewhere. Given the opportunity however, once a ship had fallen prey to the rocks and watery waste, the local population often wasted no time in filching or by outright plundering of ships timbers, fittings or cargo. It has to be remembered that the local populace often lived an impoverished existence, so the opportunity of any gain be it of a financial or material nature, was not missed hence the title of this chapter. Later with coming of mechanical propulsion and the establishment of the Coastguard Service these opportunities have virtually disappeared.

The following list of shipping casualties is without doubt incomplete in respect to the earlier centuries but does give a vivid insight of what this often, wild coastline could inflict upon seafarers. Out of necessity it includes the whole of the coastline from Seaford Head eastwards to Birling Gap, partly because some of the locations are rather imprecise and secondly, it will be of greater interest to the reader rather than stopping at an arbitrary line midway along the

Seven Sisters - this name first appearing in print in the Mariners Almanack of 1589. By today's standards the tonnage or size of many of these ships appear rather small. The vast majority of coastal shipping throughout the 18th century was of the order of 20-50 tons. By 1820 the largest vessels were nearer 100 tons. Generalising in respect to foreign-going ships, the larger proportion of this class of shipping lay in the area of some 100-200 tons until the early 19th century. The exceptions to the above would be the larger man o'wars, specialised ships of the East India Companies and in the case of our study area, the Spanish register ships all of which were of between 400 and 1,000 tons. (1).

1563. name unknown.

During November 22, a ship of unknown nationality was wrecked at Birling 'Gate' with the loss of nine of the 17 man crew. Approximately a dozen partially empty hogsheads (each having a capacity of 239 litres, 52? gallons) of wine were salvaged, but the contents were contaminated with seawater. A quantity of rope, hawsers and an anchor were also salvaged. One of the salvers was a Richard Bray of Jevington. (2).

1617. name unknown.

A wooden vessel carrying a cargo that included silver came ashore *"at Burlingate, in parish of East Dean."* The wreck was the subject of a dispute between the owner of Birling Manor and the Lord Warden of the Cinque Ports concerning the right to salvage. (3).

1702. name unknown.

A Dutch ship was wrecked at Birling Gap, her cable and cordage was valued at £20. (3).

1702. LISBON EAST.

Customs' records list the wreck of the Lisbon East at Birling Gap on June 29. She was on passage with a cargo of wine; a quantity of brazil wood was also removed from the ship. (3).

1702. JOHANA.

From the Customs' records once again, is recorded the wreck of the Dutch ship Johana, driven ashore at Birling Gap on October 2, whilst being pursued by a privateer. Her cargo was recorded as being 250 barrels of brandy, 62 of which had been damaged. During November, a quantity of walnut timber was also removed from her. (3).

1726 name unknown.

The Compton Place Muniments record the wreck of a ship of 200 tons during the month of December, bound from France for the Norwegian port of Bergen with a cargo of salt, wine, brandy and fruits. Three of the 12 crewmen died. (3).

1735. name unknown.

The Compton Place Muniments; the wreck of a ship of approximately 150 tons, laden with a cargo of French wines homeward bound from Bordeaux to Lubeck, occurred during April. About 150 hogsheads were salvaged at Birling Gap and Crowlink and more were recovered elsewhere along the coast and handed over to the Customs. (3).

1736. name unknown.

The Compton Place Muniments; yet another ship being wrecked at Birling Gap, during the month of November. The ship which was Dutch was carrying a cargo of salt, Spanish wool and a great quantity of silver, upwards of 30,000 Spanish coins of which two thirds were recovered by the Bourne [Eastbourne] Customs Officers and soldiers, and taken to the Newhaven Custom House. This source records that the ship was on passage from Cadiz to Amsterdam, and had formally been a man o' war in the Americas. (3).

1741. name unknown.

The Compton Place Muniments record a letter from Mr. Nicholas Gilbert of Birling Manor, to the Earl of Wilmington dated January 17 1741. This concerned the salvage of *"a great number of Tubs of Butter some Tallow and raw Beef Hides taken up this morning in the Manor of Bourne (which are supposed to be part of the cargo of a ship that was wrecked last night in the Manor of Birling)."* None of the crew was thought to have survived. (3).

1741. name unknown.

The Compton Place Muniments; a Dutch vessel was wrecked at Birling Gap during the month of November. The ship was carrying a cargo containing cotton and silk, presumably from the Dutch East Indies. (3).

1742. name unknown.

The Compton Place Muniments record the wreck of yet another Dutch ship, during the month of December; this ship being from Amsterdam and on passage from Bordeaux laden with 600 hogsheads of wine. Eight of crew were saved. (3).

1747. ST.PAUL.

On May 21, the 'snow' (a type of sailing brig) St.Paul, under the command of Robert Ragg on passage from London to Virginia, was at about 8am unexpectedly pursued by a French privateer that had probably been laying in wait within Cuckmere Haven. This action was witnessed by the Seaford Custom House boat commanded by Thomas Ferguson, accompanied by five crewmen, and also by two fishing boats. These three boats on seeing the situation unfold, sailed to the assistance of the St.Paul and managed to tow her on to sand lying just offshore within the Haven, so preventing the Frenchman from seizing her. On seeing the French sloop launch a boat containing 23 men, the crew of the St.Paul took to their boat and one of the fishing boats, and made for the shore. The ship, complete with a cargo estimated as being worth £20,000, was then boarded by the French; they were however, unable to refloat her. By this time, local people had begun arriving on the shore and having procured firearms, managed to pin down the boarders with musket fire, they soon receiving further shot and powder from Seaford. Meanwhile, watching upon the neighbouring cliff-top, a small group consisting of Charles Harrison, Jurat and J.P. of nearby Sutton, John Diplock, commander of the Seaford Custom House and Robert Ragg master of the St.Paul, encouraged the defenders on the shore, now aided by a one-pounder canon. Later, Robert Ragg went down to the men along the beach, and struck a deal that if they could retake the ship, he would hand them a £1,000 reward. (4).

Under a hail of covering fire the three small English boats made their way back towards the ship; the French privateer with an attached hawser was desperately trying to re-float the stranded St.Paul. With the approach of the three small boats, the French commander decided to cut free abandoning his 23-man boarding party to the triumphant English. Later, the St.Paul was re-floated and sailed on to Portsmouth under the temporary command of Thomas Ferguson. The reward was later handed over by Charles Scrase (Town Clerk of Seaford?) to Diplock and Harrison, who upon receiving the reward kept almost £365 for their selves. The remainder of the shore party disputed the disparity of the reward, pointing out that neither Diplock or Harrison, had actually assisted in the retaking of the ship. (4).

In a statement made later by Diplock, he claimed that *"when arriving on board the vessel, a dozen men were drunk, gunpowder was in evidence with a match, and a hauser for the use of towing the St.Paul free was cut by a Seaford fisherman, George Woolgar, and thought this was for the purpose of plundering the stranded ship, for which the local working classes were notorious."* Over half of the 88-man force was of local people; the three West Dean inhabitants involved were two shepherds, John Herriot and Nicholas Swailing together with William Read, a labourer. All were paid the sum of five pounds for *"assisting in firing small arms at ye harbours mouth."* (4).

1747. 'NYMPHA AMERICANA', alias NUESTRA SENORA DE LOS REMEDIOS.

The loss of the *"Nympha"* is the most illustrious shipwreck to have occurred along the entire Sussex coast; as such this saga is related at length. The only other contender being the wrecked Dutch East Indiaman Amsterdam, that ran aground westwards of Hastings in 1749. The story commences in London on March 15 1745, when one Robert Denham appeared before the Commissioners of the Office of the Lord High Admiral, to obtain Letters of Marque in respect of four ships, one of which was to be captained by himself. (5). The definition of a 'Letter of Marque' is: a licence to fit out an armed vessel and employ it in the capture of merchant shipping belonging to the enemy, the holder of the letter of marque being called a privateer or corsair, and entitled by international law to commit against the hostile nation acts which would otherwise have been condemned as piracy. This law originated during the reign of Queen Anne, when a Royal Declaration was made in June 1702 authorising the giving of such powers by the Lord High Admiral of England.

Background. The four ships referred to above were:

'King George' of about 500 tons burthen, crewed with 300 men, commanded by one George

Page from the Royal Privateers' Letter of Marque relating to Commodore George Walker's ship, the 'George.'

Walker; she was armed with 26 guns, 120 barrels of powder and 200 rounds of great shot.

'Prince Frederick' of about 480 tons with a crew of 300, commanded by Hugh Bromedge and armed with 30 guns, 90 barrels of powder and 200 rounds of great shot.

'Duke' of about 300 tons with a crew of 150 men, commanded by Edward Dotten, and armed with 20 guns, 50 barrels of powder and 200 rounds of great shot.

'Princess Amelia' of about 250 tons with a crew of 100 men, commanded by Robert Denham and armed with 26 guns, 30 barrels of powder and 100 rounds of great shot.

This squadron was to be led by the above mentioned Commodore George Walker, and was collectively known as the 'Royal Family Privateers' due to the fact that its ships all carried names of royal personages. All four ships were laying at Bristol and were victualled for a 12 month voyage; all 850 crewmen were each to be armed with small arms and cutlasses. The squadron was owned and financed by a group of City of London merchants principally, Israel Jelabert, Parnell Nevile, John Casamajor, Edmond Ironside and Valence Commyns. (5).

Privateers were particularly well provisioned, with crews enjoying relatively agreeable conditions unlike the primitive conditions and degradation that existed upon ships of the Royal Navy. The ranks were mindful in their service, for it was in their own interest to protect both ships and cargoes, as by law they stood to receive a substantial portion of the value of any captured ships and cargoes. The prestige of Walker and this squadron was very high, for during the summer of 1745 off Louisbourg, it had taken an enormously rich prize that after deduction of the owners share, had yielded £850 to each and every seaman, and to the officers in proportion. The result was that for the forthcoming voyage far more men came forward than were required, so consequently the ships were better manned than usual. (6).

Events Leading To Capture.

During the first weeks of the 1746 voyage, a French ship the 'Postillion d' Nantz' of 90 guns was seized by Commodore Walker; she was taken after being pursued close to shore in the Bay of Saffia, on the Barbery Coast of Morocco. After her capture, she was renamed the 'Prince George' and became the fifth ship of the squadron, acting as its tender. Meanwhile, the 'Princess Amelia' was sailed back to Lisbon, and was condemned as being unseaworthy and was replaced by another ship supplied by the 'Royal Family Privateer's' agents in Lisbon, Messrs. Mawman and Macey; the replacement ship took the same name. These agents were a distinguished house of credit, and

Walker had access to unlimited credit facilities through them. He personally inspected the ships comprising his squadron on a regular basis. They were frequently washed down with vinegar to maintain them in a sweet condition and were always well provisioned with greens, fish, turtle and their eggs, all of which being of fresh quality. (7).

Walker was a cultured man; to illustrate this side of his character on July 5 1746 the squadron called in at the remote Portuguese island of Tercera, and were made most welcome. During their stay, a church was due to have a consecration ceremony and Walker was approached and asked if he had any musicians amongst his ships crews. It seems that Walker was very fond of music and was more than able to oblige, with the following musicians duly being brought ashore: 2 horn/trumpet players, 2 flute/hautboy players who had been in the service of the King of Denmark at Copenhagen, a black drummer, a harpist complete with a large welsh harp (an uncommon instrument in those days), 3 violinists, one of whom was considered the second best in the whole of England. After practising together in the church accompanied by the church organ, the dignified event was carried off with unexpected flair! (7).

For intelligence, Walker employed a spy who travelled overland to the Portuguese port of Faro, which lay relatively close to the major Spanish port of Cadiz, so gaining knowledge of Spanish shipping movements. Walker elaborated on this by purchasing a small sloop his sixth ship, naming her the 'Prince Edward' which made a weekly passage to Faro from Lisbon, she also acting as a tender to the squadron. It was she that brought news that two Spanish register ships were due to sail from the Bay of Cadiz on February 14. Register ships could be likened to English East Indiaman ships, that is, their numbers were restricted under direction from the King; the ships were named as being the St.George and the Nympha. Within a few days, Walkers squadron was in pursuit of these two ships, but due to there being light or no wind, he eventually gave orders that the Prince Edward be fitted out with men to row towards the large white sail visible away to the windward, the Nympha. By the following morning the pursued ship still lay some three leagues ahead, that is, in the region of nine miles. The Spaniards fearing which nationality the slowly approaching ships were, decided to capitulate without attempting to fire a single cannon, (this probably being on February 20). (7, 8, 9).

Upon capture, the ship was found to be the 'Nuestra Senora de los Remedios', alias 'La Ninfa' or 'Nympha', built in 1730 and of 539 tons, armed with 29 guns and carrying a crew of 280 men and boys. Her dimensions were as follows: 36.56 metres (119 feet) long with a keel of 31.31 metres (102 feet), and a beam of 9.94 metres (32 feet), with three between-decks. She was owned by Da Manuela Zifuentes y Da Angela de Prado and was under the command of D. Juan Manuel Bonilla having just embarked upon a voyage to Vera Cruz in central America (now Mexico). Her mixed cargo was of great value, it consisting of bale goods such as silks and velvets, foodstuffs including canisters of nut oil, brandy, wines, pepper and citron – luxury goods and essentials for sale in the colonies. However, the item within her cargo which was of the greatest interest was 150 tons of *"quick silver,"* that is mercury, which was being shipped to mines in the Spanish colonies for use in the process of amalgamation or extracting, of silver from ore. This amount of mercury, worth at today's prices somewhere in excess of £1 million, would have been vital for approximately four months bullion production, the backbone of the Spanish Empire. Much to the captors' surprise, they found that some of the lady and gentleman passengers were from a ship the Buen Confeijo taken some weeks earlier and ransomed back to the Spanish while on passage from Cadiz to Buenos Ayres and valued at £60,000. Walker was always very civil to his captors and would issue orders that no personal possessions or jewellery were to be removed from captured ships. In the case of the Nympha, he ordered that great care was to be taken of one particular ladies lapdog, a small spaniel-type dog. He was to show much concern when a monkey on board the ship carried the dog aloft and out on to the yardarms, until tempted back down on to the deck! Incidentally, the second Spanish ship, the St.George was later seized by the Jersey man o' war 'Captain Hardy.' (7, 8, 9, 10).

Events Leading to Her Stranding.

After her capture, the Nympha was put under the command of one of Walkers lieutenants, Mr. Riddle; two days before she put in to Lisbon, her passengers were landed at Belim. Some weeks later, a diamond ring was delivered to Commodore Walker by officials of the Court of Spain, on the directions of the Register Fleet owners in recognition of his care of the ship's Spanish passengers. After being handed over to the squadron's agents Mawman and Macey, the Nympha and her cargo were initially estimated to be worth £160,000. During May, negotiations commenced on arranging insurance for £150,000, of which £105,800 was to be underwritten in London, Bristol and Exeter. Towards the end of the month, Walker was informed that his seamen were to be liable as far as the outstanding £44,000, which would be the amount of prize money likely to be shared between them. (7, 11).

Having received instructions from the owners of the Royal Family

Privateers that the ship and her cargo were to be sailed back to London, Mawman and Macey showed reluctance in carrying out these instructions. Instead, they persuaded Walker to consent to the sale of a large proportion of the quick silver at a lower price in Lisbon. He agreed this conditionally, subject to them receiving written confirmation from the owners in London. The owners response was still however that the ship and her cargo should sail to England. These instructions though arrived too late, for under Portuguese law the announced sale could not be cancelled. After this incident the owners were to place a representative in Lisbon to oversee implementation of their orders. (11).

Eventually, the Nympha sailed as part of a convoy to England arriving initially at Portsmouth, from where she joined a second convoy to undertake the final stage of her passage to London. However during the night of November 29-30 1747, the crew lost contact with the remainder of the convoy. Believing the Nympha had sailed ahead, the order was given to shorten her sails, whereas in fact the convoy was ahead. After lying for some hours under only her mizzen and foresail, they were greatly surprised by seeing breakers upon their lee. Great haste was made to get her top sail set, but to no advantage; at daybreak the crew found themselves stranded on rocks below the Seven Sisters, close to Crowlink Gap. (7).

News spread quickly far and wide of the demise of the Nympha, with many people arriving at the scene of the stranding below Crowlink, to carry off what ever they could or become drunk on brandy and wine from the ship. William Belchier, the new Member of Parliament for Southwark, who possibly had a financial interest in the Royal Family Privateers and the Nympha, *"made haste to the scene with a warrant from the Secretary of War for all the soldiers on the coast to assist him, and as he approached, he met about twelve smugglers with their loading which they abandoned at sight of the soldiers; but next day returned in great numbers to retake it, on which, the soldiers firing, killed two and dispersed the rest."* (9).

News of the wreck was reported a week later in the Sussex Weekly Advertiser of Monday, December 7 1747: *"Last Monday morning very early the Nympha Prize which was taken by the Royal Family Privateer and worth 200,000L. was wrecked between Berlin Gap and Cuck-Mare in her Passage from Portsmouth to London but was not entirely broke to pieces so that a great part of her cargo is saved. There are fourteen or fifteen of the crew missing. Her lading consisted chiefly of Bale Goods and Quicksilver the latter of which is all sunk in the sands but they are in Hopes of recovering it again. She had 5,000L. in money on board which is all saved. She was insured from Lisbon to London for 41,000L. Never was known such a Multitude of People at a wreck before, many of whom were drinking too plentifully of a Cask of Very Strong Brandy, which they found upon the Beach were intoxicated and afterwards perished by Death [not substantiated]. While numbers of others loaded themselves and some of their horses with the Goods that were thrown up by the Tide from the said Wreck tho' there is a party of soldiers sent to prevent so Abominable practice and notwithstanding they have shot one Man dead, yet People will continue to venture."* (9).

It appears that the bottom of the hull containing the mercury, was not located until almost one month later, being found over half a mile westward as supported by an entry in the salvage accounts, *"Reward for finding the Bottom."* (11). The rapid break-up and dispersal of the ship was most probably due to the great storm which swept the country the following day. For in John Wesley's Journal it is recorded that on Tuesday December 1, while on his way to Salisbury, *"It blew such a hurricane as I have scarce known in England, and that full in our teeth, so that our horses reeled to and fro, and had much ado to keep their feet."* Records show that this storm affected much of the country. The supporting report in the Sussex Weekly Advertiser on January 4 1748 states that *"There has been two loads of Quicksilver brought here [Lewes] which was weighed up from the bottom of the wrecked Ship. We are informed that there is a great Quantity lies in deeper water and cannot be got without a diver, for which Reason there is one come down from London, who purposes to undertake it by the ton weight."* Two weeks later, on January 18 the newspaper was able to report that at Lewes, *"There has been about thirty wagonloads of Quicksilver brought to this town recovered from the wreck, and there are several more to bring, each load is valued at near 800L."* (9).

Suspicion arose after the stranding beneath the Seven Sisters, as to the true value of the Nympha and her cargo, as the Spanish had only offered a £75,000 ransom for her. Lawyers brought in to deal with the loss, had after due deliberation of the facts before them, concluded that: a) had the ship and her cargo reached London, it may have fetched more than £105,800, the sum for which she was insured. b) no evidence had come to light of carelessness on the part of the crew, and that no officer on board the ship had taken out insurance against possible loss of the Nympha. c) a quantity of gold taken on board as cargo in Lisbon had been wholly accounted for by the captain after the stranding. It was not until well into the month of April 1748, that the veritable army of men engaged in salvaging the wreck and her cargo was disbanded. Goods were taken either to Lewes or Newhaven. (10).

The following is a selection of the entries within the accounts of the salvaging operation as published later in 1755. (10).

Dec 20 Salvage paid to 40 men at Seaford. £25 10 0
Jan 4 Boats at Seaford. £56 10 0
      18 Bill for Officers at The Tree. [Seaford hostelry] £4 15 6
      25 Boats and 36 men this last week £36 12 0
      31 Seaford boats. £18 0 0
Feb 2 Seaford boats. £27 0 0
      14 Seaford boats. £37 16 0
      Account to Promise to the Boats for their Encouragement for
      getting 1405 boxes Quick Silver. £2 2 0
      Reward for finding the Bottom. £2 2 0
      28 Boats at Seaford. £6 6 0
      Each boat a bottle of Brandy. 6s 0
Mar 14 Boats at Seaford. £14 14 0
      18 Dutton, carpenter, bill for cutting up the decks to get bales
      out & building house on the Battery. [Crowlink gun battery]
      £25 1 0
      22 For a coffin for the Doctor. £1 9 0
      George Sandell, cooper. £7 2 6
      23 Total of 19 farmers at Seaford, [including:] William Standford
      [of Exceat]. £16 5 0
      James Dupree. £88 6 6
      George Allfrey [of West Dean/Friston] £22 18 0
      25 Charles Harrison, Surveyor of Riding Officers. £102 14 0
      27 Boats at Seaford £15 15 0
      28 2 sloops to London via Newhaven. - Charles Cooper, for
      coopering Brandy and Wine. £3 2 0
Apr 2 Samuel Young, for fetching 5 guns and 20 tons of iron and
      putting onboard Old Sweetbland. £1 17 9
      3 Boats at Seaford. £21 5 0
      John Willard, for Officers lodging at House. £65 3 0
      9 Capt. Johnson, appointed Foreman at Crowlink from Dec 10 to
      Apr 6, @ 10s. per day. £59 10 0
      A Horse that was killed. £10 0 0
      28 Mr. Belchiers expenses and horse hire 2 servants, 150 soldiers
      for 8 days. £68 8 0
      2 sloops from Poole to Newhaven for taking
      Wreck goods to London. £138 7 0
      George Dogger, from Dec. 3 to Mar. 3, to guard Privateer and
      convoy sloops to The Downs [off Kent] £550 0 0
      Portuguese & Italian sailors in consideration of Salvage and wages.
      £277 5 0
      50 English sailors hired at Lisbon for Nympha. £432 16 6

2 packers to Lewes to sort, dry and pack goods. £108 18 0

Insurance on £9,100 from Lewes to London (goods). £271 18 6

Still to this day within the neighbourhood are cannon reputedly from the wreck of the Nympha, and a cedar wood chest made from ships timbers that were once part of her. Most intriguing of all is the bottom section of a large wooden ship's hull, located beneath the Seven Sisters cliffs at grid ref. TV 527970 and according to local tradition the remains of the Nympha. A survey carried out upon these remains gives a length of 24 metres; it is of carvel construction (planks flush jointed, not overlapping) and would have been a flat-bottomed hull. They are resting within a hull-shaped indentation of some 42 metres with a width of 8 metres and penetrating down into the chalk wave-cut platform some 1.5 metres. (11). It is generally clear of sedimentation and is accessible during low spring tides by foot from Cuckmere Haven, or can be viewed at such times from the cliff-top east of Short Brow. Nearby, are traces of concreted iron chain and considerable quantities of iron slag, possibly carried within the ship as ballast. Phillip Robertson concludes his survey by suggesting that she is of a later date and that the construction is not correct for a ship of Spanish origin. (11). Peter Marsden of the Hastings Shipwreck Heritage Centre commenting during the mid 1980's, also doubts that these remains are of the Nympha: *"Quite likely to be of 18th century construction; would more likely be of oak if of British construction. This particular wreck's construction - heavy ribs close together, makes it more likely to be of northern latitude origins. Information on Spanish and Portuguese ships built during the 17th.-18th. centuries is very scant."*

There is however, some element of doubt in relation to these two hypotheses' and we will examine these doubts here. Spain transported much of its mercury to the New World in specially strengthened ships called 'azogues,' (azogue: Spanish for mercury) sometimes termed today as 'quicksilver transports.' This type of ship would have incorporated within its design heavily constructed cargo holds low down within the hull of the ship. Mercury which is very heavy and highly subject to corrosion when exposed to the atmosphere, was poured into sheepskin bags and then sealed in small wooden casks. Each cask held half a quintal (that is, contained 51 kilograms or 1 hundredweight) of the liquid metal. Three of these casks (totalling approximately 11 litres) would then have been packed with grass matting into a wooden crate. The royal arms of the crown would have been painted on the lid, the Spanish Crown having a monopoly on this commodity. (12).

These particular ship remains lying below the Seven Sisters would appear to be constructed of perhaps a type of softwood. However the Nympha was built of 'cedar' in what is present-day Mexico; New World cedars are in fact, hardwoods and members of the mahogany family. Within that region, two species of cedar naturally occur; the specie most likely to have been used would have been *Cedrela odorata* commonly referred to as the 'central american cedar' or 'cigar-box cedar.' This is a light weight, soft timber with a distinctive fragrant scent and exhibits a wide range of variation in its general character. (13). What ever the type of timber constituting these remains, it presumably has exceptional rot-resistant properties. Moving on to consider the hulls heavy construction, this aspect would seem to point in favour of the remains indeed being those of the Nympha, as does the fact that the timber when freshly cut, imparts a strong aroma. To finally wind up the story of this ship, it would seem the only way these remains might be conclusively connected with the Nympha, would be for a sample of timber to be subjected to analysis by dendrochronology in order to establish the type of timber used and also to ascertain its age. (As a postscript to the Nympha an unsubstantiated story was that, divers working on the then new Portobello outfall off Telscombe Cliffs during the 1970's, also carried out a dive offshore of these remains. The story went that they then bought a number of rubber hot water bottles in Newhaven, presumably to collect the heavy liquid metal).

1763. GEORGE.

"On Monday morning last [March 21], about four o'clock, a Frigate of 32 guns came ashore at Cuckmere, near Seaford, in a fog; the Crew fired several guns of Distress, which were heard by people at East Dene [probably West Dean?], who went to their Assistance and saved all the Crew, consisting of nearly 100 men, and there were several Women and Children beside on board. This Ship, we are told, was formally a French Ship, taken by us, and bought by the East India Company, who let it to the Government for five years as a Storeship, but having no occasion for it, it was going to be laid up. All her guns, except two, were taken out at Plymouth."

Sussex Weekly Advertiser, March 28 1763.

Two weeks later, the following notice appeared in the above newspaper: *"To be Sold by Auction. At the Sign of the Tree, at Seaford on Thursday the 14th Instant, at Two o'Clock in the Afternoon. [This hostelry formally stood at the junction of Broad Street and High Street]. The Anchors, Cables Sails, standing and running Rigging, with sundry other Stores belonging to the George Arm'd Ship, George Gould, Commander, lately wreck'd under Cliffs near Seaford. The Goods to be view'd till Time of Sale, at Mr. Robert Stone's [farm] at Chinting; and at Mr. John Beans Warehouse, near Seaford."*

Sussex Weekly Advertiser, April 11 1763.

1778. GOLDEN FLEECE.

To have been wounded in battle, to then endure a long sea voyage home to England and that ending in shipwreck must rate as being truly nightmarish, but precisely this was to happen as the following account shows: *"Early Friday morning last [November 27], the Golden Fleece, Captain Duncan, [issued with] a letter of marque, with passengers on board, consisting chiefly of disabled soldiers from America, was wrecked at Berling Gap, near East-Bourne, in this county. She sailed about the 16th of last month from New York, with the above passengers, in number about 40, among whom were two officers, Colonel Trelawny, of the Foot Guards, (whose name we think is in the list of wounded in the late engagement at Freehold Court House) and a Captain. -As the alarm happened about four in the morning, when the greater part of the crew were in bed, many of those who escaped came up from the sea almost literally naked. Common humanity soon supplied this defect, and through the kindness of the officers, and benevolence of some worthy people in the neighbourhood, the sufferers have been amply provided with every necessary. Those who either were incapable, or could not be prevailed upon to quit the ship when she grounded, (which she did nearly at high water) were killed by the falling in of the deck, or drowned in the hold. The number of these was six, and among them a woman with child. One of those who leaped from the ship, is supposed to have lost his life by the fall of the mast, or other timbers, as his corpse was found at day-break with the skull terribly fractured. Three or four were buried on the Cliffe on Friday night: the bodies of the other unfortunate persons, it is expected will be found in the hold."*

Sussex Weekly Advertiser, November 30 1778.

1782. MARY ELIZABETH.

"In the very high wind early yesterday morning, [Sunday November 3] a Swedish brig, named the Mary Elizabeth, Jonas Hjourberg master, from Gottenburgh, to Dundalk, in Ireland, laden with iron and plank, came on shore about a mile to the eastward of Seaford. The crew are all saved, but it is feared the vessel and the greatest part of the cargo will be lost."

Sussex Weekly Advertiser, November 4 1782.

1786. name unknown.

"In the high wind on Thursday morning last [December 28], a Dutch hoy, from Lisbon to Ostend, laden with bale goods, Spanish wool, and raw hides, came on shore, on our coast, near Bears Hide. The crew and cargo all saved, and 'tis thought the vessel will be got off again." [Bears Hide is incorrect, as this was in the Peacehaven/Telscombe area; it should read 'Berlin Gap'].

Sussex Weekly Advertiser, January 1 1787.

"The Dutch galliot wrecked on our coast as mentioned in last weeks paper,

got off, and is now in Newhaven harbour, to be repaired: Her cargo, as we before observed, was all saved, but not till it had received great damage from the salt water, particularly the richest part of it, consisting of fine muslins, which have been since sent to Eastbourne to be washed. The raw hides, also part of the cargo, are lying spread out on Berlin Green to dry and sweeten, where they cover good part of an acre and emit a stench that in hot weather would endanger a pestilence."

Sussex Weekly Advertiser, January 8 1787.

   1788. name unknown.

   "Between four and five o'clock on Friday evening last [March 7], the weather being squally, a ship laden with wine and almonds, struck on the rocks on our coast, near Crowlink Gap, and in a few minutes afterwards was dashed to pieces by the violence of the waves, when every soul on board, one man excepted, perished with the wreck. We cannot say with certainty what nation the ship belonged to, as some report her to have been a West-Indiaman, and others a Dutchman. The man that saved himself being a foreigner, and among country people only, but little information could be obtained from him, he has however been sufficiently understood, to learn that the number of hands on board were twelve, so that eleven perished. On his getting to land, and seeing some persons making towards him, he fled from them like a wild man, but being very feeble, was soon overtaken, and made sensible of the friendly intentions of those who followed him, when he permitted them to conduct him to the house of Mr. Willard, of Berling, where he was put to bed, and had all possible care taken of him. The tide was at ebb, when the ship struck, and the sea, 'tis said, was reddened with the quantity of wine that was staved. The country people being at the wreck, many hours before the officers arrived, they saved and secured for their own use, a considerable quantity of the wine and almonds."

Sussex Weekly Advertiser, March 10 1788.

   The smuggling fraternity soon made capital out of this wreck for the following edition of the Sussex Weekly Advertiser on March 17 reported: *"The ship wrecked near Crowlink Gap proves to be a Dutchman. Some of her cargo has since been taken up and saved, and a great many pipes of the wine were taken off at sea by a light smuggling cutter and carried over to France."*

   "The dead bodies of several of the unfortunate men, who lost their lives in the Dutchman lately wrecked on our coast, have been since driven on shore by the tide, and taken up and buried. Some pieces of the hull of the above ship, have also been driven on shore and taken up, the decayed state of which proves her to have been a very old ship, and sufficiently accounts for her being so soon dashed to pieces." Sussex Weekly Advertiser, March 24 1788.

   1790. name unknown.

   "On last Tuesday night [January 26], a vessel with provisions from Dublin

to London, John Richards master, was by stress of weather driven on shore at Birling Gap. The master and crew were all saved."

Sussex Weekly Advertiser, February 1 1790.

1790. TWO BROTHERS.

The following might be termed something of a tangy disaster! *"On Monday night last, the brig, Two Brothers, Capt. Edward Thaker, from Malaga for London, laden with lemons, was by stress of weather, driven on shore near Burlin Gap, where she soon afterwards became a perfect wreck, being dashed to pieces by the violence of the waves. The crew, seven in number, were all saved; but the cargo was lost, eight chests only out of 600 being secured. Many thousands of the lemons have been since taken up by the country people, as they washed on shore, and sold for two shillings the hundred. The ship and cargo are insured."*

Sussex Weekly Advertiser, Monday, November 8 1790.

1790. ENINGKEIT.

"On the same night, and near the same place, the brig Eningkeit, of Mechlinbourg, laden with salt, was also driven on shore and wrecked. Her crew were all saved; but the ship and cargo were lost."

Sussex Weekly Advertiser, Monday, November 8 1790.

1792. name unknown.

"Another vessel came on shore the same night [Friday, March 16] at Crowlink, near Beachy Head. Her crew, it is supposed, had deserted her and taken to their boat, as no living soul was found on board in the morning."

Sussex Weekly Advertiser, Monday, March 19 1792.

1795. CHARMING SALLY.

The weather displayed the fact that she offers no respect for man or his beliefs, for during the season of goodwill, the following tragedy was to occur: *"In the stormy weather which we had on Saturday night fo'night at night [December 26], the Charming Sally, a small vessel, laden with Indian corn and flour, was wrecked on our coast near Berlin Gap where every soul on board perished, but the vessel and cargo have been saved."*

Sussex Weekly Advertiser, January 11 1796.

"The Charming Sally, the vessel mentioned in our last to be wrecked off Berlin Gap, has since gone to pieces. She was bound from Portsmouth to Rochester, had failed two days, and had on board the crew and one passenger, in all five persons, who perished; and their bodies have been since washed on shore, near Berlin."

Sussex Weekly Advertiser, January 18 1796.

1796. ANNA AMELIA.

Apart from the threats posed by the sea, sometimes the menace could come in an unexpected guise. *"The same morning the Anna Amelia, a Swedish galliot, Gottfried Volcking master, laden with wine, in hogsheads, from Bordeaux to Lubeck, in Germany, was wrecked near Berlin Gap.* [Tuesday, May 10 the Aurora also Swedish, came ashore at Tidemills near Newhaven]. *The crew, and more than three-fourths of the cargo are saved, but the ship is totally lost.*

On Thursday as the wreck was unloading, a number of soldiers from the Barracks at Eastbourne, attended to get a taste of the wine, which they obtained in great plenty from the seams of the vessel, by catching it in their caps, shoes, etc., and from the potency of their draughts, would soon have become troublesome if not mischievous, with their side arms, had they not been prevented by the arrival of a Sergeants guard, who compelled them to quit the wreck and return peaceably to their barracks, which may in great measure be attributed to the judicious interference of Mr. Buckley, of Newhaven, and Captain Bembridge.

On Friday, at the time of high water, when the agents and others busied in clearing the wreck, had of necessity left her, it happened there was a very large fall of the cliff, not less than 10,000 tons of chalk, which must have buried more than 150 people in its ruins, had it fell at the time of low water and when those employed in saving the cargo were at work; as the cliff gave way exactly at the spot where all the spectators were assembled.

The remains of the wreck, were on Friday sold on the beach for seven pounds, but before they could be broken up and removed, there was another fall of the cliff which nearly buried the whole."
Sussex Weekly Advertiser, May 16 1796.

Lloyds' Register records that the Anna Amelia had a length of some 26 metres (85 feet) and a tonnage of 184 tons and owned by Stettin of Sweden. (3).

1797. LITTLE MARY.

"In the fog on Saturday morning last [January 14], the brig Little Mary, of Great Yarmouth John Brown, Master, laden with lumber from Admiral Mann's fleet at Gibraltar came on shore on our coast of Berlin Gap. The crew were saved; but the fate of the vessel remains doubtful." Two other ships were also reported as being in distress locally on the same day. Sussex Weekly Advertiser, January 16 1797.

1797. PTOLOMEUS.

The following account is of heart-rending proportions, and graphically captures the macabre scene. *"Last Tuesday [December 12] the ship Ptolomeus, of between five and six hundred tons burthen, laden with salt and coffee, bound from Liverpool to Dantzic, (to which latter port she belonged) Michael Blanck, Master, was, by the violence of the wind and waves, wrecked on our coast, off Cuckmere, near Seaford. The vessel struck about ten in the forenoon, on a ridge of rocks half a mile from the shore, when the sea made a free passage over her, and soon afterwards drove her farther in by violent lifts, which beat her rudder, and stove in her bottom and lower part of her side; the scene that followed, was shocking beyond description, as the unfortunate crew, were then in a situation that denied them any assistance from the shore, where a great number of people had assembled, but could only witness and lament the horrors which surrounded the despairing sufferers; who every minute expecting that the ship would go to pieces, launched their small boat into the breaking billows, but instantly sunk with three men in it, one of whom was drowned, but the other two recovered the wreck; they next tried the same experiment with their long boat, but that also filled and broke adrift; the main-mast was then cut away, but it afforded no relief, for the extreme violence of the gale, carried the fore and mizzen masts by the board, and completely broke up the vessel, before which six of the crew had perished; the survivors, consisting of the captain and nine hands, clung to different parts of the wreck, and all but one, (who was jammed between a part of the hull and the anchor stock) thus sustaining themselves, till about four in the afternoon, when they were washed among the rocks and saved.*

The situation of the above poor wretch was lamentable indeed, having supported himself by help of the cable, for nearly three hours, the sea beating over him the whole time, except at intervals, when he, in vain, sent forth the most piteous cries for help. But about seven in the evening, at the ebbing of the tide, Mr. Langridge, of this town, Mr. Chapman, of East Bourne, and several privates of the Worcester Militia, in praise of whose humanity too much cannot be spoken, resolved on braving the waves to gain the wreck, and if possible, rescue him from the horrors of his situation; they accordingly embarked on board a raft, and after several fruitless attempts, succeeded; but the miserable man on being relieved, exhibited a broken thigh, and legs most shockingly lacerated. He was floated to shore on a plank, and carried by the soldiers on their backs to Seaford, where he was put to bed, and had the immediate aid of a surgeon, but being almost perished, it proved too late to save his life, for he languished till the next morning, and then expired. His remains, with four of the drowned bodies, which had been picked up, were interred the next day in Seaford Church-yard. The captain and those who had escaped the wreck, attended them to the grave. The distress of those unfortunate men, we were sorry to hear, was to some degree aggravated on learning that part of their clothes had been taken up and kept as lawful plunder, by some unfeeling wretches, and for whom no punishment can be too bad."

Sussex Weekly Advertiser, December 18 1797.

1800. JULIANA PROSPERA.

"Last Saturday morning [May 17] the brigantine Juliana Prospera, of Stetten, John Michael Bunger, master, from Bourdeaux to Embden, laden with wine, was wrecked near Crowlink. The crew were all saved."

The following update upon the wreck appeared in the following

week's edition: *"The Prussian brig, mentioned in our last to be on shore at Crowlink, is now a complete wreck. Her rigging, and nearly the whole of her cargo, consisting of upwards of 800 half hogsheads of red wine, from [to] Embden, have been saved. The hull of the wreck, the rigging, and part of the cargo, will shortly be sold to pay for salvage."*
Sussex Weekly Advertiser, May 19 & 26, 1800.

1807. name unknown.

The following incident is the only account recorded in this chapter, in which cowardice is to play a part in the unfolding drama: *"About five o'clock, on last Friday morning [January 9], a vessel, in ballast, by some means not to be accounted for, as there was little or no wind at the time, got inbayed, and came ashore, near Berlin Gap. The crew, in their eagerness to save themselves, left a woman-passenger on board, who was afterwards obliged to be dragged from her alarming situation through the water by means of ropes. It was expected the vessel would be got off again without any material damage."*
Sussex Weekly Advertiser, January 12 1807.

1807. ACTIVE.

"Last Monday [February 2] night as the brig Active, John Langford master, was proceeding up Channel, bound from Swansea to Chatham, laden with timber, for the use of Government, she was driven on shore by a gale of wind, on our coast, between Seaford and Cuckmere, where she lodged upon the rocks, and received so much damage, that but little hope is entertained of getting her off again [this being confirmed in the following weeks newspaper]. *Happily no lives were lost. Five of the crew, being Portuguese, and consequently Aliens, after making the usual declaration at the Customs-house, at Newhaven, came to this town [Lewes], on Saturday evening."*
Sussex Weekly Advertiser, February 9 1807.

1807. MARGARET.

A few days after the demise of the *Active*, another shipping casualty was to occure: *"The brig Margaret, laden with slate, stranded a few days afterwards near Berling Gap, was so much damaged by the accident, that her hull has been since sold to be broken up. Her crew and cargo, were all saved."*
Sussex Weekly Advertiser, February 16 1807.

1808. THREE BROTHERS.

"In the violent gale of wind, on last Monday night [April 4], a large ship, supposed to be an homeward bound West Indiaman, struck upon rocks, opposite the Signal Station [below Seaford Head?], *near Seaford, and was in a very short time, so completely dashed to pieces, that not an atom of her cargo, consisting chiefly of coffee, could be saved; and we are sorry to add, that every soul on board perished. No document has yet been found, whereby her name and description can, with certainty, be ascertained; but as some casks, exhibiting the words, Three Brothers - Surinam, have floated on shore, with fragments of the*

wreck, the loser, it is feared is a Jew-merchant, in London, he being now known to have had a ship in the West India trade, so named, Macauly, Master. The most valuable article belonging to her that has been saved, we believe, is an anchor and cable almost new. The unfortunate crew, it is supposed, consisted of from 16 to 20, and as some female apparel, of different descriptions, has been washed on shore, there is no doubt, women and children were on board. The bodies of six men and a boy, were on Saturday morning picked up, and the same day decently interred, in coffins provided for that purpose, by C. Harrison, Esq, in the church yard at Seaford. Being all nearly naked, when found, it is supposed they had, in the moment of danger, cast off their clothes, with the hope of saving themselves by swimming."

Sussex Weekly Advertiser, April 11 1808.

1808. INTEGRITY.

"On Thursday last [December 22] the Integrity, of London, a merchant vessel of 230 tons burthen, Jon Gardner, Master, from Rio Janeiro, to London, laden with rice, coffee, hides, horns, and Brazil wood, was stranded at Berling, near Beachy Head in this county, where she now lies a complete wreck. The rice is nearly all spoiled, and the coffee is much damaged, the rest of the cargo, it is expected, will be saved. The lives of the crew were all preserved. The vessel must be broken up. Mr. Atkinson, of Seaford, is part owner, with the Captain and others."

Sussex Weekly Advertiser, December 26 1808.

1842. name unknown.

Some questionable practice comes to light in the story of a wreck that took place at Birling Gap at the beginning of April 1842, concerning a vessel loaded with timber. Apparently, Eastbourne fishermen salvaged the copper sheeting and bolts from the vessel, and their agent Edward Maynard, sold the metal valued at nearly £200, to Ebenezer Morris of the Lewes Foundry. In an article published in the Eastbourne Gazette in about 1897, Ebenezer's son James, recalled that much of the metal fetched 10d [5 pence] a pound.

Two or three days after the copper had been conveyed to Lewes, Maynard sent word that there was some dispute as to its ownership, and urged Morris to 'lose' the copper as soon as possible. Workmen at the foundry were just finishing for the day, and Morris hurriedly arranged for a night shift to be worked. The horse employed in operating the bellows was given an hours rest, while the men rigged up the largest pair of bellows at their disposal. By the end of a long nights labour, all the copper had been transferred into unrecognisable ingots. (3).

1876. REUBENS.

In an attempt to save a ship, debatable decisions were sometimes taken in the heat of the moment, which would later be challenged during subsequent inquiry, as to why that particular course of action had been taken. *"The vessel ashore off Beachy Head, we are informed, is the screw steamer "Rubeus" [Reubens] from Liverpool, and was bound from Bunes Ayres, to Antwerp with a cargo of wool. The vessel is about 1,240 tons burthen, has one funnel, and is schooner rigged. She ran ashore during a very heavy fog that prevailed at the time, about three o'clock in the afternoon of Monday [January 17]. The boatman in charge at Birling Gap, coast-guard station was soon on the spot together with several other men, who heard her whistle just before she went aground. There was a very heavy sea running at the time, but no serious danger was feared for the safety of the crew, which numbered about 42 hands, on account of the ship resting on a smooth though rocky bottom. The captain was landed in order that he might proceed to Eastbourne to telegraph to the owners and make other arrangements. The coastguards went on board, and at the request of the captain, who returned as quickly as possible, remained there all night. At an early hour yesterday morning, two steam tugs arrived from Newhaven, and every effort was used to get the vessel afloat, but in vain, and it is now thought that she will become a complete wreck, as the bottom is stove in, and she is also broken amidships, while large quantities of stones are being forced into her, and she has been driven several feet further ashore. During the following day, the crew, and the coastguards were engaged in throwing the cargo overboard, so that it might be washed ashore, and a great number of people have visited the scene of the catastrophe."*

Eastbourne Gazette, Wednesday, January 19 1876.

The insurers, on becoming aware of the cargo being jettisoned overboard, were highly critical, for in the following weeks edition it was stated that: *"Captain C.S. Knight, (Lloyds Agent at Newhaven) has entered a protest on behalf of the underwriters of the cargo, and all persons concerned. On Monday some divers arrived, and from inquiries made late yesterday afternoon of Captain Ferguson, it appears that the ship will in all probability, in a few hours, be rescued from her late perilous situation."*

"During the afternoon of Thursday, two powerful steam tugs arrived from Dover, and at high water succeeded in getting the vessel off her "rocky bed" and towing her safely into dock, at Southampton, where we are informed she will undergo the necessary repairs. It is reported a court of inquiry into the conduct of the captain, will be held at Southampton on Thursday."

Eastbourne Gazette, Wednesday, January 26 & February 2 1876.

1876. COONATTO.

The early months of 1876 proved to be an eventful period for both rescue services and salvage operators along this stretch of the Sussex coast, for within weeks of the stranding of the Reubens, came news of the stranding of the Coonatto. For the following account, the author is indebted to Mr. John Wareing who has meticulously researched this particular wreck. (14). The Coonatto had been on passage from Adelaide for London with a cargo consisting of almost 3,000 bales of wool. In addition, she was also carrying a consignment of 1,232 copper slabs and some 7,000 ingots; she was also carrying a quantity of kangaroo skin and bags of bark.

Her demise began seven hours after her master, 31 year old Captain John Eilbeck Hillman took his last navigational reading, when off Selsey Bill. This was to lead to the Coonatto becoming stranded at 4-45am on the morning of Tuesday, February 21, in heavy seas within the sandy cove below Crowlink, her bows facing landward. Within hours of her demise, the steam packet Brighton was summoned. However, the ensuing salvage attempt only succeeded in swinging the stranded ship through 90 degrees so that her bow was facing seaward; during the attempt, the Brighton came close to becoming a victim of the nearby rocks, herself. After this failure, the Coonatto's bows partially swung back towards the land, so she was now broadside to the heavy seas, and wind. By midday, her position was described by the Receiver of Wrecks as *"very dangerous"* with a *"strong wind dead on land."* The Coonatto had grounded on a half tide, and with the tide cycle increasing in height toward springs, she was driven further inshore on each successive high tide.

The following day, reports spoke of 13 inches of water within her hull. On Thursday the heavy surf was heaving against her, driven by a strong south-westerly wind; this was causing her to be bumped heavily causing significant damage to her keel. By now, the crew had unbent her sails and managed to land them ashore. Her bower (spare) anchor had been paid out and secured to the confining rocky bar seaward of her, in an attempt to stop her drifting further inshore with each successive high tide. Later, her crew which had suffered no casualties departed by train from Eastbourne for London.

By Friday, February 24, with her hull now badly damaged, she was taking in a great deal of water; a cliff-top derrick had been erected in readiness for use in the proposed attempt to salvage her valuable cargo. Work commenced upon unloading part of her cargo under the supervision of Lloyds' Newhaven agent, Captain Knight; bags of bark and 567 copper ingots were landed and put into the charge of the coastguard. By Saturday, the hooding ends, that is, where the planking along her hull narrows to form her bows, had sprung allowing water to freely flow in and out. Work had also commenced unloading her several thousand bales of wool but there was now concern about working beneath her main mast, which was now in a dangerous state.

Sunday, February 26, following a night of yet more heavy weather, work commenced on transferring bales of wool on to both lighters and the Coonatto's ships boats; also on hand was the tug Anglia, loading wool for shipment direct to London; by Monday evening 100 bales had been salvaged.

Tuesday 28, saw work move apace with bales being taken off via ship and also landed via the cliff-top derrick. The Coonatto had by now been aground for one week, having endured heavy seas through much of that period; she had by now begun parting amidships on her starboard side. Copper ingots were washing out from her bilges. Wool was being washed in along the coast, with 228 bales being salvaged at Birling Gap, 80 of which were forwarded by rail from Eastbourne. A bulk of the wool however was being despatched initially to Newhaven; loose wool from broken bales was being salvaged as far away as Holywell near Eastbourne. The salvage of cargo, ships fittings and stores continued throughout March, with the employment of ships carpenters brought in to cut into the hulk of the ship where necessary and also the use of divers. Reports for March 6 stated that she had finally broken up, with her parting amidships and the lower section of the hull parting from the upper. The Eastbourne Gazette of April 15 reported an auction held on the beach by J.C. Towner, of ships stores, 90 metres (300 feet) of chain; ropes, sails, anchors, blocks, three ships boats, copper sheeting and several tons of iron and brass.

The Coonatto had been built in 1863 by Thomas Bilbe and Sons, of Rotherhithe, originally as a clipper, with an overall length of 48.77 metres (160 feet) and with a gross tonnage of 633 tons. Her owners were Anderson & Company, founders of the famous Orient Steam Navigation Company. She was of composite construction but uniquely, her framing was of both iron and timber. Also, Bilbe had experimented by cladding her hull with diagonal planking. In 1874, she was modified from clipper rig to that of a barque, presumably to reduce her crewing requirement, a common practice with schooners well into their working lives. She had spent her life in the Australian wool trade, carrying emigrants and general cargo on the outward voyage and mainly wool on her return passage. Although one of the smallest clippers on this trade, she was renowned for some fast passages: *"Her best run to the Semaphore Lightship was 66 days, and she once did a 69 day passage out after broaching to off St. Paul's Island and losing both helmsmen and the wheel itself overboard."*

At the Lloyds' inquiry into the loss of the Coonatto, it was never established as to why the loss occurred: *"The distance from the position of the ship at 00.20a.m. of the 21st to Beachy Head was 27 miles... At 4.30 a.m.*

Coonatto berthed in Australia with her sails being dried. (Courtesy of Newhaven Maritime Museum)

bright shore lights were seen, the ship having then run a distance of 27 miles. Yet the light of Beachy Head is stated not to have been seen. The discovery of these bright shore lights, probably the gaslights of Newhaven or Seaford, appear to have been the first indication of danger, but even this warning does not appear to have awakened the captain to a sense of his position, five valuable minutes were allowed to elapse before the vessel's course was altered, ...nor was the lead [the taking of depth readings] then or before resorted to, a circumstance that appeared to the Court inexplicable, seeing that the vessel had run her distance, and the fine light of Beachy was still invisible." Capt. Hillman was blamed for faulty navigation, having veered off course by some twelve miles over a distance of only 27 miles. Hillman had his Masters Certificate suspended for three months. There were local rumours that the Coonatto, then well on in her working life, had been deliberately wrecked, for by coincidence her owner was on holiday in Eastbourne at the same time. Whether coincidence or otherwise, within a few years, Anderson & Company had replaced their small fleet of ageing sailing ships with faster steam ships.

1881 FAIRFAX.

Gallant efforts were often undertaken by the coastguards stationed along our coastline as is witnessed in the following drama. On Thursday, February 10 before dawn, the screw-driven collier, Fairfax, in excess of 1,000 tons, ran aground just to the west of Crowlink, her bowsprit almost touching the cliff face. Built at Glasgow in 1863, and under the command of Captain C.F. Butler and with a crew of 18, she hailed from London and was owned by the General Steam Collier Company of London.

She had embarked from Le Havre on Wednesday morning after discharging coal and was on passage for South Shields, when she encountered a storm. The Fairfax being light in ballast, drifted easily before the wind; also, she was handicapped by a defect in her steering gear causing difficulty with steering her. Driven before the storm, she eventually became stranded beneath Rough Brow, this being witnessed by the Crowlink coastguards. Station Officer John Jessey sent a messenger to the Birling Gap station stating he required assistance from the rocket apparatus. Meanwhile, Jessey with four men and equipped with cliff ladders with a total length of some 40 fathoms, hurried to the cliff-top overlooking the stranded ship. Iron stakes were then driven into the ground, and the ladder literally hung in chains down the cliff face to the shore. Unable to communicate with the ship, S.O. Jessey and two men equipped with surf lines proceeded via Crowlink Gap across the rocks to near the ship. These were attached to the bottom of the cliff ladder, and thrown out to the ship enabling the crew to haul the cliff ladder out to the ship. Attaching themselves to this, the crew were then hauled to safety, the captain and first mate being last to leave the ship. Both the coastguards and the crew then had to stay for 3? hours upon a fallen rock only some five feet square until the tide receded, before walking to safety. The crew were given quarters at Crowlink coastguard station for the night before leaving the following day by train for London from Seaford. (During the same storm, the packet SS Normandy on passage for Dieppe took in tow the dis-masted schooner the Secret of Truro, bound from London to New Quay with 155 tons of super phosphate).
Sussex Express, Saturday, February 12 1881.

"On Saturday and Sunday, hundreds of persons visited the spot where this vessel lies stranded beneath the high cliffs, westward of Crowlink coastguard station and the Tiger, at Eastdean, the nearest public house within several miles. The vessel remains in the same position as we reported on Friday, but an inspection at low water showed a large hole in her stern. She is, however, said to be built in water-tight compartments, and on Saturday hopes were entertained that, being light in ballast, she might be got off on the top of the approaching high spring tides. With that view workmen have been engaged in clearing away some of the boulders and chalk debris under her stern to ease the way, but on Sunday the wind which had previously been from the north, shifted to the south-

east and freshened, and it is now feared a total wreck is unavoidable. The ships papers, the clothing of the seamen, together with other portable property, have been rescued, but if the southerly gales, with which our coast is threatened, set in, soon, well-built as is the Fairfax, the 'sister' into whose arms she has thrown herself will quickly gore her to fragments. "

Sussex Express, Tuesday, February 15 1881.

The weather it would seem, thought it fit to finish off what it had begun, for the following weeks Sussex Express carried news that *"Messrs. Easter & Wright sold the wreck of this steamer, by auction, on Friday. The price realised, we understand, was £665, and the purchaser Mr. Cohen of London.* "

Sussex Express, Tuesday, February 22 1881.

1883. NEW BRUNSWICK.

What must surely be one of the most gallant and determined rescues undertaken by the Eastbourne lifeboat, occurred during one of severest storms that the then inhabitants of Eastbourne could recall. After consultations following news of the plight of the New Brunswick, Lloyds' Eastbourne agent sent a telegram to Newhaven, believing the Newhaven lifeboat would be able to arrive at the scene more speedily, taking into consideration the severe south-westerly gale blowing; however:

"It was a question whether it was advisable to dispatch the Eastbourne boat at all. Mr Emary, local secretary to the Lifeboat Institution, and Charles ['Bones'] Hide, coxswain of the boat, were consulted, and it was determined to take the boat overland. It was very fortunate this decision was arrived at, because, [for] the Newhaven boat never left the harbour. It is only fair to the Newhaven life-boat crew to state, that when they received the telegram from Eastbourne, they promptly manned their boat, but in the face of the terrific gale, were unable to leave the harbour. The steam tug on which they generally rely to tow them out of the harbour, was quite unprepared and it would have taken some time to get her steam up.

While the consultation was going on, the Eastbourne crew mustered at their post, and received the announcement with hearty cheers, and at once set to work to drag the boat out of the house, and had actually pulled it by manual labour to the end of South-street before the horses could be attached. In the first instance six horses were supplied by Mr. Newman, of the Anchor hotel, but these were supplemented by four more supplied from other sources. The tug up the new road to Beachy Head was a terrible struggle, and it required the full power of the ten horses... On, however, they went, and in two hours reached Birling Gap, down which it was necessary to take the boat before it could reach the shore. At that time the vessel could be dimly seen, amid the drifting scud, some three-quarters of a mile from the shore, with the sea at times breaking completely over it. The crew, lashed to the rigging, drenched to the skin with every passing wave, were observed waving signals of distress.

It was now about half-past one o'clock in the day, and there was every appearance of the storm increasing in violence, as the tide had just turned. At this point, however, a difficulty arose, which it was thought at one time would render useless all the labour which had already been expended in bringing the life boat to the edge of the cliff. Those who know Birling Gap will remember that in ordinary times it is a narrow roadway just sufficiently wide to permit the passage of a cart, leading from the top of the cliff to the beach, but those who ventured down, found that in consequence of the severe storms which have lately prevailed, at the lower end the water had washed away the sloping road, and there was a fall of fully ten feet between the end of the road and the beach... Somebody discovered not far from the spot a load of timber, and with these a temporary path was rigged out by the aid of numerous by-standers, who had by this time gathered on the scene. It was a remarkable sight to see gentlemen, fishermen, coastguardsmen and visitors of all classes tugging and pulling and hauling away in bringing this wood to the spot, and erecting a temporary roadway, down which the lifeboat was safely lowered. Reaching the water's edge at length, the dangers and difficulties were by no means surmounted ..."

"To those standing on the beach it seemed impossible that the boat could ever reach the wreck, again and again it appeared overwhelmed by the waves and was lost from view altogether, and the bravest men on the shore watched with bated breath, expecting every moment to see the lifeboat thrown back on the shore a helpless wreck. Slowly but surely, Charles Hide and his gallant crew, approached the ship. At times they were forced back, their boat filled with water, but the valves and other apparatus worked perfectly, and the boat was soon again clear. For fully one hour did this struggle continue, it seemed almost beyond endurance, but British pluck at length prevailed, and the wreck was reached.

It was impossible to take the boat alongside, and a rope therefore was made fast, and the life boat allowed to drop astern. One by one the crew of ten men with the captain, were dropped into the water and dragged into the life-boat. One poor fellow we are sorry to say, got his ribs crushed while being thus transferred, but all were saved, and at length the life boat was once again turned to the shore, with its precious cargo of human lives. The beach was safely reached, where scores of ready hands were ready to drag it out of danger. The injured man was carried to one of the coast-guard cottages, where his immediate wants were attended to by Mr. Scanlan, assistant to Dr. Colgate, who fortunately happened to be present."

After a great deal of effort from the small army of bystanders and coastguards, the lifeboat *"William and Mary,"* was finally hauled back to the cliff-top. Fortunately, Lloyds' Eastbourne agent John Bennett, had arranged with the Devonshire Hotel for, *"...a copious supply of bread and meat and ale, which was very acceptable not only to the crew but to all those who had been working so indefatigably in getting the lifeboat launched. The crew reached the shore about half-past four o'clock in the afternoon. The ship from which the crew was rescued was called the "New Brunswick" belonging to Berwick [Bergen], Norway, 480 tons burthen. Captain Tobeason was in command assisted by a crew of ten men, all Norwegians, she was laden with deals [softwood timber] from Canada. It would seem that in approaching the English Channel, that they were caught in the terrific gales which have now prevailed for some days. Day by day they struggled with their difficulties, their main topmast and the foretopmast being carried away, and all their principal sails blown to rags. On Sunday morning they found themselves on a lee-shore off Newhaven; they attempted to weather the Head, but in their weakened condition they were unable to do so. In this extremity they cast anchor. To their great dismay they found that their anchors dragged, and their total destruction appeared inevitable. They hoisted signals of distress which were promptly seen by the coast-guard, who at once telegraphed to Eastbourne for assistance... Fortunately..., their anchors held. Every wave broke over their vessel, carrying away everything portable, and the crew could only retain their place on the deck by lashing themselves to the rigging. In this dilemma they remained seven hours...*

Among the gentlemen present on the beach was Mr. H.P. Hughes, a well-known friend of the sea-faring community in this town, who worked himself most heartily, and very liberally supplied the lifeboat crew with a supper at the Anchor hotel..." This particular storm caused extensive flooding throughout the lower lying areas of Eastbourne that Sunday. After the gale had subsided, the Newhaven steam tug went out to her, and managed to tow her into Newhaven harbour.

Eastbourne Gazette, Wednesday, November 28 1883.

1890. POLYNESIA.

For over 100 years the wreck of the Polynesia, a three-masted sailing ship owned by the Laeisz ('Flying P') Line, defied the seas ceaseless assault by the revealing one of her masts during spring low tides, just off the mouth of the Cuckmere River. She is listed as being built in Hamburg during 1874 with a tonnage of 985 tons and a length of 59.44 metres (195 feet), and of timber construction with steam auxiliary power. (2).

The story of the Polynesia which was on passage from Iquique in Chile unfolded thus: *"On Thursday morning [April 24] at about 10-45, information was received at Newhaven that a ship was ashore at Beachy Head. The lifeboat was promptly launched, and the tug "Tipper" with Mr. J. Bull, Lloyds' agent, on board, left for the scene. The vessel was found to be the full-*

rigged ship "Polynesia," Capt. Rightman [Reitmann], of and for Hamburg, with a cargo of nitrate of soda. The vessel is now broadside on at Birling Gap. The captain and crew landed at Newhaven in the lifeboat at about 5-30, and will be in readiness to proceed to the vessel, should there be any operation of getting her off."
Sussex Express, Saturday, April 26 1890.

The pleasure steamer based at Eastbourne did good business, for on the following Tuesday she took over 100 passengers to within 20 yards of the stranded ship. The report continued: *"...if they cannot pump out the water from the vessel, they will have to break her up. If they succeed in pumping her dry she will be towed to Newhaven. The crew, about twenty in number, are very hard at work..."* It was stated that she lay about 300 yards eastwards of Birling Gap and that the salvers had arranged for pumps to be sent down from London.
Eastbourne Gazette, Wednesday, April 30 1890.

"During the past week, advantage has been taken of every opportunity to save the cargo, boats from the harbour have made several trips. The cargo saved is being loaded into the Bull Line vessel Commerce, by which ship it will be taken to its destination, Hamburg. All of the ships boats together with the sails, yards and other material have been brought to the harbour... Pumps have been taken on board, and should the weather continue fine there is reasonable hope of saving the ship and bringing her into port. The National Lifeboat Institution sent a sum of money for each of the crew of the lifeboat and the tug Tipper for their assistance rendered."
Sussex Express, Saturday, May 3 1890.

Luck though finally ran out for the crippled ship for: *"Whilst being towed from Birling Gap to Newhaven the Polynesia was so leaky that she had to be beached at the mouth of the Cuckmere river. It is rumoured that she will have to be broken up. ...the wreck was offered for sale by Mr. John Easter (Easter & Wright, auctioneers and house agents, Eastbourne) at Newhaven, Friday last. There was a large company including people from London, Liverpool, Portsmouth, Southampton and other ports. Mr. Easter conducted the sale in his usual agreeable fashion. The hull was sold for £125 to a Newhaven firm, and the fittings realised good prices. The vessel will now be broken up."*
Eastbourne Gazette, Wednesday, May 14 & 28 1890.

1899. INTERNATIONAL.
The last significant shipping casualty of the 19th century was the 1,004 ton steamer International, which was under tow to a breakers yard in Cherbourg. *"A heavy gale of exceptional violence raged round the South Coast... During Friday night the boat was found to be leaking. Signals of distress were made; but, owing to the tremendous seas and the fog, they were not seen by the tug. At daylight, when the condition of the International was*

discovered by those on board the Gauntlet, it was decided to make for Newhaven. Off Beachy Head however, the tow-line parted and the steamer drifted before the wind, with heavy seas breaking over her. At some time the line was made fast, but again snapped. She drifted about until she was driven ashore at Birling Gap. When she struck the crew (9 men) managed to launch a boat, and they were picked up by the tug."

Sussex Express, Tuesday, October 3 1899.

"A curious circumstance in relation to the loss of the International is that she was employed in the laying of the telegraph cable from Birling Gap to France, and that when she grounded last week she severed this cable." Built at Stockton-upon-Tees in 1870, she had been used by the India Rubber and Gutta Percha and Telegraph Works Company, of London. She had a length of 73 metres (240 feet). She was auctioned on the beach by Easter and Wright and sold to Messrs. Blackmore and Company of London for the sum of £225.

Eastbourne Gazette, Wednesday, October 4 & 18, 1899.

1899. name unknown.

"Early on Sunday morning [October 1] another large steamer was observed to be on shore near the same spot [as the International], but before assistance could be rendered she floated with the rising tide and proceeded westwards, showing two red lights, suggesting that the ship was not under control, from which it is assumed that her steering gear was damaged."

Sussex Express, Tuesday, October 3 1899.

1902. CITY OF BENARES.

There must have been an element of humiliation for the captain concerned with this incident, being in command as he was, of a recently launched cargo liner. *"At 6.30 a.m. on Wednesday, [April 16] The City of Benares, of 4,316 tons burden, belonging to the City line, went ashore in a dense fog near Birling Gap, about 300 yards from the Coastguard Station, on soft chalk and rock. The sea was very calm, and the vessel in no danger. The liner was on her maiden trip from Calcutta to London, and had a general cargo [of 6,000 tons].*

The Coastguard report that a dense fog prevailed in the Channel, and the lights from the Bell Toute lighthouse were practically invisible, certainly to a vessel a quarter of a mile away, where the City of Benares found herself in difficulties. The vessel was invisible from the shore, but at about six o'clock the Coastguard were able to hear her movements, and by means of gun signals ascertained that she had grounded. Chief Officer Gorbyn, of the Coastguard, and a boat's crew immediately put off to the vessel and found she was shipping no water, and had apparently sustained no damage. There were 48 [38] passengers on board and 107 officers and men, Captain Edward Halley, of Glasgow, being in command. The passengers were, of course, very eager to hear

the latest news, and the Coastguardsmen sent newspapers on board.
The vessel was only launched in October 1901, having being built at
Glasgow. She last touched at Malta, where her passengers were taken aboard.
The vessel got off at about four o'clock [2-30pm], with the assistance of her own
steam and of two tugs from Newhaven, the Alert and Belle of the Usk."
Eastbourne Gazette, Wednesday, April 23 1902. [Sussex Express,
Tuesday, April 22 1902].

1905. MILLGATE.

The impression is sometimes gained when reading the account of
a disaster, that fate never intended otherwise; on reading this gripping
episode one is forced to ask the question, why did the vessels master
not defer embarking? During a week in which the Sussex coast was
beset with south-westerly gales, the coaster Millgate: *"...was driven by*
force of wind and water on to a dead lee-shore, and she now lies four fathoms
deep off Crowlink, the coastguard station between Birling Gap and the
Cuckmere, the buildings of which are the only sign of life on what is perhaps the
most desolate part of the Downs in East Sussex. The ill-fated vessel - the
'Millgate,' a small Manchester steamer - foundered on Thursday [November 2]
morning and the news, which soon became known in Eastbourne, created a
considerable amount of excitement. Undeterred by the drenching showers which
came down at intervals, many set out over the Downs to view the wreck, but
naturally, there was little to be seen, the steamer being quite under water.

The voyage of the 'Millgate' was a short, but eventful one. She started from
Guernsey, laden with a cargo of granite, for London on Tuesday evening.
Immediately on getting clear of the harbour the vessel encountered the full force
of the tremendous gale then raging. It gradually increased in violence, until at
four o'clock on Wednesday morning a crisis was reached, when a huge wave
struck the vessel and flooded the engine room. This affected the boiler, and an
hour later, when the boat was off Barfleur, the cargo shifted. Capt. Proctor set
his course across the channel, but barely enough steam could be maintained to
keep the vessel on her course; and seas kept washing across the decks, so that it
became an absolute impossibility for the crew to obtain any food. On Wednesday
evening the vessel was off Shoreham, and gradually edged along the coast past
Brighton. The captain attempted to beach the vessel at Brighton, but such a
terrific sea was running that he was unable to do this. The boiler gradually
became useless, and the captain finding that he should not be able to weather
Beachy Head, when off Newhaven burnt a flare. This was about 7 o'clock on
Thursday morning. The alarm was given to the Newhaven lifeboat crew at once
and within fifteen minutes of the call the lifeboat "Quiver No.1" was speeding
on her way to the disabled ship. This was an exceptionally smart piece of work,
seeing that the majority of the lifeboat's crew had nearly one mile to go, and the
coxswain of the lifeboat, E. Eager, is to be congratulated on the promptitude and

smartness of his crew. This is the first time Eager has commanded the lifeboat when on rescue work. There was a tremendous sea running at times and especially when crossing the bar the lifeboat was absolutely covered by sea and spray and hid to the view of the anxious watchers on the pier. The lifeboat reached the disabled vessel just before ten. She had in the meantime drifted to eastward and eventually come to anchor just inside Beachy Head, but this proved of no avail, for the seas continually broke over her. It was seen that she was gradually foundering and, though at first the captain was averse to leaving his ship, he, the crew of nine men and a puppy, the pet of the men, were eventually removed to the lifeboat. The 'Millgate' foundered soon after. The 'Quiver No.1' arrived back at Newhaven just after noon and was received with rounds of cheering. The crew lost all their belongings and several had no shoes.... This is the first time the 'Quiver No.1, Reserve No. 3,' has done any rescue work since she has been stationed at Newhaven. She is only there temporarily whilst the 'Michael Henry' is being converted into a motor lifeboat."
Eastbourne Chronicle, Saturday, November 4 1905.

1907. NEWSTEAD.

"Early on Monday morning [March 18] a vessel went ashore westward of Beachy Head. The stranded proved to be a steamer of 2,300 tons, carrying a general cargo. She is registered at Newcastle in the name of 'Newstead,' and was bound from the Tagus [Portugal] to Hamburg. After fighting a fierce south westerly gale all night in the Channel, the 'Newstead' ran into a thick fog, and was stranded on the low foreshore rocks off Cuckmere, about two miles from Seaford.

When her predicament was noticed by a coastguardman at about six o'clock in the morning, soon after she had stranded, a heavy sea was beating over her, and vessel and crew appeared to be in considerable danger. It was impossible, owing to the thick fog, to discern the vessel clearly, and the first tidings that reached Newhaven were of an alarming character. The harbour lifeboat [Sir Fitzroy Clayton] immediately put to sea and was followed by the tugs 'Alert' and 'Belle of the Usk.' A rocket apparatus was carried from Cuckmere and fixed in position on top of the cliff ready to fire a line across the ship if necessary.

When the lifeboat and tugs arrived they found the crew of the 'Newstead,' numbering between twenty and thirty, in no immediate danger. The vessel was laying broadside to the tide, and almost parallel with the shore, and later in the morning the sea moderated sufficiently to enable the lifeboat to hitch on to the lee of the stranded steamer. Throughout the morning the two tugs were doing their best to get the vessel afloat, but were unable to move her.

When a special correspondent of 'The Tribune' reached the scene in the afternoon, the 'Newstead' was hard and fast on the submerged rocks, not more than one hundred and fifty yards from the shore, opposite Cow Gap [this should read Hope Gap]. *There was a slight haze at sea, but the sun was*

SS Newstead aground to the west of Hope Gap. Newhaven lifeboat Sir Fitzroy Clayton alongside. (Courtesy of Newhaven Maritime Museum)

shining brilliantly on shore. At the top of the three hundred feet of sheer cliff was the rocket apparatus in readiness, and the lifeboat still clung to the lee-side of the vessel. The two tugs had left, with the intention of making another attempt to refloat the vessel on the next high tide. [Last] Sunday was the highest of the spring tides, and each succeeding tide being lower the task of refloating the vessel was rendered more difficult."

Eastbourne Gazette, Wednesday, March 20 1907.

"The cargo steamer 'Newstead' (bound for Hamburg) which went ashore last week at Cuckmere a few hundred yards west of the Haven, still remains hard on the rocks, despite the efforts of four tugs to disengage it. The work of salvaging the cargo has been undertaken by Mr. Collard, of Newhaven, and on Thursday afternoon the hulk 'Wallands' with forty men aboard, was towed to the wreck by the tug 'Belle of the Usk,' where derricks were rigged up and work of salvaging the cargo proceeded as quickly as possible."

Eastbourne Gazette, Wednesday, March 27 1907.

1916. OUSHLA.

This incident is the shipwreck referred by Len Jeffery in the previous chapter, when he was a child. *"One of the victims of the extraordinary southerly gale of Sunday, November 5th, is the ss. 'Oushla,' which lies against the cliffs a short distance beyond Birling Gap and which, according the 'The Times,' has been abandoned.*

Visiting the scene of the wreck on the 7 inst., one was struck by the

remarkable position of the vessel. She lay broadside on against the high chalk cliff, the second of the Seven Sisters from Birling Gap, with her bow heading to the north-west, so close to the headland, towering some 300 feet above her, that a biscuit could scarcely be inserted between the bluff of her bow and the cliff... 'The Times' says she is of 2,514 tons, built in 1891, and valued at £24,000; but this was probably only her book value, and in war-time she was likely to be worth two or three times that sum. A close inspection from the heights showed that the vessel was two-masted, iron-decked, and that every paintable portion of her was of a slate grey colour. The only outward signs of the terrible time through which the vessel had passed were a loose derrick on the fore deck, the apparent loss of one anchor, and a boat and davits missing from the port side. One noticed her rudder was hard over to starboard. At half-ebb the ship was high and dry, completely out of reach of the seas still breaking heavily on the beach. Inquiries made locally elicited the fact that the steamer was what is called at sea 'flying light,' with no cargo aboard. She reached St. Catherine's, Isle of Wight, but the storm compelled an attempt to return up Channel. On Sunday morning (November 5th) the vessel appears to have become unmanageable, and to have grounded between 10 and 11 a.m. On the night tide she was swept against the cliffs and on November 6 the crew were able to walk ashore and seek shelter at the Birling Gap Hotel. It is stated that the pilot was still on board when the ship grounded. The crew of 21 Chinamen passed through Eastbourne on November 7 on their way to London. On Wednesday the captain and officers were still staying at the hotel, and could be seen at half-tide walking back to the wreck along the beach, accompanied by the coastguards..."
Eastbourne Gazette, Wednesday, November 15 1916.

    1919. UB 121.

After the armistice of 1918, the captured German submarine UB 121 was assigned to France; while she was being towed to Cherbourg during April 1919, the tow line broke and she was driven ashore, her bow smashing into the engine room of the Oushla. Upon the following tide, she floated free and drifted a little to the eastward. (3). She was one of the UB III class of submarine of which some 107 were built and having a surface displacement of over five hundred tons, powered by powerful twin diesels and armed with five 500mm. torpedo tubes. These coastal boats were at least as powerful as the standard U boats at the beginning of the war. (15). The vast bulk of these two vessels were salvaged during two episodes, in 1928 and 1959, the second involving a light railway beneath the cliffs to Birling Gap. (3).

    1923. BOY DANIEL.

"The crew of the Eastbourne motor lifeboat [coxswain Henry Boniface] were called out at 10.15 on Wednesday morning [February 21], news having been

received that a steam drifter trawler had gone ashore near the mouth of the River Cuckmere, east of Seaford Head. The lifeboat had rather a stormy passage, for a heavy sea was running and wind and tide were against her. For a short time the crew were able to hoist a sail, but this became useless as the wind veered round to the west dead in their face. It took the craft two hours to cover the distance - about seven miles - and it was plainly demonstrated that her 12 h.p. engine is not powerful enough in a choppy sea. In other respects the boat behaved splendidly.

On reaching their destination the lifeboatmen found that the stranded vessel was the 'Boy Daniel,' belonging to Mr.Daniel Rolf, fish salesman, of Brighton. At the time of the mishap, about 5a.m., she was making for Newhaven Harbour with her catch of fish, and it is understood that she ran into a heavy squall of rain, which made observation difficult. When the Eastbourne lifeboat reached the scene she found that the Newhaven lifeboat had passed a hawser aboard the trawler from the Newhaven tug 'Alert,' which was trying to tow the fishing boat off. This lasted for two or three hours, but the rising tide only carried the vessel farther ashore, and at low tide she stood high and dry close to the cliff. The Eastbourne lifeboat stood by the 'Boy Daniel' for several hours, in case of emergency, but her services were not requisitioned, as the trawler's skipper (Captain Medhurst, of Margate) and crew of eight remained aboard for the rest of the day and during the night.

At 2.30p.m. the Eastbourne lifeboat set out on her return journey.... The Newhaven lifeboat returned to harbour about 4p.m. and the tug about half-an-hour later.... It is believed that nothing can now be done to refloat the vessel until the next spring tide, in about a fortnight's time."

Eastbourne Chronicle, Saturday, February 24th. 1923.

1925. COMTESSE DE FLANDRE.

The grounding of the Comtesse de Flandre is the first shipping casualty within the study area in which use was made of wireless to transmit a SOS message for assistance. The following account is composed from two separate articles which appeared in the Eastbourne Chronicle, the following Saturday. *"During Tuesday night one of the heaviest south-westerly gales experienced for many years was general all along the South Coast, and, accompanied by heavy banks of drizzling rain, which is often worse than fog, made it extremely risky for vessels passing up and down the Channel.*

At 4.30 a.m. on Wednesday the shore wireless station at Newhaven Harbour picked up a S.O.S. message from the Belgian steamer 'Comtesse de Flandre' (1,886 tons) to the effect that she was ashore about seven miles to the eastward of Newhaven, and asking for the assistance of tugs. When the ship grounded, the lifeboats were quickly made ready, but were not launched. Lifebelts were also issued. The stranded vessel was laden with a general cargo (including a considerable quantity of fruit), and was bound from Naples to London and Antwerp, the latter being her port of registry.

The information that the vessel was ashore was passed on to the local lifeboat authorities, and about six o'clock the lifeboat (Sir Fitzroy Clayton) put to sea under the command of Coxswain Richard Payne.

Terrible seas were experienced, and after the lifeboat was clear of the breakwater and in broken water she was frequently swamped, with the result that baling had to be resorted to. The heavy seas also extinguished all her lights. After a very rough passage, the lifeboat located the 'Comtesse de Flandre' ashore off Crowlink Point, which is situate at about the second Sister from Cuckmere. [In actual fact, she was probably in the vicinity of Rough Brow or Brass Point]. *The vessel was then broadside on the cliff and the waves were dashing right over her, to such an extent that she was frequently hidden from view. The Coxswain of the lifeboat got into communication with the captain of the stranded vessel, but at that period the latter decided that he and the crew would stand by the vessel and would not leave her.*

The lifeboat stood by, and shortly afterwards the Newhaven tug 'Foremost 22' (Cpt. L. Pascoe) arrived on the scene. It was then decided to make an attempt to re-float the 'Comtesse de Flandre.' With the assistance of the lifeboat a line was got aboard the stranded vessel and a thick hawser was fixed. At first it seemed that the tugs efforts would be successful, but when she succeeded in getting the vessel's stern to sea the hawser parted, the vessel's bow being too firmly grounded. Further efforts were unsuccessful, and the vessel drifted back to her original position - broadside on.

Some of the Coastguards were on the cliff head from 5 a.m. until dusk, provisions and hot drink being brought to them by their children. Later the rocket apparatus (superintended by Lieut. Simmons, District Officer) was brought from Birling Gap and communication was established from the top of the cliff, which at this point is 150-ft. high, a single rocket sufficing for the operation. The landing of the crew by the suspended lifeline (breeches buoy) commenced shortly before noon, the work of rescue then being facilitated by the use of a rope ladder hung down the face of the cliff. The dramatic proceedings, which took place amid blinding rain and tempestuous wind, were an entire success, no personal injury or other mishap marring the well planned scheme of those responsible. Seven of the 27 members of the crew were landed on the beach, whence they trudged slowly to Cuckmere and afterwards to East Dean.... With the exception of this minority the crew were conducted from the cliff to Birling Gap coastguard station, where they received hospitable treatment..." Eastbourne Chronicle, January 2 1926.

The mainly Belgian crew left Eastbourne next morning for London, en route for Antwerp. The captain and officers however, remained behind and returned to the vessel to exploit possibilities of floating the ship, to which they seemed somewhat optimistic. Several weeks later, two men were apprehended by the ship's Chief Officer and escorted to Birling Gap coastguard station, for breaking through custom seals aboard the ship and stealing. The accused appeared before the Hailsham Magistrates court.

1929. MOGENS KOCH.

The weekend of December 7-8 proved to be one of the stormiest that southern England had experienced since accurate records had been kept; at intervals the wind very nearly reached hurricane force, often accompanied with heavy downfalls of rain, hail and thunder. During this storm, the four-masted schooner Mogens Koch was driven ashore beneath Haven Brow. She was Danish and of 385 tons and on passage from Haparanda, Sweden, to the port of Villa Garcia in north-west Spain, with a cargo of timber. During Saturday morning, the Newhaven lifeboat Sir Fitzroy Clayton had to struggle through heavy seas for some hours; eventually she successfully managed to rescue the crew of ten, who had to jump from the deck of their vessel down on to the lifeboat.

On the return journey a great wave struck the lifeboat, washing overboard Charles Holder, one of the lifeboat crewmen; luckily he was dragged back aboard. The wave dashed the rescued crew into the bottom of the boat, and two of the men were injured and required

Mogens Koch in distress beneath Seven Sisters, showing her deck cargo beginning to break loose. (Courtesy of Newhaven Maritime Museum)

hospital treatment. Most serious of all, Coxswain Payne sustained serious injuries which brought about his premature death. The Mogens Koch was eventually re-floated at 11pm. on Monday, December 16, and taken into Newhaven harbour. Sussex Express, Friday, December 13 1929. Eastbourne Chronicle, Saturday, December 14 1929. Eastbourne Gazette, Wednesday, December 18 1929.

1933. ELLIN.

The Ellin is the largest casualty to occur along this section of coast; fortunately she was safely re-floated with an impressive show of strength: *"In foggy, rainy and squally weather the Greek cargo steamer, Ellin, 4,577 tons bound for Hull with a cargo of grain from South America, ran aground on a reef off the Seven Sisters on Saturday morning [February 4].*

The crew of the Eastbourne lifeboat, under Coxswain Mike Harding, had a busy time standing by the ship, ready to lend assistance. The crew assembled quickly and were afloat at 8-30. They reached the Ellin about an hour later, after a somewhat rough passage, and stood by [the first of several trips to her]. The ship was undamaged and on an even keel, almost broadside to the coast, and about 500 yards out.

Meanwhile the Birling Gap coastguard under Station Officer Dashwood, had assembled with the lifesaving apparatus, which, drawn by two horses, was taken to East Dean and Friston and across the Downs to the top of the cliffs near Crowlink, 150 to 200 feet high. Signals were exchanged by the coastguards with the lifeboat, and the party remained on the cliffs until a late hour in case their services were required...

They [the Eastbourne lifeboat] went back to the Ellin the same night and stayed until nearly mid-day on Sunday, when, as the weather became worse, the captain asked the coxswain to put half the crew [which totalled 29 men] ashore. Actually, 20 men were brought to Eastbourne in the lifeboat." Eastbourne Chronicle, Saturday, February 11 1933.

"The incident had a happy ending yesterday morning, when at the peak of high tide the Ellin was successfully floated. No fewer than six tugs were engaged in the operation. They were, Seafalke (Bremer Haven), Schlde (Rotterdam), Goliath (Antwerp), Sampson (Hamburg), Foremost (Newhaven) and Lady Brassy (Dover). The Ellin was got off the rocks at five minutes to 10, and with two tugs towing and two in attendance, the slow journey to London (or Dover?) began. She was being towed stern foremost from which it is assumed that she was damaged forward in striking the ledge." Eastbourne Gazette, Wednesday, February 8 1933.

1943. AVANTURINE.

The last remaining account in this chapter, although neither a wrecking nor stranding, did result in the loss of one brave life. On November 23, the Newhaven lifeboat Cecil & Lillian Philpott, put to sea after a request was received by the coastguard service from the Admiralty, requesting the services of the lifeboat to go to the assistance of the armed trawler HM Avanturine, in difficulties off Hope Gap. Lifeboat cowswain Leonard Pendlesden and his crew put to sea having been told that further information would be relayed to them. Owing to the severe conditions this was not possible and the lifeboat had to return to port before once again embarking on her mission. (16).

After rounding Seaford Head, the crew observed through the black of night, red distress flares. Upon reaching the vessel, the coxswain realised that there was little time left in which to prevent a disaster. He found she was in the lee of a reef 'The Mares' in about 5.5metres (18 feet) of water; in his estimation he thought the trawler was probably drawing in the region of 4.6m (15 feet) of water. At this point, he decided to drop anchor and ride in close to the stricken vessel, wrongly believing due to the poor visibility, that the trawler was also riding at anchor. (16).

As the lifeboat reached her, the trawler unexpectedly proceeded ahead towards the much smaller lifeboat. In the ensuing collision the lifeboat sustained severe damage, her hull receiving a hole in excess of 0.7 x 0.17 metres (five feet by two feet). Due to the impact, the lifeboats mast crashed down causing the lifeboats signalman, Benjamin Clark to be lost overboard and was drowned. Coxswain Pendlesden dazed and suffering a severe back injury, on finding only three of the remaining seven man crew uninjured, signalled to the trawler and escorted her out into deeper water where she rode out the remainder of the storm. One and a half hours later the crippled lifeboat finally reached the shelter and safety of Newhaven. Subsequently, Coxswain Pendlesden was awarded the R.N.L.I.'s silver gallantry medal; lifeboatman Clark was posthumously awarded the institutions bronze medal for gallantry. (16).

SOURCES.

1) McGowan, Alan. The Ship – 'The Century Before Steam.' HMSO. 1980.
2) ESRO AMS 4606.
3) ESRO. Shipwrecks of the Seven Sisters. Richard Gilbert. Unpublished.
4) SAC vol. 42.
5) PRO HCA 26, piece 24.
6) Dictionary of National Biography.
7) Walker, George. 'Voyages and Cruises of Commodore Walker During The Late Spanish and French Wars.' Published in Dublin, 1762.
8) Archivo General de Indias, Seville. Contracts File no. 1513.
9) Astell, Joan. 'The Spanish Prize.' Seaford Museum of Local History. 1977.
10) Magens, Nicholas. 'An Essay On Insurance.' Publishd in London, 1755.
11) Robertson, Philip. The Seven Sisters Voluntary Marine Conservation Area – A Maritime Archeological Perspective. University of St.Andrews. (unpub. thesis). October 1993.
12) Bass, George, ed. by. 'Ships & Shipwrecks Of The Americas.' Thomas & Hudson Ltd. 1988.
13) Farmer, R.H., 'Handbook of Hardwoods.' H.M.S.O. 1981.
14) John Wareing, per. comm.
15) Guston, B. 'Submarines.' Blandford. 1976.
16) Newhaven Museum of Local & Maritime History.

CHAPTER 7.

AGRICULTURE.

INTRODUCTION. This chapter sets out to describe and explain the study area's main industry, agriculture; we look at its background, methods of operation and external economic influences; of the farmers themselves who managed the industry and to whom the small local community depended on for their livelihood. The original intention of this chapter was not an exhaustive account of Downland farming, rather an in depth look at the study area. However, that would have created a somewhat blinkered, out of context portrayal; therefore this chapter does look at the wider picture. In order to keep this chapter to within a reasonable length and to maintain the strong local theme, this chapter only deals with the past two centuries or so, a period in which significantly more information is recorded and for which the word of mouth could also be called upon. Indeed a notable portion of this chapter would not have been possible but for time given to the author by former members of the farming community, in relating life and work before the period in which the tractor became the main source of power on the land. Much of the chapter deals with Exceat Farm but with references to the surrounding farms where applicable.

SETTING THE SCENE. Agricultural production upon the Downs was based upon the 'Sheep-Corn System' and was concerned with the large scale production of wool and mutton from sheep and cereals, largely wheat. The origins of this system date back to the medieval period, being refined and improved during succeeding centuries culminating in the *"golden age of high farming"* spanning the century 1780-1880. During the 18th century this led to cessation of the practice of leaving ground fallow, this being replaced by the introduction of new crops such as turnips and legumes (crops belonging to the pea family). This trend led to complicated crop rotations where perhaps up to 12 different crops might be grown upon a single farm often involving 'catch-cropping,' that is, quick-growing successional fodder crops for sheep. Discounting the heavy input, industrialised era of farming practised during the latter part of the 20th century, the heyday of Downland agriculture occurred during the period 1855-1877. The layout of farms within the study area arose from the abandonment during the 16th and 17th centuries, of the 'open field system,' long before the Enclosure Acts were envisaged. These farms often cover substantial areas of their respective parishes and in the instances of Exceat and Chyngton the farms were indeed the entire parishes. Downland farming required a relatively small workforce; reliance was placed upon the large size of families and lodgers for supplying the necessary labour, keeping to a minimum the amount of housing required. These large farms due to economic advantages of scale, were able to produce substantial profits for both their tenant and landlord, particularly after the substantial rise in cereal prices from the mid-18th century and the increased value of the Southdown wool clip from the 1780's. (1).

As with most situations involving trade and its market forces this situation was not to continue. From about 1870 an upward spiral of costs had begun due to increased exports of manufactured goods leading to a consequent rise in wages and living standards; this in turn pushed up farm labour costs and rents beyond reasonable levels. Above all else, in return for these exports of manufactured goods, Britain increasingly received large imports of cheap foodstuffs from her expanding Empire and the Americas. Until this period the British farmer had been protected from overseas competition by sea and distance. With the large scale construction of railways abroad coupled with advances in marine transportation, British farming was about to receive a severe body blow. Between the mid 1870's and 1890's shipping rates were slashed by some 75%, while contemporary wheat prices were virtually halved. Britain's cereal farmers assumed this decline in profitability to be short lived and initially took no fundamental action until too late for any actions to have any effect. (2).

Towards the end of the 19th century but to a lesser degree, livestock producers were also becoming increasingly affected by the 'Great Agricultural Depression' as it became known. Over the period 1873 to 1903 wool prices tumbled by approximately 50%. During 1882 the first cargo of frozen mutton embarked upon the long voyage from New Zealand; by 1899 this new trade had grown to a staggering 175,000 tonnes. The now acute situation of British farming was compounded by extremes of the British climate; the period 1875-79 was characterised by wet summers, while the 1880's were mainly fair. However the proverbial tap was turned to the other extreme with the period 1892-96 experiencing prolonged periods of drought. (2).

Through the duration of the Depression, large acreages of arable land were converted to pasture for livestock production. This allowed for economies in labour to be made; nationally, somewhere in the order of one third of the farm labour workforce left the land during the final quarter of the 19th century. (2). The situation during the opening decades of the 20th century showed little sign of improvement; by 1907, the value of rents upon Downland farms had tumbled by somewhere in the order of 50%. Creasey and Ward's work sums up the situation so: *"The rise of manufacturing industry led inexorably to the decline in the importance of agriculture and the traditional rural industries, leaving the countryside progressively denuded of people, their skills and vitality. Britain became a nation of town-dwellers, dependant for food supplies not from her own farmers, but on low cost producers from overseas, the Americas, Australasia and parts of Europe. As increasing numbers of steamships unloaded foodstuffs from all five continents at the great ports, for rapid distribution by rail to every part of the United Kingdom, agriculturists bemoaned the ruin of their industry and appealed in vain to successive Governments for protection against foreign competition. But by this time free trade and cheap food were such powerful vote-winners that no party could champion protection and hope to succeed at the polls. By 1914 the contraction of British agriculture had gone so far that only some 30 per cent of the country's food requirements was home-grown, a deficiency that was to have serious repercussions following the outbreak of war with Germany. During the early years of the war agricultural production continued to stagnate, primarily because the Government offered no incentives to farmers to raise output. By 1917, however, sinkings of British merchant ships by German U-boats, were so numerous that a serious food shortage ensued, forcing a change in Government policy. For the first time, farmer's incomes were directly supported by the state; the 1917 Corn Production Act guaranteed prices for wheat, oats and potatoes - a stimulus that resulted in a considerable expansion of the cultivated acreage. By 1918 centralized control had been established over all food supplies - both domestic and imported."* (3).

After the cessation of hostilities free trade resumed and Government made the concession of continuing the guaranteed price system under the Agriculture Act, 1920. This ray of light was however very short lived for in 1921 world prices were to slump. Saddled with the sudden soaring cost of a food support policy, the Government repealed the Act. This resulted in both production and wage cuts leading to Britain becoming a dumping ground for the world's food surplus. By 1932 this had reached an alarming level and the Government realised that action was imperative. Creasey and Ward again: *"This action took the form, principally, of a return to the subsidies so successfully pioneered during the First World War, supplemented by the creation of Marketing Boards to promote more efficient marketing, and a number of trade agreements with overseas exporting countries. State intervention, however, was introduced on a piece-meal basis and did not represent a strategy for British agriculture, or long term commitment to the prosperity of the industry. At best, legislation offered only limited assistance to farmers, and helped sustain incomes until a general economic recovery in world trade was effected in the mid 1930's. The real significance of the 1930's legislation is that it provided the mechanisms for permanent state control, adopted during the Second World War and later incorporated in the 1947 Agriculture Act."* (3).

During the inter-war years, as cereal farming became less profitable especially on more marginal land such as parts of the South Downs, large acreages were put down to grass or simply left to grass over naturally. The Downland arable-sheep farmers were badly affected; they could no longer afford to fold their flocks in the time-honoured way on a succession of fodder or catch crops, the system being too expensive in terms of labour. Nationally, the situation continued to decline with the area of arable land together with the number of agricultural workers employed, reaching an all-time low. By 1938, with agricultural output at an all time low, Government action was again imperative as it was now realised that should another war break out, Britain would be in an extremely vulnerable position.

With the darkening clouds of war again looming over Europe, War Agricultural Committees were set up again within each county, composed of leading men from that county's farming community. They in turn formed district committees, so that in every county a body of between 50 and 100 persons steered that county's agricultural war effort and disseminated the latest technology. The committees also became directly involved in wartime production on land where the owner was unable or unwilling to contribute to the war effort themselves.

THE FARMERS THEMSELVES.

Exceat. The first reference to 'Exceat Farm' as a consolidated farming unit, as opposed to separately farmed parcels of land within the parish was at the beginning of the 18th century. Recorded in the West Dean parish register is an entry for August 26 1708 concerning the baptism of Richard, son of Edward Stanford. Edward Stanford, who was born at Itchingfield in West Sussex in about 1660, was the tenant of Exceat Farm. Here follows part of his lease when renewed on March 27 1722: *"Term, 14 years; rent , [£]210. The leasee to be allowed a half of all Wreck goods salved by him. Leasor to allow 10 cords of wood out of Abbots wood yearly for fuel. To repair the Causeway leading towards and over the River from Exceat House to Seaford. To keep in repair the wall of 49 acres of the Salt Marsh which had been Inn'd from the sea.*" His grandson William became Lord of the manor of Preston and Hove, and High Sheriff of Sussex in 1808; in turn, his grandson was Thomas-Stanford, M.P. (4, 5).

Between 1751 and 1766 Exceat was tenanted by William Hanford. During the years 1766 and 1780 the farm was taken in hand and farmed by its owner, Lord Gage of Firle. In 1780 the farm was tenanted to one Peter Martin possibly hailing from Ditchling. From 1787, the farm was in the name of George Allfrey, a member of a well known local farming family. (6).

On October 11 1794, a lease was entered into by Messrs. John, Thomas and Richard Ellis, all of Newhall, Henfield, for the tenancy of Exceat Farm which totalled 407 hectares (1,007 acres) plus 21 hectares (53 acres) of Pevensey Marshes, for 13 years at a rental of £596 per year. (7). Five years later the lease was made over solely to John who we learn from the parish burial register died in May 1843 at the age of 74 years. The Ellis' continued to farm at Exceat it passing to John jnr. until his death in 1874. Between 1878 and 1895, the farm was worked by a George Homewood, who did not reside on the farm. According to the 1881 census, Exceat House was occupied by William King born in North Nibley, Gloucestershire and recorded as being the manager of Exceat, employing 15 men and 9 boys.

On October 11 1895, Edward Joseph Gorringe who already farmed Chyngton Farm took on Exceat at a rent of £150 per year. He was described by Alfred DeBock Porter of Cluttons, land agents for the Ecclesiastical Commissioners as *"a substantial tenant who has sufficient capital"* to stock and manage Exceat. (8). During the previous year, 41 year old Gorringe had been elected a committee member of the Southdown Sheep Society in recognition of his work in furthering the breed. By way of his fathers second marriage, his step brother was Rowland Gorringe (b. 1885) who went on to establish the well-known local estate agents still trading under his name. (9).

In 1909, the tenancy was transferred to his oldest son Edward Percy Gorringe; in May of that year the Ecclesiastical Commissioners received a bill for expenses incurred by E.J. and E.P. Gorringe for amongst other items, painting and repairing Exceat House where 'Percy' was shortly to live. (Permission had been granted in the original Gorringe tenancy agreement of 1895, to sublet this house to Kemp the wheelwright.) Further light upon Percy's forthcoming marriage appeared in a communication received in October of that year by the Commissioners from their agents. It contained a request from his father for an earth closet to be installed and that a passage room be converted into a bathroom complete with bath, lavatory basin, and hot and cold water services. His wife was the beautiful Eleanor Schor known to the family as 'Nell;' local children came to know her well for they would regularly visit Exceat House where she held a Sunday School. (8, 9).

In 1925 Percy Gorringe gave notice to Cluttons of his intention to terminate his tenancy of Exceat the coming October 11. Cluttons remarked that *"we anticipate considerable difficulty in reletting this large sheep farm owing to the amount of capital required to stock it at present prices."* After gaining assistance from land agents Messrs. Powell & Co. of Lewes (subsequently absorbed into Strutt & Parker?), who were formally involved with Exceat as agents for Lord Gage, several names were put forward as possible tenants. From these, Charles Schwier of Hands Farm, Writtle in Essex was selected. *"The proposed tenant is recommended to us as a keen and energetic farmer who is at present farming a small farm of some 187 acres, of which he owns the freehold - This farm is at the present time in the market for sale and he proposes to reside at Exceat. He is some 35 years of age, married and has 4 children. The father is a successful farmer possessed of a considerable amount of capital and is, we understand, prepared to support his son financially should it be necessary to do so."* The Commissioners on receiving the above recommendation from Cluttons together with a suggested annual rent of £475 gave their approval. (8).

Eleanor and Percy Gorringe relaxing in garden of Exceat House. The garden originally stretched to the road.

Having acquired the tenancy of Exceat Farm, Schwier was particularly loathe to have members of the public wandering at will across his land and there ensued a incensed controversy between the public and ramblers on the one hand and, Schwier and Cluttons on the other. In December 1925 Arthur Beckett, an Eastbourne newspaper proprietor and president of the Society of Sussex Downsmen, wrote to the Commissioners registering the following complaint. That two people were recently stopped on the cliffs west of Crowlink by two aggressive men. The walkers were told that they had no right of way and that they were trespassing; when asked what authority they had, one of the men stated that he was Schwier, the farmer. The walkers were then escorted back to the Crowlink boundary, Schwier adding that in future nobody would be allowed to walk across the Seven Sisters. Beckett pointed out that he had walked the Seven Sisters cliff-tops for 40 years; a month later he wrote again reporting a similar incident. Cluttons considered the situation had arisen during the days of the Crowlink coastguards, there then being a ferry across the river which also took members of the public. On January 21 1926, the Commissioners wrote to Cluttons stating that they *"...were not prepared to sanction any action by the tenant, nor any action to stop the public entering the land."* The dispute swiftly became very emotive with letters and articles appearing in both the local and national press. (8).

In March, Cluttons received a letter from the Reverend Lawrence, rector of West Dean and chairman of the parish council. He wrote that access to the beach via Exceat Farm was *"...regarded as a general right of way on foot until recent enclosure by wire fencing."* He considered the cliff-top path was the property of the Admiralty, there still being piles of chalk along the path to show the way during dark. He went on to say that during the latter part of Gorringe's tenancy, there had been a great increase in the number of people visiting the beach, especially in motor cars and several camping parties. A great many people were now being turned away. (8).

The Rev. Lawrence wrote again in July on the issue of access from Exceat to the beach; attached to his letter were statements from 13 people who stated that access to the beach had been uninterrupted until recently. Four of the statements are reproduced here for they contain other facts of interest (8):

"B. 70 years of age. Has known path following the above course for 60 years past and used it originally without interruption and no gates. Heavy vehicles used that track for collecting beach for road repairs. He brought timber that way after a wreck. No gates."

"C. Born 56 years ago in the district. Used path for 40 years seen track used for haulage of beach no gates originally and at times has seen residents and strangers using the path. He remembers erection of gates after which pedestrians could still go as before but wheeled traffic were required to obtain the key from tenant."

"H. Has lived in district about 50 years been Fly Proprietor for about 35 years. Has used path and driven down it many times. Has seen people on foot and with vehicles using it and has not been stopped. Cannot recollect any gates being locked."

"J. Was Wheelwright at Exceat started work about 34 years ago and remained 16 years. Put up gates on farm when he first went to Exceat people could go where they liked if they closed gates. No gates between Exceat Farm on the Eastbourne side of the river and the sea until he put them up and then only for enclosing grazing land. Anyone on foot or in a cart or wagon could use track without being stopped."

"M. Was employed at Exceat from about 1884 to 1896. Knew of path there were no fences between road and cliff end. Has seen visitors as well as local people going that way for bathing. He has not heard of any one being stopped."

Shortly afterwards, the Commissioners re-stated their position and presumably because of the strength of public opinion and a wish to settle the dispute amicably they issued the following compromise. That notice boards be placed ten feet inland from the cliff-top path at intervals asking people to keep to the path and that the land beyond was private. There was to be no access to or from Exceat Farm to the coast; people who had or were about to cross the Seven Sisters would be allowed to pass along the embankment to Exceat Bridge via land belonging to Chyngton Farm. (8).

Being financially guaranteed by his father who had recently bought Dittons Farm at Pevensey, proved to be Charles Schwier's downfall for during October 1927 his father died. Due to the winding up of his father's estate Schwier had to relinquish his tenancy of Exceat. Upon leaving the farm and the public access controversy, he introduced Lt. Col. Alexander Watson of Radway in Warwickshire to Cluttons, who was willing to take over tenancy of the farm. Watson was assigned the tenancy as from September 1927 and continued to farm there until his death in January 1945. During Watson's time access and camping was permitted together with the siting of caravans overlooking the Haven and within the Exceat Newbarn area, until the outbreak of World War Two when the caravans were largely abandoned. (8).

Some considerable time after Watson's death, Cluttons in July 1946 wrote to the Commissioners: *"Messrs. A.S. Pattenden, D.A.*

Butterfield and A.R. Malcolm who duly signed a memorandum giving effect to the agreement as from 31st January 1945 under the terms of the previous Agreement and from which date we have been collecting the rent in full. Mr. Pattenden is 32, married with two children and resides in the farmhouse, being a practical and enterprising young farmer of somewhat limited means for a farm of this size; the other two partners are substantial business men who have no previous farming experience but with the necessary capital and we consider this a satisfactory combination for the working of the farm." (8). Arthur Pattenden came to Exceat from the Gatwick area and was of a forthright, resolute character, indeed a man who 'called a spade a spade;' hard working and with a good business acumen he became a well-respected cattle dealer at local markets. Under him the farm prospered, diversifying into pigs, race horses and in particular a thriving camping and caravan site. Indeed camping flourished too well for in the late 1960's a closure order was placed upon it after a public inquiry, due to its huge, sprawling nature and inadequate facilities, usage being far in excess of the site's licence. Arthur Pattenden died in February 1970 and was to be the last mixed arable/livestock farmer on Exceat.

West Dean. Inventory of known tenants (6):

1751 George Allfrey	1871 William Bannister
1766 Lancelot Harrison	1880 A.D. Mannington
1790 William Harrison	1887 H.M. Simmons
1797 John Durrant	1895 Tom Ayles
1806 Richard Saxby	1900 Duke of Devonshire
1850 Charles Saxby	1907 Eastbourne Waterworks Co.
1859 Charles Waters	

Charlston. Inventory of known tenants (6):

1653 Thomas Read	1843 Charles Ade
1668 Edward Allfrey	1845 Ann Ade
1696 Edward Allfrey	1848 Charles Ade
1729 George Allfrey	1875 Charles Bradford
1752 John Bean	1882 J.S. Richardson
1794 William Packham	1888 A. Richardson
1808 John Hitchens	1890 John Brook Bray
1825 James Hall	1918 Alan Richardson
1827 Messrs. Ade & Newman	1921 Richard Canning Brown

Chyngton. In 1839, the tenant of Chyngton Farm is recorded as being Thomas Chambers. From the 1851 census we learn that the tenancy was held by James Turner, born at Southwick in 1802; he continued to farm Chyngton until 1867. At this point in time, Edward Joseph Gorringe enters on to the scene. He was a firm, authoritive gentleman; when he became chairman of the board of governors of the Seaford Board School, he inherited a history of frequent teacher turnover that is, until he dealt with the head teacher! During the first 31 years of the newly created local authority, known as the Seaford Local Government Board, later becoming the Seaford Urban District Council, he was continuously a member and served as chairman from 1896 until 1914. Gorringe initially worshipped at the small parish church at West Dean, but did not take to being locked in while the service was in progress as was the habit of the rector! In due course he had part of the large tythe barn at Chyngton converted with use of wood panelling into a small chapel. (9).

From 1918, Chyngton was tenanted by Messrs. Wells & Wakefield until approximately 1925 when Daniel Paul took over the tenancy of the farm, having moved over from the then adjoining Frog Firle Farm near Alfriston. With the break up of the Chyngton estate after the untimely death of its recent new owner Hugh Northcote, the land to the north of the A 259 was later to be owned and farmed by the Wyniotts until bought in the late 1970's by Mary White. Chyngton Farm nowadays comprises of two land holdings; the southern half being the property of Lewes District Council and the northern half which was owned and farmed by David Paul and family until 1993; when he retired from farming the Paul's sold their land to the National Trust.

Crowlink. Inventory of known tenants (6):

1752 John Willard	1877 J. Baker
1766 Nicholas Friend	1881 Thomas Carey
1795 Thomas Rason	1895 Frederick de Costabadie
1811 Charles Willard	1896 John Hole
1823 George Buckwell	1898 executors of John Hole
1834 Mrs. Buckwell	1905 Edward Joseph Gorringe
1843 John Guy	- Edward Percy Gorringe
1871 Matthew Mockett	1922 K.A.H. Thomson

ARABLE FARMING. With the exception of parts of Chyngton and Dymock Farms, much of the land within the study area is of relatively poor quality, which during the early decades of the 20th century in the main consisted four large sheep farms. A report prepared by Clutton's for the Ecclesiastical Commissioners in 1896 stated that: *"The Lands included in this Report are of a purely agricultural character and comprise two Sheep Farms on the edge of the Southdowns adjoining the coast. The greater portion of the land is thin especially Crowlink Farm, and much of it used merely as Sheepwalk... The exposed bleak situation of the Farms and the poor character of much of the land make the property less desirable than its compact character would otherwise render it.* "Two leases drawn up in 1850 state that of the 198 hectares (489 acres) of Crowlink Farm, 87 hectares (216 acres) were composed of *"Sheep Down."* In regard to Exceat Farm, of the 407 hectares (1,006 acres), some 132 hectares (326 acres) were made up of *"Sheep Down."* By 1922 these figures for sheep down or sheep walk, had altered slightly to 200 and 344 acres respectively and were fetching a rent of between 5s 0d and 7s 6d (25p and 372p) per acre/year. (8). The sheep flock was vital to the downland farmer; the famous agricultural commentator Arthur Young referred to them in 1813 as a *"moving dunghill."* Geographers sometimes refer to this system as a 'robber economy;' basically, during the day sheep removed nutrients from the sheep walk and deposited them on the arable lands during the night, this being referred to as 'foldtail or foldings'.

James Caird writing in 1851 about foldtail or as he referred to it, *"tenant-right or compensation for unexhausted improvements,"* made the following critical observations: *"The only counties in which the custom of tenant-right is fully recognized are Surrey, the Weald of Kent, Sussex, Lincoln, North Notts, and parts of the West Riding. In these counties the custom has been so long in operation as to have become binding in law. The amount of the valuation varies between ,3 and ,5 an acre. A tenant entering to a farm is thus obliged to pay over a large sum to his predecessor for operations which he has had no voice in. The advance of so much capital over and above the ordinary stock of the farm often hampered their own tenancy. In counties where this system exists, the agriculture is on the whole inferior to that of other districts."* (10). When E.J. Gorringe took over Exceat Farm in October 1895, the low rent of £150 per year increasing to £180 after two years, was to take account of the outgoing valuation or foldtail amounting to £700. During Gage's lease of Crowlink *"the old Sussex custom"* for the incoming tenant paying for the dung and foldtail to the outgoing tenant was extinguished with a large single payment by Lord Gage. E.J. Gorringe asked if this arrangement could also be agreed for Exceat; accordingly, the Commissioners agreed to pay the sum of £360 - 14s - 10d. (£360.74). (8).

Chalk itself was often applied upon the Downs as 'manure,' not on the typical chalky soils but on the heavy clay with flint deposits frequently found. This helped to ameliorate the heavy and somewhat acidic character of these clay soils benefiting the production of wheat;

evidence of quarrying can be seen in the study area by the presence of abandoned chalk pits upon Exceat and Gayles Farms. They are often mistakenly claimed to be bomb craters from the Second World War but as they are shown on the Tithe Map of 1840, this is obviously not the case! Sometimes, chalk was burnt or roasted in kilns to produce lime which was even more beneficial to producing wheat. The practice was expensive when taking into account the coal or wood required to fuel the kilns; Arthur Young writing in 1813 questioned this additional expense. (11). Running inland from between Short Brow and Rough Brow is Limekiln Bottom, the name inferring that a lime kiln was once situated here and which to this day contains several disused chalk pits. On the 1874 edition of the 25 inch O.S. maps covering the Exceat area two lime kilns are shown; one sited between the two later Second World War pillboxes near to where the floodbank adjoins Cliff End and another where the present day cliff strikes the shingle beach. They may have also been involved with the production of lime for mortar for use in the building trade.

On one occasion sometime during the late 19th or early 20th century, an unusual form of manure was used upon Chyngton; it seems there was a snowstorm which blew in from the south-east. During this spell of cold weather a large quantity of dead fish were washed ashore and deposited along the strand line between Cuckmere and Seaford; these were loaded on to carts and spread upon the land. (12). The first recorded use of artificial fertilizer in the study area was during 1920 when the Eastbourne Waterworks Company agreed to allow its use on part of their West Dean Farm.

Until the 1930's, flint picking was carried out upon the arable lands during slack periods by the farms labour force. Bottomless one cubic yard-capacity boxes were used as measures; two were held at Exceat and one at Crowlink. These were placed in the field and work proceeded to fill them to the brim; when full the 'box' was lifted from around the flints and the process repeated. Much of the flint from Exceat went for road making in Eastbourne. The County Council also purchased flints; for example an advertisement placed in the Sussex Express of April 26 1890 invited tenders for Land Picked Flint in quantities of between 50-400 tons in particular parishes, to be dropped in 2-6 ton 'lumps' for use on main roads. Quantities were also required to be delivered to railway depots. Locally for example, during the early 1920's flint was delivered to the lay-by just east of the entrance to The Gayles. Here, a 'stone-breaker' using a hammer and wearing goggles for eye protection, proceeded to reduce the size of the flint prior to its use. The reduced flint was used by placing a layer along a section of road, it then being covered with a blinding of soil which was then watered in, and steam rolled. The surface was then brushed clear of dust, followed by a liberal coat of tar which was applied using brooms and lastly, surfaced with gravel which arrived by rail at either Seaford or Eastbourne goods yards. (13).

During the Gorringe period, there were three corn binders or reapers which worked their three farms. Preceding entry of the binder into a field, men would cut a swathe around the headland of the field using scythes, in order that upon cutting the first swathe, the horses would not trample the standing corn. Once safely incorporated into the form of a rick or stack the corn would await the arrival of a contractors thrashing outfit during the following months; this would comprise of a steam traction engine, thrashing machine and caravan. Bert Etherton recalled when a young lad working on Chyngton Farm during the 1890's, being asked to accompany a thrashing outfit: *"One day the foreman Mr. Carr said, "Bertie, you're going to earn sixpence this morning, but you must keep your eyes open. We're shifting the threshing tackle to Exceat by road. Here's a flag, you've got to walk in front, and when you see cattle coming, or horses or sheep, stop the machine till they get by. When you get to Exceat, hand over the flag to the driver of the thresher and come home!"* (14).

George Levett who was born and lived until aged 27 in the hamlet of Milton Street near Alfriston, recalled how when 16 years of age he worked for two winters (possibly 1924-25) for French's of Seaford. Ben and Burt French kept their thrashing outfit in a yard on the site now occupied by The Seven Sisters public house; Jack Goacher was the traction engine driver. George usually walked to work from home, often to Exceat, Foxhole, Newbarn or Chyngton, for which he earned four shillings (20 pence) per day, work commencing at seven o'clock. When thrashing, sheaves were pitched up on to the top of the thrashing machine where George acted as bond-cutter before passing the sheaves on to the feeder, Arthur Simmons. When thrashing at Foxhole once they were nearing the floor when suddenly a large rat ran from beneath the remaining stacked sheaves, negotiated the wire mesh put across the barn doors to contain rats and began running up the nearby hillside, with George armed with a piece of wood in hot pursuit. Suddenly, the rat abruptly turned and jumped at George, hitting him square in the chest! (15).

On another occasion they were taking the thrashing outfit over hill from Exceat to Foxhole when, nearing the crest of the hill, the outfit became stuck on the steep, greasy trackway. This occurred at about 4 o'clock on a winter's afternoon. After a struggle, they eventually got the engine on to firmer ground and plying out a steel cable attempted to extract the thrasher and caravan, but the cable broke under the strain. By this time the daylight had completely gone and so they decided to stay the night in the caravan. During the long night however, the wind strengthened considerably; being on the exposed hilltop and fearing the caravan may blow over, they decided to lash it down with rope! (15).

On two occasions, they worked at South Barn, Chyngton, once to thrash a crop of linseed out of the barn and stack back within, this taking a fortnight; the other occasion was to thrash a crop of field beans, the sheaves being fed into the thrashers drum whole, the beans flying in all directions! George frequently found other seasonal employment on a casual basis carrying out a variety work for a number of farmers. Crops of mangolds and turnips had to be hoed along between rows and then with a six inch wide hoe, cross ways along the rows in order to thin out the plants. Later in the season bolters and forked plants required being pulled by hand. (15).

In closing this section concerning arable farming, we will briefly look at the Agricultural Returns for the parish of West Dean. These have been compiled annually since 1866; however West Dean's records appear to be incorrect or incomplete. The acreages do not tally with that of the parish, they only appearing correct for the period 1880-1910. From the 1930's Exceat Farm appears not to exist! Taking the figures from the correctly recorded period, the total recorded acreage varies between 777 to 797 hectares (1,920 and 1,970 acres). Crops listed as grown include wheat, barley, oats, rye, peas, potatoes, turnips, swedes, mangolds, cabbage, rape, vetch, lucerne and sainfoin. (16).

SHEEP. For hundreds of years the South Downs were famous for their sheep and wool production, indeed the local breed the 'Southdown,' has been of outstanding significance both in its own right and that of assisting the improvement or creation of new breeds.

Introduction. The Southdown occupies a position among the 'short-wool' sheep akin to that of the 'Leicester' among the 'long-wools,' i.e. it was the first short-wool breed to be systematically improved and contributed greatly to the improvement of many other breeds in that group. One of the smaller British breeds, Southdown ewes reach a mature weight of 55 kilos (120 lbs), with lambs becoming gradeable or marketable at 32-36 kilos (70-80 lbs) liveweight. The general conformation is compact and blocky with a wide firm back and an exceptionally thick leg. The head is short and wide, the ears small. The face and short legs, which are partially wooled over are of a uniform light greyish brown. The wool is of 60/65 quality, exceedingly dense on the pelt, very short and is the finest wool from any breed native to Britain. The clip is not heavy, reaching ordinarily only 1.5 to 2.25 kilos and is used in a wide range of quality fabrics including hosiery, hand-knitting wools, dress fabrics, flannel and light tweeds. Wool of this fine quality made first class lightweight underwear in which soft texture, elasticity and insulating properties were combined, an important use in years gone by! The Southdown is early maturing and produces sheep meat of unsurpassed quality.

Origins. *"Although the Southdown is undoubtedly the oldest of the short-wool breeds, its early history is more or less wrapped in a veil of mystery, but through this veil appears one undeniable fact, that upon these chalky hills, an active, short-wooled breed of sheep flourished from time immemorable."* The records of medieval and later times are full of references to flocks both great and small which ranged over the Downs. For example, in 1341 the monastic sheep farmers of Alciston Grange, part of the huge Battle Abbey estate, had a flock numbering in excess of some 3,000 sheep. (17).

Those sheep were certainly not recognisable as the Southdown which we know of today. A connecting link with those early ancestors would appear to be given by the Rev. Gilbert White who wrote in 1773, *"One thing is very remarkable as to sheep: from Westward till you get to the River Adur, all flocks have horns, and smooth, white faces, and white legs, and a hornless sheep is rarely to be seen, but as soon as you pass that river Eastward, and mount Beeding Hill, all the flocks at once become hornless, or as they call them 'poll sheep;' and have, moreover, black faces with a white tuft of wool on their foreheads, and speckled and spotted legs."* (17).

Breed Improvement. Towards the end of the 18th century, Sussex farmer John Ellman commenced upon work which was to ensure his place in history, namely the improvement of the local Downs sheep which then thickly populated the east Sussex Downs, into the modern Southdown breed. John was born in 1753, the son of Richard and Elizabeth Ellman. His father farmed in the wealden parish of Hartfield until 1761, when he became the tenant of Place Farm in Glynde also known as Great Farm, which like most of the parish belonged to the Trevors of Glynde Place. The farm's account books suggest that Richard had already established the grazier business which John was to make very prosperous; this meticulous management of accounts was also considered important by John. When his father died in 1780, John aged only 27 became tenant of Place Farm. (18).

It was at about this time that John began his improvement of the breed on the 202 hectares (580 acre) farm, which had initially carried a breeding flock of 500 ewes. He has been credited with pioneering work in many aspects of sheep husbandry, the flushing of ewes, folding and the housing of ewes during bad weather; though more than likely he was following good contemporary practice, significantly he was publicising it. The native Down breed was being improved at this time by several other breeders but again, Ellman probably did rather more in publicising, including the sale of improved stock to such noble farmers as Thomas Coke of Norfolk and the Duke of Bedford. By selective breeding, he managed to fix the breed on the best of the existing types of the old breed: the best standard of the pre-Ellman days became the common standard of the new Southdown. His fame as an improver was however, to be steadily nurtured by his friend the agricultural commentator Arthur Young. From about 1790 his reputation grew rapidly until his retirement in 1829, he passing away the following year. He was to become a farmer of such repute that his presence at important agricultural gatherings was reported in the national agricultural journals along with that of such noble agriculturalists as the Duke of Bedford and the Earl of Egremont and he entered into regular correspondence with other well-known improvers such as Coke and Robert Bakewell who improved the long-wool Leicester breed. (18).

Ellman took special care in choosing his breeding ewes, paying particular attention to the quality of wool and carcass conformation; the same criteria also applied to his selection of rams. He wanted stock with *"thick, curly wool with depth of staple, and even topped, such wool as will best defend the sheep in bad weather, from being very thick and even topped, will not admit the water to penetrate it, as it does a thin light loose wool. I believe I grow the heaviest wool between Brighthelmstone and Eastbourne, and sell for the highest price of any wool on the South Downs."* Whilst paying attention to the conformation of his sheep and quality of wool, he accepted that he could not inbreed as this would lower the standards he sought to maintain. To introduce new blood into his flock Ellman selected fifty of the best ewes from neighbouring flocks which he judged to be of suitable quality and drafted out thirty to forty of his own ewes that failed his criteria of conformation or had become barren. (18).

By 1799, Glynde rams were held in the highest esteem nationally and were hired by other enlightened farmers for breeding purposes; the rams were numbered and their age and parentage carefully recorded. One ram was hired that year for 100 guineas (£105). They appeared to have provided Ellman with a considerable income, as the prices they commanded continued to rise for much of his life. Hiring had the advantage in that he could have more rams working per season and therefore able to select more rapidly the very best rams for future use on his own flock. Young when commenting upon the area observed, *"Between Eastbourne and Steyning, which is 33 miles, the Downs, are about six miles wide and in this tract there are, it is said, about 200,000 ewes kept. I am inclined to think, that this is the highest stocking that is known in this kingdom, and ought to give us a good opinion of the Breed, whatever it might be, that can be kept in such numbers on a given space of country."* At the Lewes Sheep Fair of 1793, 30,000 sheep and lambs were sold, large droves of them being bought by dealers from Essex. (11).

Jonas Webb. Later during the 19th century Ellman's pioneering work was further enhanced by Jonas Webb. Born November 10 1796 at Great Thurlow in Suffolk, he was the second son of Samuel Webb who later moved to Streetly Hall, West Wickham in Cambridgeshire. Jonas Webb began business as a farmer at Babraham near Cambridge during 1822. After experimenting, he rejected the local Norfolk Horn breed and devoted himself to the breeding of the Southdown. He first of all purchased *"the best sheep that could be obtained from the principle breeders in Sussex"* and then by a vigorous system of judicious and careful selection, he produced a permanent type in accordance with his own ideas of perfection. He staged a series of lettings which became a major event during the agricultural year. These were held in a small meadow near the Hall, the rams being on view around the field from early morning. Each bore a ticket indicating the weight of its fleece, they being introduced one by one into a roped enclosure in which both auctioneer and bidders stood. The average price of the lettings was nearly £24 each with some rams bringing in the large sum for those days of £180. At full strength, the Babraham flock numbered some 2,400 ewes, divided into five 'tribes' indicated by marks which Webb kept strictly secret despite banter from his friends. (19).

Webb began his career as an exhibitor at the second meeting of the Royal Agricultural Society of England held at Cambridge in 1840, when he received two prizes for his Southdown ewes. This success was followed up on practically every subsequent annual meeting at which he exhibited until at Canterbury in 1860, when he took all six prizes offered by the Society for rams and sold the first prize ram *"Canterbury"* for 250 guineas (£262.50). He was also a consistent prize winner at other shows. In several instances however, these successes were bought dearly as his ewes and aged rams were rendered useless by over fattening, a prerequisite for showing during that period. The result was that he resolved in the future to only exhibit his younger rams. He had great success with his shearling rams exhibited at the French International Exposition in 1855, for which he received a gold medal of the first class. The Emperor Napoleon III congratulated him on his success, admiring the beauty of the rams he had exhibited. Webb responded by presenting him with the choicest specimen, receiving in return some time afterwards *"a candelabrum of massive silver with appropriate devices."* (19).

But age and gout were beginning to tell and Webb decided to retire from sheep breeding. On July 10 1861 there was a great dispersal sale at Babraham. A special train was laid on from London and well over a thousand people, including visitors from France, Canada, America, Australia, Switzerland, Sweden and the German states sat down to a huge feast. In all, 358 rams and 1,049 ewes were sold for a total sum of nearly £17,000. A year later in June at an equally prestigious event, the remainder of his flock was sold, 969 sheep being sold by auction for a total of £10,926. Webb died at Cambridge on November 10 1862, his birthday; his end being accelerated by the death only five days before of his beloved wife. (19).

Other New and Improved Breeds. The improved Southdown was by the end of the 18th century, establishing for itself a pocket of influence in the centre of the Norfolk Horn country. The Norfolk was a *"notably derisory"* sheep, difficult to confine and lean in its conformation. Another well known farmer and commentator, Marshall of Suffolk, believed that with careful internal selection these could be converted into as good sheep as would thrive on the heaths and barren sheep walks of the Brecklands. Norfolk breeders however, paid more attention to preservation of the breed's distinctive points than taking advantage of its great gift of prolificacy. So began Marshall's work, the first of a number of new or improved breeds incorporating the qualities of the improved Southdown. The result came to be known as the Suffolk; the breed today is this countries most popular sire for fat lamb production. The use of the Southdown to manufacture other Down breeds began during the period 1830 to 1840. The motive behind this multiplication of British breeds was a simple one, the continual search for more and better mutton, more quickly. The use of the Southdown was to lead to the creation or improvement of the following breeds: Hampshire Down, Oxford Down, Dorset Horn, Dorset Down and Shropshire Down. (20).

By the period 1850 to 1870, the characteristics of all these new breeds had become fixed and accepted. The Southdown went on to become the country's most popular breed of sheep throughout the 19th and early 20th centuries. At London's Smithfield Show of 1920 (John Ellman incidentally was a founder member of the Smithfield Society), Southdown's won the Championship for both dead and alive, for the 23rd time out of the 49 shows held between 1869 and 1920. In this respect as if a consolation prize, the nearest rivals were Hampshire

Downs and Suffolks, both winning the above coveted distinction eight times each. (21). Changes in the outward characteristics of the modern breed, the lighter face and short legs are relatively recent; the breed in France still retains the dark face and longer leg of the earlier improved breed.

Folding. Traditionally, Southdown sheep were associated with 'folding,' together with the close-grazing of the Downland sward, so revered by today's conservationists. Folding can be best described as the penning with hurdles (panels constructed from interlaced hazel or split ashwood), of a large number of sheep upon a limited area of fallow or purpose-sown crop, for a short duration. The practice originated date back to the Middle Ages when sheep were confined at night within folds to prevent straying into crops. Before the 18th century, no specific crops were grown for folding; with the adoption of legumes and green fallow crops, there followed the improvement of the sheep themselves. By day, the flocks would graze the open, un-fenced Downland 'sheepwalk,' accompanied at all times by a shepherd; when returned to the fold at night, manurial residues (dung) referred to as 'foldtail,' was transferred from the sheepwalk and deposited on the to be cultivated land; a 'robber economy.' This system gave rise to that unique English pastoral spectacle, the Downland shepherd tending his flock, so evocatively chronicled during its closing days by the great naturalist and writer, Barclay Wills.

Southdown sheep folded within wooden hurdles on Chyngton Farm.

The agricultural authority and sheep folding advocate James Thomas, termed this 'The English Folding System;' the following description was published by him in 1945. *"Arable sheep farming is costly. A full-time shepherd is necessary every day of the year for flocks exceeding 250 ewes. He will require additional help during the lambing season; he must be waited on, because from time to time his folding equipment must be moved from one part of the farm to another. During the summer, water must be hauled for the flock if they have not access to a natural supply, and the shepherd may expect considerable amounts of hay and trough food to be provided, particularly if he is in charge of a ram breeding flock. Some of the rotations used on arable sheep farms are very complex; catch crops have to be introduced for consumption during the late spring and summer months to fill up the gap that exists when roots are finished and aftermath clovers and sainfoins are not ready. In some of the older rotations practised, three successive crops were folded off in preparation for wheat; here is an example of such a rotation - first year, wheat; second year, autumn-sown catch crops, such as rye, winter barley, vetches, followed by swedes, and swedes and kale; third year, rape or rape and turnips; fourth year, wheat; fifth year, oats; sixth year, seeds mown [hay]; seventh year, seeds folded off by sheep in preparation for wheat again.*

It is perhaps advisable here to summarize various crops of tillage land which can be fed-off by sheep. First, the cruciferous [cabbage family] crops. Early-sown rape, turnips, and marrow-stem kale are best fed during December and January, after which period swedes, thousand-headed kale, and certain late-flowering rape hybrids can be used until the end of April or early May. Certain leguminous [pea family] crops are specifically grown for sheep; in addition to sainfoin, red clovers, and lucerne, mention must be made of trefoil, trifolium, and vetches for the early summer period. As to cereal crops, rye and winter barley have a very limited value for sheep folding, as they so quickly bolt into ear and become fibrous; they must in fact be regarded solely as stopgaps following the root crops and preceding the summer fallow crops. The maintenance of an arable flock does greatly complicate the farm cultivation programme, for crops for sheep must be sown at the right time and, in addition to the ordinary cropping programme; the provision of arable crops for a flock of three or four hundred ewes is no simple matter; but it is still done [1945], and where it is done properly, light arable land is producing better crops of corn than on comparable farms where the root-break has been eliminated and heavier applications of chemical fertilizers are made." (22). By contrast, during the early 1800's, the flock of John Eards of Alfriston consisting of 450 ewes, lived on the *"native Downs"* plus eight acres of turnips, eight loads of hay, and five acres of rape. (11).

Summing up, the three main advantages of sheep folding were: i) improvement of the moisture retaining quality of soil during dry weather. ii) a reduction of leaching of nutrients from porous soils. iii) an increase in the reserves of organic plant food. The acknowledged American authority on sheep W.C. Coffey, made the following observation: *"anyone who has seen the sheep of England within hurdles cannot question the efficiency of the hurdling method for bringing sheep as nearly as possible to their perfection."* (23).

The Southdown Sheep during the 20th Century. The earlier Southdown Sheep Society Flock Books of which volume one was published in 1893, read like a who's who of the Downland farming scene, as many Downland farmers owned pedigree Southdown flocks. For example, to take the flock on Exceat Farm, flock number 305, this was founded during 1895 by Edward Gorringe with a draft of ewes from his Chyngton flock (flock number 76), having just taken on the tenancy of Exceat. Purchases were also made from the flocks of the Countess of Chichester and W.P. Ashby of East Dean; further purchases were made from Mr. Brock of East Dean and G. Winter of Seaford. By 1908, the flock is recorded as numbering 906 breeding ewes. In the following year, ownership of the flock transferred to his son Percy, when 709 ewes were put to the rams. One of the rams used that year was from the highly respected Eartham flock, its sire being a Sandringham ram, the future King George V being Patron of the Southdown Sheep Society. Percy Gorringe's sheep were to win two

Southdowns being trough fed just prior to lambing. Note blocky shape, short legs and short dense fleece. Late twentieth century.

prizes at the 1921 Lewes Sheep Fair. During the early 1920's all registered Southdown flocks were given a suffix, usually the name of the farm or parish e.g. 'The Exceat Flock;' others were 'Birling,' 'Frog Firle' and 'Litlington.' 'Aquarius' was the name chosen by the Eastbourne Waterworks Company for their flock which grazed upon land where nowadays stands Friston Forest. (21).

To continue with 'The Exceat Flock,' in 1923 Gorringe bought six rams from the famous 'Flansham' flock of John Langmead of Ford near Arundel. Two years later on September 3 1925, the flock was disposed of when Percy Gorringe terminated his tenancy of Exceat. The flock dispersal of 246 ewes and 100 lambs, included the following sales:

R.C. Brown, Clapham House, Litlington.	48 ewes.
Viscount Gage, Firle Place, Firle.	25 lambs.
J.E. Gallup, Birling Farm, East Dean.	18 ewes.
Major Harding, Birling Manor, East Dean.	25 ewes.
Henry Harris, Perching Manor Farm, Fulking.	50 ewes.
Hole & Davis, Waterhall Farm, Patcham.	25 lambs.
G. Holeman, Tarring Court Farm, nr. Newhaven	25 lambs.
Scrase & Baldock, Wayfields Farm, Pyecombe.	60 ewes.
E. Turner, Skipton Oliffe Manor, Andoversford, Glos.	50 lambs.
J. & E. Wadman, Yew Tree Farm, Sompting.	20 ewes.

The next registered Southdown flock upon Exceat, flock number A8, was that of Col. Alexander Watson founded in 1928 as the 'Seven Sisters' flock and consisting of 274 breeding ewes. This flock was disposed of during 1940 after a disastrous lambing season, with much of the farm having been requisitioned by the military authorities. (21).

The number of Southdown breeding ewes in the 20th century peaked during 1911 when there were a total of 114,495 within the 359 registered flocks in the country. Being a rather small breed of sheep, lambs nowadays weigh about 15 kilos deadweight compared to a preferred deadweight in the order of 18 kilos, farmers began to look towards the northern hill breeds of sheep which also required less shepherding. The Southdown having become primarily an arable sheep, also suffered during the inter-war years from the rise in labour costs and the introduction of chemical fertilizer. Finally, the large post-war increase in cereal farming upon the Downs sealed the breed's fate in its native domain. Some idea of the crash in the fortunes of the breed may be gained from the following figures (21):

1927 263 flocks 58,769 ewes put to the ram.

1933 206 "   45,917 "
1937 157 "   30,344 "
1946 75 "   9,696 "
1951 40 "   4,420 "

Today, the breed languishes close to being a rare breed within this country, with a total number of registered breeding ewes in the region of some 1,500. Its main use commercially is as a 'terminal sire' for the production of quality lamb for discerning palates, it producing a succulent carcase of excellent quality and flavour. The breed also withstands drought conditions well.

Returning to the study area, the following events will help colour in the scene. During November 11 1776, heavy snow fell burying sheep at Exceat belonging to farmer Martin. Three unaccounted sheep were found by a dog 11 days later, while 23 days after the snow fell two more sheep came to light during the thaw. All five animals survived being nursed at his house on 'caudle,' (hot gruel with spiced wine!). (24). A common sight on the Downland farm was the shepherds hut or caravan; during the 19th century they were constructed of wood, but were later clad with corrugated iron. An average model made by a firm in Westbury, Wiltshire cost about £46 in 1925. During Gorringe's time at Chyngton, a shepherds caravan would be situated during the lambing season in Hope Gap Bottom, near to where today's steps descend the cliff.

Gorse which is to be found growing on the more acidic clay with flint deposits upon the Downs, was put to good use with the approach of construction of the lambing folds. This entailed the upright placing of cut gorse approximately 2 metres (6 feet) in height against the encircling hurdles, kept in place with twine secured to poles; this formed a windbreak around the lambing folds. Arthur Mewett while a carter upon Chyngton Farm for Edward Gorringe, was one day told by the farms foreman Mr. Crowhust, to go and fetch between 200-300 faggots of gorse from down in Brock Hole Bottom. Approaching the coombe from the south-west, his team of horses managed to hold the wagon until about halfway down the steep hillside until their hooves began to lose control due to the frozen nature of the ground. Arthur had to unhitch his team and withdraw, the wagon remaining in its precarious position for some time. (25).

A sheep wash was situated at Exceat across the horseshoe bend of the river opposite the old farm buildings and the present day car park. It consisted of a 'race' or penstock constructed of timber through which sheep were made to swim. Alongside the race ran a platform from which men could assist the sheep with 'dipping crooks,' a 'W'-shaped crook mounted upon a long shaft. The reason for washing sheep in those days was that washed fleeces commanded a higher price from wool merchants than equivalent unwashed fleeces. Beside sheep from Exceat and Chyngton, sheep came from West Dean and even from as far as Firle. This practice gradually fell out of use and by the late 1930's had completely ceased.

During part of the 1920's, the senior shepherd at Exceat was Dick Fowler who resided at 2, Foxhole Cottages, with whom lodged another shepherd Charlie Picknell. Dick was one of the last of the traditional Downland shepherds to work on Exceat. He would always carry a piece of emery cloth to polish his crook with and a needle and cotton secured behind his hat-band to enable him to sew on any loose buttons. He had three sheepdogs: an Old English, a Rough-Coated or Bearded Collie and a Welsh Collie. (26). The traditional companion of these Southdown shepherds were the Rough-Coated Collies and to a lesser extent, the Old English type sheepdogs. They were essentially droving dogs, capable of working the docile native sheep of the Downs, but also capable of a day's droving work when sheep were taken to fairs or sold. With the introduction to the Downs of more agile northern hill sheep, a dog with matching agility followed, the Border Collie, a dog with an insatiable lust to work at break-neck speed combined with an ability to 'fix' or 'head' sheep with its piercing stare

Southdown sheep being washed in river adjacent to Exceat farm.

and stance. Dick finished his working life at Birling Manor Farm where witnessed the introduction of Cheviot sheep, much to his disgust! (26).

Dick had a fine collection of sheep bells comprising of thirty in total including some which belonged to his grandfather. Sheep bells were mainly employed for the pleasure of the shepherd. They also had practical uses; the shepherd could tell whether the flock was grazing peacefully or not, even if out of sight. During the thick fogs which cloak the Downs at certain times of the year, the shepherd could locate where the flock was as it grazed across the un-fenced Downland.

The shearing gang was composed of local shepherds (at least six in all) who came from as far as Milton Street and East Dean. On Boxing Day, the local shepherds would congregate at either The Pelham Arms (later called The Hole In The Wall) in Seaford, or The Tiger in East Dean, sometimes all returning to Dick's cottage afterwards. During the lambing season, Dick would live in his shepherds caravan up at the old Foxhole Barn, he only coming home for a hot meal and a change of clothing. On leaving Exceat he worked at Birling Manor where he saw the Cheviot breed of sheep introduced, *"much to his disgust."* (26). Dick was visited on many occasions by the great chronicler of the South Down shepherds, Barclay Wills.

Arthur Duley a well-known local Sussex shepherd born at Firle in the 1860's, wrote the following account for the Sussex County

Shepherd Harry Fowler on hill above Foxhole. Note his crook and rough-coated collie.

Magazine during a spell of illness in 1930. (27). The following extracts are reproduced with original spellings. *"...The next move for us was to Glyndebourne, not a very big lot, about 30. I use to take the sheep on the hills by day then. The school managers made me go to school again; then I had to work night and morning. I thought it was a bit hard as I was only between 9 and 10 years old, but it was no use grumbling; they had there way about it.... I was on the hill one day and I had a bitch and I sent her after the sheep and she cut one off and drove it in the pond in Oxingdean Bottom. When I saw it in the pond I cried; I was afraid I should lose it, but it came out all right. I felt very lonely up there all day by myself. It use to be a very good hill in those times; it was kept down more than it is now. My wages was 3/6 [17.2p] a week. My father use to let me have his watch, but if I see any one I use to ask them the time just to start a yarn.... My bitch had 6 puppys in a rabbit hole. She was gone 2 or 3 days then came home for some food; then we watched her back. That was how we found them. I am very fond of dogs. I had some good and some bad. When you get a good one it is company when you are on hills by yourself; if it is not a good one I don't have it long. You don't find many bob-tails now; they make the bob-tail after they are born by taking the tail off; I have done it and I know others have. I had 18 born in 2 days.*

The next move was to Alciston. There was a flock of sheep there nearly 1,000, made in 3 flocks; my father had one, my eldest brother had one, and I had the other. Then I had 9/- a week; but when I first went there I went with father as shepherd boy; then I had 4/- a week. Now the wage is 35/- [£1.75] for a shepherd and only the same work now as then. In 1881 there was a big snow storm. Our sheep were over the hill and when we got to them they were nearly covered in, so we set to and cleaned their coups out and put hay in for them. After they had eaten that we turned them out, put clean straw in for them to eat, then we made for home. My father tied a cord round his waist and I held on to it; that is how I got home. When I got home I was nearly done. My Mother laid me down by the fire and rubed me and got me round.

In 1887 we got back to a place called Folkington, Nr Eastborne, and my father thought I was old enough to look out for myself. I think I was about 20, and so I went as under shepherd at Firle. The money was not very big: 13/- a week [£0.65], 1/6 to keep my dog, 6/1? once a quarter for my club, 2/6 for lodgings, tea and sugar. I use to buy a loaf of bread a day and a pound of beef made into a pud-ding lasted Sunday and Monday, and a little peice of bacon; some times a rabbit for the rest of the week. I manage to get a glass of beer some times.

The next move from Firle was to West dean Nr Seaford [1889]. There I took another young flock about 300; my brother had a flock of 400 on the same farm. Then there was another flock 250 what they called tegs [sheep less than one year old] and a few fat sheep, and about 12 rams. The master [H.M. Simmons] kept very well the first 3 or 4 years. We sent some Wethers [castrated male] tegs to London fat stock show, but they were to course. They would not look at them; they like little sheep and fat and not much bone. We showed some at Lewes show, Lambs & tegs and took 2 first prises, and we took first prise at Lewes fair with 100 best Lambs. That wanted some doing as there were a lot of sheep to show against; more than now. I don't think they use to dress them as much as they do now; they were more their natural color, but dressing them so much does not make any difference to the man that as to buy them... While I was at West Dean we had a lot of snow in the Lambing time; we had nearly half done and it made us have very bad luck. We lambed up under some links and the snow drifted over the top and nearly covered us in. As fast as the lambs droped we had to pick them up and put them in the warm. We had about 30 lambs in the morning and a lot of their mothers we did not know. That started us having bad luck. Then the scours set in and that was worst than the snow. I should think we lost nearly 100 through it and big lambs after they were cut [castrated]. The forman came round at night and I asked him if he would get us some gin; that was about 6 in the evening and we never got our gin till 6 next morning and then he was drunk. He said he lost his way and had to put up for the night. We heard something when he did come - plain Sussex; you could understand what he said; he did not wrap anything up. He would drink a bottle of gin besides beer. I earnt a bit of money while I was there; I use to wire for rabbits, but the foxes use to play me up. There was some 2 legged foxes. You had to lay up by them and go for them as soon as you heard them cry or the foxes was there befor you. Some use to go to Eastbourne, some to Seaford. Those that went to Seaford was what the 2 legged foxes got." With this personal account by a South Down shepherd we finally draw to a close our examination of sheep and shepherds on the Downs.

Children And Casual Labour. Referring once again to the reminiscences of Arthur Mewett, he recalled that he had a rather bizarre method of earning money for himself. Often on Good Fridays he together with some other boys, would walk up on to the Downland laying behind the Seven Sisters to catch adders for which they would receive two old pence for each snake killed. Ratting in and around Foxhole Barn also earnt a bounty for each rat dispatched. By far the most dangerous source of income was the collecting of sea gull eggs from cliff-tops or any cliff falls along the Seven Sisters. This he carried out without his mother's knowledge! He would sell this precariously harvested crop to Dr. Jarvis who resided in Broad Street, Seaford for 2s 6d (12? pence) per dozen! (25).

George Levett remembered the occasions as a child when he and others would be truant from school to assist with seasonal work such as harvesting. Occasionally the School Attendance Officer would appear in the neighbourhood on his motor cycle, adorned with goggles and a cap worn back to front. Upon the sound of his approaching machine, children would hide beneath hay-cocks endeavouring not to giggle or sneeze. *"The Kid Catcher"* as he came to be known was of Dutch descent and would stop to ask the field workers if they had seen such and such; after his departure the children would emerge from their places of hiding. (25).

During January 1923 the school master at East Dean Edward Drew, informed his pupils that Mr. Gorringe wanted two boys for work on Exceat. Jim Wickens who was aged 13? years of age, was picked and told that if he behaved for the rest of the week he would be allowed to leave school. He worked for three years on Exceat employed as carter boy to Bill Holter. (28). However the transition from days at school to days earning a wage were not so straight forward for Harry West. In 1916 when eight years old Harry's family moved to 2, Foxhole Cottages at Exceat, his father being a shepherd. That same year, all able bodied males over the age of eight in country areas were called up for work on the land. He continued to work until the war effort was wound down in 1920, but due to a rise in the school leaving age he was required to return to school for one more year. Harry was *"like a fish out of water"* and spent much of that year carrying out work in the school masters garden! (29).

Some tasks on Exceat were carried out by individuals not employed on the farm; cleaning out of the ditches that dissect the valley meadows was one such task. During the early 1900's two brothers from Milton Street, George and Jack Fears carried out this chore. The technique was to cut the reed root mass and underlying mud with a hay knife attached to a long shaft, and then to throw the detached spoil over their shoulder using a long narrow scoop again attached to a long shaft. Work was paid for by the rod length (5.029 metres) completed. The two brothers also undertook thatching on the various barns and cottages as required on local farms. When working on cottages at Foxhole they would spend the whole week there, lodging at one of the cottages. (25). During the First World War and succeeding years, essential maintenance of Exceat's buildings including thatching was undertaken by Gorringe's own labour force. Initially this was due to a shortage of labour because of the war effort. Casual labour was relied upon during the busy periods of the summer; a gypsy family by the name of Baker from the Worthing area, would set up camp on Ewe Down upon Chyngton Farm, or alongside the hedgerow that once ran alongside the road at Scabs Island, Exceat. They were hired for such tasks as setting up or stooking of the sheaves of corn. (30).

Rabbits were fair game for everyone whether legal or illegal. Popes who lived at Exceat Newbarn Cottages would retrieve the 'starters' (young rabbits) which their cats brought home allowing the cats just the livers, they repeating the exercise until they had acquired enough rabbit to make a family-size meal. The young boys would set snares for rabbits thus also helping to stretch their father's meagre income. (12). An unusual way of obtaining rabbits occurred during the early part of Second World War, while one of the Stutchbury's sons was feeding the chickens at Gayles. A German aircraft appeared unexpectedly and droped three bombs; one exploded beneath the cliffs, another near a bren gun unit and the third exploding upon a rabbit warren. From this situation the opportunist son collected three rabbits! (31).

Oxen. To provide a background to the subject of oxen, the following extracts are taken from John Creasey's *"The Draught Ox"* (32), followed by their status in the study area. *"Cattle were the earliest draught animals employed in agriculture and have remained in use longer than any other. Although in Britain the horse was first put to the plough before 1100 it did not generally replace the ox until the middle of the eighteenth century. Thus almost on the eve of mechanisation a new form of animal power superseded the traditional draught beast used in most areas of Europe and Asia from the third millennium B.C. Since the Second World War, the horse in its turn has been completely superseded by tractors to the point where it is no longer included in official agricultural statistics. The replacement of oxen by horses in Britain was an uneven one and indeed at certain points this process may even have been temporarily reversed. There existed considerable regional differences in the speed and timing of the transition, which meant that in some counties draught oxen remained in use perhaps two or three centuries longer than in others. The Domesday Book, compiled in 1086, used the full eight ox team as a standard unit in the assessment of land values. It is possible that although a full working team may have consisted of eight oxen, no more than four of these would have been attached to any one implement. After the Domesday Book, the ox was joined by the horse for draught purposes, at first only to pull the harrow where speed of operation assisted the final pulverization of the soil. The comparison between the two animals was to raise questions that practical farmers must have had to consider until the end of ox traction in this country. They had to place the economy of the ox against the greater speed, longer endurance and flexibility of use of the horse. The ox could be fed on straw throughout the winter, supplemented by hay when worked and pastured from May to October, while the grass grew. His equipment, the yoke, was cheaper and simpler to make than the horses harness and he required no grooming or attendance. When his working life was over, a sixteenth century writer pointed out, 'he may be fedde, and thanne he is mannes meate, and as good or better than ever he was. And the horse, when he dyethe, is but caryen.'*

We must, however, assume that during the period from about 1500 to 1750 an increasing number of farmers faced with this decision decided that the horse held a greater advantage for them. It was certainly in these two and a half centuries that the horse replaced the ox as the major draught animal on the majority of English farms. Cultivation, especially after-cultivations, such as harrowing and rolling, became more extensive, the arable acreage increased, crop rotations followed each other more rapidly and the amount of fallow was reduced. In consequence, the demand for draught power increased and became more spread over a longer working season; the effect was to encourage the use of the more efficient animal.

Improvements in the breeds of both horses and cattle served to lesson the ox's importance as a draught animal. Heavier and more powerful draught horses widened the performance gap between the two animals and specialised cattle breeds for beef and dairy purposes, rather than draught, now came to be recognised. Once the longhorns of the north west and midlands and the shorthorns of the east and north east coast had been taken in hand by the improvers, the middlehorns remained as the most important draught animals, maintained as part of an agricultural system in which they worked for several years and then sold to a grazier for fattening. These middlehorns were the Devon, Hereford and Sussex breeds. In addition, the Welsh Glamorgan, Pembroke and the Scottish Aberdeenshire breeds were valued as draught animals. The home territories of these breeds corresponded closely to those areas of Britain where the use of draught oxen survived into the nineteenth and twentieth centuries: the south western counties of Cornwall, Devon, Somerset and west Dorset; the Cotswold areas of Gloucestershire and Oxfordshire; Herefordshire; the Weald of Kent and East Sussex. In the counties where the use of oxen was traditional their numbers declined steadily throughout the nineteenth century. By 1900 they were practically extinct in the south west and only a limited few survived in the Cotswolds, Wiltshire, Dorset and Sussex, and in Scotland in Deeside."

Moving from the national scene, we will now focus our attention down to the part played by oxen upon the east Sussex Downs. James Caird an agricultural commentator writing in the mid-19th century, made the following vivid though caustic observations upon having watched oxen working upon the Downs. *"Very old-fashioned clumsy ploughs are used, made of wood, with a bit of flat wood for a mould-board, which is shifted from side to side at each turning; the beam, a thick, strong, straight piece of wood, set on to the head of the plough at an angle of 45 degrees, and borne up in front in a very solid and substantial manner on a pair of wheels from 22 to 3 feet in diameter. This implement is drawn by three or four*

Oxen ploughing east of Foxhole in about 1890 with Len Flint and ox-boy Albert Burton.

horses, or six bullocks [oxen]. Within a couple of miles of Brighton these ploughs may be seen in use every day; and we saw in that neighbourhood a working team, which, for waste of opportunity, of power, and of time, could probably not be matched in any other county in the United Kingdom. At the end of a ploughed field were a lot of bullocks all crowded together, but which we presently perceived were in the yoke, and being turned round. Slowly the crowd separated, each team wheeling about; and steadily advancing up the hill came eighteen heavy bullocks, two and two abreast (six in each plough), drawing three ploughs following each other, one man guiding each plough, while another, armed with a long pliable stick, like a fishing-rod, kept the team under his charge at their duty." (10).

Arthur Young writing in 1801 (11), drew up the following table for the comparison of costs in operating a team of oxen as against a team of horses:

Eight oxen @ £12	£96 0 0
Yokes & chains for six	4 0 0
Six mths. summer work @ 2s. per week	20 16 0
ditto winter @ 2s 6d	26 0 0
	£147 0 0
If they rest 2/3 mths. may cost £8	8 0 0

£139 0 0

Four horses @ £1 5 0	£100 0 0
Harness @ £1 5 0	9 0 0
Oats, 2lb. per week	52 0 0
Hay & herbage @ 6s. per week	15 12 0
Farrier, wear and tear	4 0 0
	£180 0 0

An ox-team will plough one acre per day per year through @ £2 2 0 per week	105 0 0
Horse -team the same	105 0 0
Cost in favour of oxen	£41 12 0

From the Invasion Return of autumn 1801 (33), we learn that there were within the parish of West Dean a total of 56 draught oxen. Upon Exceat towards the close of the nineteenth century three teams each consisting of six oxen were kept.

Arthur Beckett, a newspaper proprietor, rambler, author and one of the earliest to demand preservation measures for the Downs wrote the following in relation to oxen in 1927: *"Mr. Gorringe and his father had worked oxen on Downland farms for some 60 or 70 years. The animals had a distinct advantage over horses on the steep gradients of Chyngton, being better at a dead pull than the latter. Half a century ago upwards of twenty oxen were worked on this farm. Mr Gorringe was of the opinion that his Welsh 'runts' had more pluck than most breeds. Frederick Jones, formerly land agent to three Earls of Chichester writes: 'Oxen were formally used for farm work because of their strong steady pull. Though slower than the Suffolk punch or shire horse they ploughed deep, and their hoofs, with a screwing tread, pulverised and consolidated the soil, making the 'season' the Downland farmer loved.''* An oxman interviewed in July 1924 on Exceat, related how the oxen were worked from 7am to 3pm and then grazed on the Downs. From October-November to about April-May they were kept in the yard and fed with hay and straw - nothing else. They required no grooming or shoeing, and their harness was much less expensive being merely the yoke and 10ft. chains."* (34).

Percy Gorringe would boast that for many years he had offered to back his ox 'span' (team) against any tractor over a period of one year, but was never taken on. Oxen yokes were made of ash timber and had two loose iron links attached to the iron yoke shackle; these links were connected to the oxen yoke in front or behind by chains with hooks at either end. Brass knobs were often screwed on to the tips of misshapen horns of the more lively animals. Oxen were probably never shod within the study area during the 20th century; however an ox shoe or 'cue' as they were termed was found at Exceat Newbarn and is in the author's possession. When oxen were shod, they were 'thrown' on their side using a large tripod consisting of wooden poles. The nails were placed in a thick piece of pork fat, the theory being that if the nail hurt the animal the fat would counter the pain.

Oxen were docile, easy to train and to control as former ox-boy Ray Kemp recalls: As the ox-boy he usually stood to the left of the team. To turn them right he would point the long stick he carried termed a 'goad' to the right and give the command *"Gee"* followed by the name of the leading beast on the right. To turn the team left the same procedure was followed but with the command *"Hay."* If he placed or laid the goad in front of them they would not attempt to cross it; if *"hit"* by a fly they might move around it. On several occasions while yoking up oxen near to the present day entrance to The Gayles, a fly would make one of the oxen take flight, it eventually being caught up with towards Friston! During harvest time school children would take over the leading of the oxen from stook to stook and were known as 'stand hard kids,' that being the command to stop and *"hard up"* being the command to move on. (13). Sticks for use as goads were collected once a year from Abbot's Wood where coppice workers converted the hazel into sheep hurdles; carter Bill Holter while collecting hurdles would also collect a bundle of straight hazel rods. Upon the end of these was fixed a nail, *"a half length of barley corn"* to use as a prod in case the oxen proved stubborn. (35).

The last person to break-in and drive oxen on Exceat was Charles *"Curly"* Pope; he was born at 'Pincham' on Rathfinney Farm near Alfriston and worked on Exceat for 21 years. By the early part of the 20th century oxen were becoming something of a curiosity. During 1908 Curly took an ox team to appear in the Eastbourne Pageant being staged at Pevensey Castle. During this period pageants were in vogue and viewed as a good advertising vehicle for a town. Pageants took the form of a spectacular founded on events in local or county history and presented together with music and dance. During January 1914 he was called upon to take his ox team by rail from Seaford, to take part in a trade procession in Manchester, their particular role was helping to promote *Camp Coffee*. They were housed at a local army camp. (12, 36).

If a crop of wheat showed signs of damage from an infestation of wireworm, the order was given for a team of oxen to be taken on to it; for this purpose they were not harnessed to any implement, thereby

Curly Pope with his ox team and wagon loaded with hazel sheep hurdles opposite Exceat Farm.

they tending to tread in different places and so destroying many of the wireworm. During or after periods of prolonged or heavy rainfall, ground conditions would become very soft. If this coincided with the need to take a wagon loaded with 40 117 kilo (23 cwt.) sacks of recently thrashed corn over the hill from Foxhole to Exceat, it often called for a 'pickaxe team.' This comprised of a team of horses being hitched to the wagon and in front of the horses, a team of oxen were attached. Oxen tended to work in 'low gear' and they would set the pace; as the team together with the heavily laden wagon (in excess of 5 tons) proceeded uphill the oxen would sink up to their hocks, their tails stiffening under the strain. (35, 37).

Between Curly Pope and the head carter Bill Holter, there existed a certain amount of professional rivalry, as manifested itself in the following incident. Whilst working at Exceat Newbarn, French's thrashing engine became stuck fast in the bullock yard next to the barn. At this, Bill Holter drew his team of horses up to the front of the engine and attached them. The horses were given a hearty command to pull, but to no avail. Now Curly Pope and his ox-boy Ray happened to have four oxen yoked up; off came the horses and on went the oxen. After taking up slack on the chains, they were given the

Harvest time and a wagon hauled by oxen is being loaded with sheaves in Newbarn Bottom.

command to pull; with the engines driving wheels slowly revolving, the oxen extracted the engine from its predicament with ease, much to Bill's annoyance! (13).

The last oxen to work on Exceat, indeed the last to have been seriously worked in England (38) were sold on October 15 1925. Their names were Lamb, Leader; Duke, Diamond; Quick, Nimble, all being red Sussex cattle and, Gallant and Goldring which were Welsh Blacks. They were all sold to Major Harding of Birling Manor but were not seriously used, and may have been sold after just six months to a buyer in Oxfordshire?

Before leaving the subject of bovines, Col. Watson maintained a dairy herd totalling some 60 cows which to begin with were of the Sussex breed; during the mid 1930's they were replaced by the higher yielding Ayrshires. These were apparently not as easy to milk as they had shorter teats. On one occasion while Arthur Miller was bringing the herd across the road at the bottom of Exceat Hill, an Austin 7 containing two old ladies, instead of waiting attempted to weave through them. One cow refusing to move and instead, *"just s- - - all over the radiator"* much to its occupants consternation! Having complained to cowman Miller, he went and fetched a bucket of water and threw it over the offended parts of the car! (39).

HORSES. A typical days work for a carter and his boy on Exceat would start at 5am with the feeding of the horses and turning of their bedding after which, the carter would return home for breakfast. Following this the horses were groomed and harnessed up, given a further feed and made ready for work at 7am. Work stopped at 9am for a short snap or bite, with lunch being taken between 11-30am and noon. (13). While serving as a carters boy, Harry West reached the end of one day in a rather damp state after watering a horse in the pond which used to be opposite the buildings at Exceat (just behind the present day telephone box). A plank ran out into the pond, so that the horses could be held while mud was soaked off the feathering on their legs and hooves. For some reason this horse was startled and took flight across the pond dragging poor Harry through several feet of water! (29). Sometimes while taking their lunch break while working in the vicinity of the Seven Sisters an old trick would be played on one of the cliffs resident Jackdaws. A single hair would be taken from one of the horses tails; to one end would be attached a piece of bread crust while to the other end was tied a brown paper bag, weighted by a small stone. After awhile, an unsuspecting Jackdaw would approach the crust and fly off with it closely pursued by the fluttering paper bag! (12).

The steep gradients encountered on some of the roads and trackways crossing the Downs presented a formidable challenge to both the carter and his team. There were two methods of braking a farm wagon when descending a hill; on the hard rough road surfaces, 'wagon shoes' otherwise known as 'skid pans' were used. These consisted of cast iron rectangular blocks with a groove along the centre, wide enough to accommodate the width of the iron wagon tyre, and open at one end only. These were on chains and were placed in front/beneath the two rear wheels, and so effectively locking them. Alternatively on grassy or greasy slopes, an extra chain was kept on the wagon and was looped through the spokes of the rear wheels so as to lock them. (12). Jim Palmer could recall taking carts down Exceat Hill with the horse in the shafts nearly on their buttocks, sparks issuing from under the wagon shoes! When still only 13 years of age his driving skills were to prove not so lucky; while using a hay rake upon The Gallups, the shafts broke. The horses took fright and with the reins wound around his hands, Jim was dragged along and had to receive hospital treatment. (40). Woods of Polegate delivered the coal to the Friston pumping station and would sometimes after unloading come on over to Exceat for a return load of flint (some three cubic metres). Occasionally the horses experienced difficulty ascending Exceat Hill and so the team was doubled up with a team of farm horses. Arthur Mewett and his team often found the steep descent down from Friston into East Dean tricky, when loaded with forty sacks of wheat, destined for Eastbourne. The horses would have difficulty holding back the weight even with skid pans beneath the wheels, the wagon sometimes slewing sideways across the road. (25).

There appears to have been three blacksmiths practising within the study area during the early years of the 20th century. Luther Hill and *"Brassy"* at East Dean, Mr. Phillips who was employed by Kemps at Exceat and Mr. Brooks who came over from Alfriston and operated a small forge opposite the West Dean pond.

During the First World War, tens of thousands of farm horses were requisitioned by the military authorities. The following account from those dark days was written by Frank Blackwell who then lived at Sessingham Farm, Arlington, and though under age before the outbreak of war, signed up to the cavalry section of the territorial army: *"The three batteries at Eastbourne, Bexhill and Hastings had their guns and ammunition wagons, but as an ammunition column we had nothing, and were badly under strength. The latter was soon remedied as there was a mild stampede to enlist, but to acquire the necessary horses and vehicles to carry the tons of ammunitions that we drew from the fort at Newhaven, we raided farms for miles around and deprived the farms of their only means of carrying on their trade and cultivation. Obviously a very short sighted policy as the country was soon to depend so much on home production for the next few years. The procedure for this ravaging of the countryside was for an army officer, a policeman and a veterinary surgeon to travel round in a car to commandeer horses and vehicles suitable for their purposes. A party of selected men followed in a bus to bring in the days spoils. I was dropped off on one of these expeditions at a farm at Friston to carter back to Hailsham a complete team of three beautiful horses, together with their harness and wagon. Can you imagine my feelings when the old carter, with tears streaming down his face, threw me his whip, saying: 'Here, take this as well. I won't be needing it any more.' I could easily have cried with him and I have often wondered how the old chap got on later - learning to drive a tractor!*

I think this demonstrates the heartbreak and hardship the "calling up of horses" must have caused the farming community in general. Horse lines had been erected in the old "Deer Paddock," and when that spilled over, in part of the market. With the expert aid of the "Vet" we collected the cream of the horse population for miles around, from great hairy legged "Shires" to a pair of high stepping carriage horses."

To put this in perspective Captain Sidney Galtrey writing in 1918, estimated that the army possessed some 25,000 horses in 1914; by the end of the war however numbers were in excess of one million. The resources of the United Kingdom were quite unable to supply such quantities; *"colossal numbers"* were bought in the Americas, Australia, New Zealand, India, Spain, Portugal and South Africa. For horses as for men, Flanders mud was the great evil; horses at and near the front lines were hock-deep for much of the time. Mud said Galtrey was a pernicious carrier of disease; when the strain became too great, horses were regularly taken out of the line and moved back to rest camps. Veterinary hospitals appear to have treated as many cases of disease caused by the mud as they did horses wounded in action. Veterinary surgeons would work day after day in operating theatres extracting shrapnel and bullets using chloroform as an anaesthetic. Great pride was taken in looking after the horses and in nursing back to health those that were sick or wounded; it was not true that wounded horses were simply left to die. (41).

Following the war, horses became extremely cheap due in part to: i) the saturation of the market by ex-army horses, ii) a fall in demand as arable farming declined, iii) by large numbers of town draught horses being displaced by the advent of the motor lorry. Until the 1930's tractors due to their fickle reliability were seen as more of an aid rather than a substitute for the horse; their chief advantage was speed, especially on heavy soils and during wet seasons when time was of the essence. (3).

As seen earlier, carters (or 'teamsters') became very fond of their charges and would sometimes pamper them; Ray Kemp would each week collect 1? bags of oats from George Patching, the foreman on Crowlink Farm in Gorringes time. Ray found that he could collect an extra ration through a hole in the granary floor, at least until the foreman made the discovery! (13). Bill Holter would often enter his team and a wagon into the Sussex County Show; on these occasions he would use his own tack emblazoned with horse brasses; these are now held by the Country Park. The finishing touch on these occasions was effected by the placing of four sets of turret bells upon the hames of each horse. Each set of these bells were housed on an iron frame or turret with each bell inscribed with the name of their maker 'R. Wells.' These were probably cast during the 19th century at Aldbourne in Wiltshire; they were passed from one Exceat farmer to the next. Sometime during the second half of the 1930's, Bill who was responsible for the breaking in of new horses and Jim Palmer, went up to Seaford railway goods yard to collect some 10 or 12 Suffolk Punch's; they were not broken in and one was led while the others were driven. Before this the farm used Shire type horses. (40).

Once during the early days of Second World War, teenager Brian Cornelius helped out as a carter on Exceat after many young men had

Andrew Holter working a 3-horse team ploughing on Exceat Hill.

been called up for the Territorial Army and had a harrowing experience! While harrowing with a pair of horses somewhere in The Gallups/Hard Link area, a German bomber flew over quite low, perhaps as low as 150 feet. As it passed over he *"saw the tail gunner swivel his guns"* and the next moment a trail of bullets was raising the dust between the horses and himself! (42). When Arthur Pattenden took on the tenancy of Exceat Farm in 1945 the farm was still powered by Suffolk Punch horses with no tractors. (43).

The study area had a connection of some substance with the horse racing industry; the ride running parallel with the present A 259 was used as gallops during the 1920's by a trainer based at Sutton Corner Seaford; Mr. Hackett. Another string of race horses were trained in the Charleston Bottom area by James Batho of Alfriston, one of whose horses won the 1912 Lincoln race. Pattenden also owned and trained race horses, with as many as 20 mares and 2 stallions; they were trained on the area known as The Gallops on what is today part of Gayles Farm. Pattenden's greatest success albeit after his death, was the foal called Ben Nevis out of Ben Trumiss and sired by Casmire. It went to America as a young horse and eventually returned to this country and won at the second attempt, the 1980 Grand National. He was trained by a Mr. T. Forster and ridden by Charlie Fenwick; he won partly due to a number of other horses having fallen and came in at 40/1! (43).

IMPLEMENTS. The most in depth surviving source of information concerning equipment and tackle used upon Exceat

Farm is contained in a small green paperback pocket book. Upon the cover is hand written: *"Sale of Live Stock, Farm Implements, Utensils & Household Furniture at Exceat Farm by order of the Exors. of the late Mr. John Ellis"* and dated October 7th. 1875. The auction realised the sum of £2,215. Items sold included:

Hand tools	Mowing Machine
2 Corn Sowing Barrows	2 Reapers
Horse Harness & Chains	2 Winnowing Machines
4 Rollers	Ladders
2 Furrow Presses	Sheep Equipment inc. Marking Irons
3 Scarifiers (cultivators)	4 horse Thrashing Machine
6 Sets of Harrows	Wheelwrights Shop Equipment
12 Dung Carts	Beer, Dairy & Butter Utensils
12 Waggons	268 Wattles (hurdles)
Dog Cart	13prs. Oxen c/w Yokes & Chains
Gig with cushion	14 Draught Horses
8 Sussex Wheel Ploughs	13-coulter Corn Drill

Mick Balkham and Tony Parsons with one of Pattenden's racehorses. (Stable building is today's gent's toilet).

The wooden ploughs, which were probably in use until the end of the First World War, needed periodically to be repaired due to abrasion from the flinty nature of the soils. From time to time, ploughmen would walk to East Dean to arrange for wheelwright Jessy Kemp to repair their plough. Usually it meant the replacement of the foot or 'chip.' Next day the wheelwright would make up a replacement and that evening after consulting his book of field names, drive out to where the plough was in use, turn the plough on its side and carry out the repair. This service was carried out upon farms from East Dean to

Jevington to West Dean; gradually these wooden ploughs were replaced by 2-furrow metal ploughs. (13).

Wheelwright Walter Kemp, a cousin of Jessie Kemp, traded from workshops situated behind Exceat House. This was a modest-sized business, he employing his two sons and a blacksmith; here, various types of wagons and carts were built to order. Sussex farm wagons would cost in the region of £60 and would weigh in at 1 ton 1cwt. (1067 kilos) and took two men six weeks to construct. Logs of timber were bought and seasoned in the river meanders opposite the farm buildings, with the butt end in the water so as to drive out the sap and counter any twisting. Paint was made upon the premises, milling together lead dross (scum) with whiting, linseed oil and pigment. When varnishing took place in the paint shop, water was sprinkled upon the floor and the doors kept shut until the varnish was dry. (44).

By the 1850's, the use of traction engines to haul ploughs by means of wire cables was becoming practical. In 1856, John Fowler a well known agricultural engineer from Leeds, patented his system of ploughing with two 'ploughing engines,' one at each side of the field. With the cost of the equipment beginning at several hundred pounds, it meant that most steam cultivation came to be carried out by contractors and so the use of steam power in the fields remained scarce. During 1866-67 a mere 200,000 acres, less than 2% of the arable acreage was steam tilled; at the height of steam cultivation during the First World War there were 450 twin-engined ploughing sets in England. (45). On open landscapes such as the South Downs ploughing by this method was the fastest option when dealing with relatively large acreages; Gorringes annually ploughed approximately 60 hectares (150 acres) by this method, calling in Lewes contractors Tom and Albert Fuller. Ploughing engines were large steam powered traction engines each weighing 18 to 20 tonnes, with the specialised addition of having a large drum attached beneath the boiler section of the engine, upon which was wound somewhere in the region of 4-500 metres of steel cable. The engines were positioned on and parallel with the field headland and power was transferred to hauling the drum holding the cable. The cable from the two engines would be attached to a 'balance plough' of four to seven furrow, balanced because it was in effect two ploughs mounted at approximately 120° to one another upon a two-wheeled carriage upon which was seated a driver with two opposing steering wheels, one for each plough. When the plough reached the headland on which the engine then hauling stood, the plough driver would then tilt the other half of the plough down on to the ground. The nearby engine would then give a blast on its whistle to signal to the driver of the engine situated at the far side of the field to take up tension on the cable and haul the plough back across the field. This was repeated with the engines moving in tandem a few feet at a time along the field headland, finally finishing with ploughing the two headlands themselves. Sometimes a man had to walk with the plough to clear trash from the plough shares with a type of dutch hoe. A horse and man had also to be employed to haul water and coal to where the engines were working.

On Exceat, while working the expansive slopes of Newbarn Bottom the plough was worked across the hill rather than up and down, termed 'contour ploughing.' Following steam ploughing would be oxen or horse teams pulling harrows; this work was termed 'tining' or, 'wenting' if work entailed harrowing the piece just harrowed, again. After Gorringe's left the scene steam ploughing was no longer carried out upon Exceat. (13). This was due to the decrease then in the amount of land under cultivation. In a wider context the tractor was becoming more reliable; a local exception however were Willett's who farmed Manor Farm, Bishopstone just to the west of Seaford, where steam ploughing continued into the Second World War. (46).

The first combine harvester to be used within the study area was on what is now Friston Forest, when most of it came under the control of the counties War Agricultural Executive Committee. (47). Due to the initial high investment, farmers usually considered it cheaper and

'War Ag' workers posing in front of a Massy-Harris combine on forestry land.

easier to use a horse-drawn or tractor-drawn binder and then to use or hire in a thrashing machine. A drawback for many farmers was that with a combine they ideally required some form of a corn drying plant, this all at a time of depressed corn prices or during war time shortages. In a nationwide census carried out during 1942, there were 940 combine harvesters in operation as opposed to 101,970 binders. (3).

SOURCES.

1) Brandon, Peter. 'The Sussex Landscape.'
2) Perry, P.J., ed by. 'British Agriculture 1875-1914.' Methuen & Co.Ltd. 1973.
3) Creasey & Ward. 'The Countryside Between The Wars, 1918-1940.' Batsford Ltd., 1984.
4) S.A.C. vol. 57.
5) E.S.R.O. SAS G.
6) E.S.R.O. Land Tax Assessments.
7) E.S.R.O. SAS & Additional.
8) Chichester Chapter Estates of West Dean and Friston management files. Church Commissioners archives.
9) Mavis Lister, verbal comm.
10) Caird, James. 'English Agriculture In 1850-51.' 1852. new ed.1968.
11) Young, Arthur, Rev. 'General View Of The Agriculture Of The County Of Sussex.' 1813. repr. David & Charles., 1970.
12) William 'Bill' Pope, verbal comm.
13) Ray Kemp, verbal comm.
14) Bert Etherington file, Seaford Museum of Local History.
15) George Levett, verbal comm.
16) P.R.O. MAF 68.
17) Walford-Lloyd., ed. by. 'The Southdown Sheep. Southdown Sheep Society. 1933.
18) Farrant, Sue, Dr. John Ellman Of Glynde In Sussex. Agricultural History Review 26. 1978.
19) Cambridgeshire Records Office.
20) Trow-Smith, Robert. 'British Livestock Husbandry, 1700-1900.'
21) Southdown Flock Books. Southdown Sheep Society.
22) Thomas, J.F.H. 'Sheep.' Faber & Faber Ltd. 1945.
23) Thomas, J.F.H. 'Sheep Folding Practice.' Vinton & Co. 1931.
24) Seaford Museum of Local History. ref.43/95.
25) Arthur Mewett, verbal comm.

26) Grace Taylor, verbal comm.

27) Sussex County Magazine, vol. 5.

28) Jim Wickens, verbal comm.

29) Harry West, verbal comm.

30) Ilene Chant, verbal comm.

31) 'Winky' Stutchbury, verbal comm.

32) Creasey, John S. 'The Draught Ox.' Museum of English Rural Life, Reading. 1974.

33) E.S.R.O. Sussex Lieutenancy Papers.

34) Sussex County Magazine. October 1927. p462.

35) William 'Bill' Holter, verbal & recorded comm.

36) Eastbourne Gazette. April 10 1907.

37) Work With Oxen by Kathleen Holter. The Countryman. 1971.

38) John Creasey, written comm.

39) Bert Miller, verbal comm.

40) Jim Palmer, verbal comm.

41) No Ribbons To Wear by Gordon Winter. Country Life. Jan.7 1988. p.368.

42) Brian Cornelius, verbal comm.

43) Vera Wilson (formally Pattenden), verbal comm.

44) Wilton Kemp, verbal comm.

45) Mingay, G.E., ed. by. 'The Agricultural Revolution - Changes In Agriculture 1650-1880.' Adam & Charles Black. 1977.

46) Howard Barnes, verbal comm.

47) Herbert Vickery, verbal comm.

CHAPTER 8.

FRISTON FOREST - WATER FOR EASTBOURNE.

The establishment of Friston Forest by the Forestry Commission during the second quarter of the 20th century brought about a significant change to the Downland landscape within the neighbourhoods of West Dean and Friston. An area in excess of 808 hectares (two thousand acres), once cultivated by teams of oxen and horses where, shepherds tended their flocks of Southdown sheep and where extensive areas of gorse, heather and partridge thrived, has now evolved into a relatively vast tract of beech woodland. Today, the shepherds are replaced by protectively-clad chainsaw operators and the sheep and partridge by deer and tawny owl.

To encompass the whole story of Friston Forest, we have to first step back to the late Victorian era, when Eastbourne was rapidly expanding and demand for mains water was approaching the limits of the Eastbourne Waterworks Company's wells within or close to the town. For much of the first element of this story, the author is indebted to the former Eastbourne Waterworks Company for allowing access to the Minutes of the Company's Board Meetings. Secondly, the creation of the Forestry Commission in 1919; it's main objective was to replace a strategic reserve of general purpose timber for use the next time there was a world war, grown on cheap land to offset another onslaught by enemy submarines. An additional objective appeared during the 1930's, that of job creation due to the Depression.

By 1896, serious thought was being given to finding an alternative source of water by the Company's Engineer, Mr. Stillman; his deliberation focused upon two sites, Wannock and Friston. The latter had conflicting qualities; it was disadvantaged by having a lift of nearly 61 metres (200 feet) greater than the alternative site at Wannock. The ramification of this was that fuel consumption for lifting say 18 million litres (four million gallons) would be 8 tonnes of coal at 22s 8d (£1.13) per tonne. At Wannock consumption would only be 4 tonnes at 18s (£0.90) per tonne. However Friston had the advantage of being on land owned by the Company's chairman the Duke of Devonshire, whose family had nurtured and profited from Eastbourne's growth into a major seaside resort. By November of 1896 an application had been laid before Parliament to execute works for *"additional water supply from Charlestown in the neighbourhood of Friston."*

Events proceeded rapidly. During January 1897, the Company's Board agreed to the commencement of tunnelling where necessary, due to the high elevation of the downland crests along a route between Friston and the Meads area of Eastbourne, for the purpose of laying a temporary pipeline. The connecting trenches were to be completed that same month and the laying of pipes had already commenced. Later that year, it was agreed to completely overhaul two stationary steam engines from the company's Bedford well in Eastbourne and house them at Friston within a temporary engine-house, rather than proceed with the proposed permanent structure. August saw the rather grand official *"Opening of the new auxiliary water supply from Friston Valley"* in a marquee by the Duke of Devonshire, attended by numbers of various civic dignitaries from Eastbourne, dress including top hats, wigs and gowns. At their meeting of October 26 1900, the company agreed in principle to purchase the whole of West Dean Farm from the Devonshires. In actuality the purchase was not completed until December 13 1922 when both West Dean and Friston Farms were purchased, so enabling the Company to safeguard the purity of their water catchment area. This was several years after

Duke of Devonshire officially opening the new pumping works at Friston in August 1897.

the Duke of Devonshire had reduced his interest in the Company.

In November 1906 farmer John Bray of Charlston Farm presented a claim to the Company for damage caused to the Charlston 'roads' by the company's contractors in the course of carrying out excavations on the 'adit' or 'heading' over the preceding few years. This adit consists of a tunnel deep within the chalk measuring several metres in height and approximately one metre wide; it commences beneath the Friston pumping station and extends to northern end of Charlston Bottom, east of Litlington. Water from within the chalk strata, which acts as a huge sponge termed an 'aquifer,' drains into the adit and flows towards the pumping station. January 1936 saw work commence on extending the heading to beneath the beautiful Deep Dean south of Wilmington, giving the heading a total length in excess of 2 miles. The contract was awarded to George Stow & Co. Ltd. who employed Welsh miners to carry out the tunnelling. Work included the sinking of the No. 6 shaft to enable access and removal of excavated chalk, thus creating the fine view point which today overlooks Lullington Heath. Chalk and men were lifted within this deep shaft (in the region of 60 metres deep) by steam crane. The miners reached the working face each day by boat, the water level being kept down by pumping at Friston. During 1990, all six shafts were inspected and all had new concrete cappings placed upon them.

During 1912, provisional agreement was reached for the purchase of Friston Place Farm, recently acquired by the Duke. That same year also saw the appointment of Maurice Williams as working Bailiff for the two farms at £1-18-0 (£1.90) per week, replacing the late Mr. Burgess. A varying proportion of the estate was grazed by Charlston Farm; shooting and sporting rights were also let as were several areas for use as gallops for local race horse trainers such as Zorgis Michalinos of Jevington. As a major landowner, the company would make selected annual donations towards such organisations as the East Dean, Friston and West Dean Rat and Sparrow Club, which consisted mainly of local farm workers who kept in check vermin such as rats and sparrows with nets. Others were the three villages victory Celebrations Committee Fund and the local Nursing Association. During the summer of 1918, agreement was reached with the East Sussex Agricultural Executive Committee for the hire of a tractor and two pairs of horses and implements, the company having been coerced into ploughing up 115 hectares (285 acres) in order to help stem the worsening food shortage situation.

At the Board meeting on December 16 1920, consideration was given to a letter received from the newly formed state Forestry

Commission, enquiring about the possibility of afforestation of parts of the company's West Dean and Friston catchment area. The General Manager was instructed to reply that almost the whole of the ground not under cultivation, was sheep grazed Downland and not suitable for afforestation but, he would be willing to meet a representative from the Commission. By a year later, the company had had a change of heart and it was resolved to let as much as possible of the sheepwalk on the two farms and that an increase in the size of the company's flock of sheep be made together with expediency in restoring as much as possible of the cultivated land to grass. A decision was taken during April 1922 to set a side in the region of £500 from the past half years profits to bolster the company's farming account. This was most likely because of the dramatic fall in market prices due to cheap imports and removal of government subsidy.

During July 1922, the company's Board discussed the option to buy the two farms; agreement was reached to purchase the farms under section 11 of the Eastbourne Waterworks Company Act, 1920. The money was to be borrowed from the Duke of Devonshire by way of a mortgage, West Dean for £6,000 and Friston for £5,000; the company's seal was affixed to the conveyance of sale on December 13 1922. Deliberation as to whether to lease their estate for afforestation was furthered. At the Board meeting of September 25 1923, Charles Allix a director who carried considerable influence within the company, reported upon a meeting he had held with Mr. Taylor of the Forestry Commission, who were still seeking a location along the south coast of one thousand acres (405 hectares) for afforestation. It was agreed that he should show Mr. Taylor over the two farms with a view to obtaining an offer for the whole estate.

Grave concern was expressed by the directors during 1925, upon learning of the Hastings Water Bill which proposed purchasing Rathfinney Farm situated to the west of the Cuckmere between Alfriston and Seaford leading to the construction of wells, headings and a pumping station. After receiving a report commissioned from consultant geologist J.B. Hill, former Geological Advisor to the Ministry of Health, the Board decided to formally oppose the scheme upon the grounds that it would reduce the water table east of the Cuckmere. Subsequently, the scheme was never pursued.

As of September 29 1926, the Forestry Commission were assigned a lease of 200 years for the company's estate at West Dean and Friston. Five days previously, an auction of live and deadstock was conducted by auctioneers A. Burtonshaw & Co., including the disposal of 600 Southdown sheep and lambs, 10 draught horses and a Fordson tractor.

That same autumn news reached the company that Mr. R.C. Brown of Clapham House, Litlington, was considering selling part of his estate within the parishes of Litlington and Lullington for building development. The company viewed this as a further threat to the purity of their catchment area. Following negotiations, the company purchased in May 1927 a further 284 hectares (702 acres) for the sum of £10,540. A lease was drawn up at the same time for Brown to continue to train his few race horses and keep the sporting rights for a period of 21 years at a yearly rental of £80. A further 34 hectares (84 acres) were also purchased from Brown during the same year, followed by yet another purchase in Lullington of 140 hectares (347 acres) during September 1934 for £1,650. During 1928, the company sold off West Dean Brooklands, the meadows bordering the river, to Mr. E.C. Arnold, head master of Eastbourne College and a well-known ornithologist for a sum in the region of £800 to safeguard its wild birds.

On November 19 1929, the company exchanged contracts with Messrs. Davey Paxman & Co. to the sum of £25,371 for a new pumping station at Friston, capable of lifting and pumping in excess of 13 million litres (three million gallons) per day. In October of 1938, with the ominous clouds of war approaching, instructions were given for the fitting of blinds to the roof lights upon the new pumping station as a precaution in the event of possible air raids.

Having now looked in some detail at the acquisition and management of West Dean and Friston Farms by the Eastbourne Waterworks Company and their eventual leasing to the Forestry Commission, we will now look into the establishment of this major beech plantation upon the South Downs. The following account detailing the early history of Friston Forest has been abstracted from an unpublished report by Thomas Aston, who served as Forester in charge of operations during the period 1928 to 1943.

Upon being posted to Friston, Thomas Aston was immediately confronted with a planting programme which in its first 17 months had not proceeded at all well. *"It had then already been seen that the P.27 [1927] Plantations were not making immediate growth and for administrative reasons the Labour had been "stood off" with the exception of The Warrener and one Forest Worker since it had been decided to cut down the Programme considerably. The Forest Workers affected, ensured that the reputation of the Forest should not remain untarnished. The local residents and many visiting Foresters pronounced it to be a "bad egg" but this has never been the Writers opinion... On arrival at Friston, this was found to be the local opinion. Arriving by road in the dark over night, the first clash occurred early in the morning when we met the Parson. Apparently his desire was the reinstatement of the Workers but he managed to convey many things uncomplimentary to the soundness of the venture. The Barber also seemed to be an Expert in Forestry and thus we endured quite a few lectures before he, becoming rather personal, lost a customer. The Doctor asked many shrewd questions and the Bank-Clerks seemed to require a fortnightly Progress Report which, though sometimes tiresome, was more often humorous. The various Tradesmen seemed to think that as local Citizens they had a right to the latest information and so all this continued for a period of many years."*

The following is a chronicle containing some of the more important and interesting events as the Forestry Commission strove to establish the forest. The planting operation started in 1927 under Forester Telfer. His first priority was to establish a major wind-belt along the southern boundary from west of Scabs Island eastwards to Friston, to secure the forest planting against the salt-laden winds sweeping in from the coast. Below this on predominantly north facing slopes clothed in springy chalk grassland, commenced planting of a mixture comprised of 25% european larch and 75% beech, the larch acting as a nurse crop for the main beech crop.

By the 1928 planting season, it was realised that a 25% nurse crop was insufficient and so a 50% inclusion of larch was planted, this being on the south facing slopes between West Dean and Friston. During the following growing season the thin soils overlying the chalk were proving detrimental to the young trees. However, a significant event occurred during this season, when an area was planted using a 25% beech, 75% corsican pine mixture; the use of pine was to become the predominant nurse crop.

Two entries of significance appear concerning the 1929 season and the problems faced. *"This planting season has been a most difficult one, cold and windy, with a low rainfall, long continued frost accompanied by bright sun and a further period of continuous and biting wind lasting until mid-April, ruined the Spring and made it necessary to leave the programme unfinished. This, followed by May frosts, again left us without positive development upon which to reconsider our Silviculture... Another point, rectified, this season, was that of prices for planting - previously 6d. per hundred for Pines - now raised to 9d. (in screefed patches: screefing 9d., planting 9d., making it a total of 1/6 [72p] per 100.... when it was seen that this had produced no visible results Planting Methods were investigated."* Screefing was the technique of clearing the ground vegetation using a mattock and creating a cleared area approximately 18 inches (46cms) square. After experiments using various digging and planting techniques, it was considered that the hand fork was, after screefing, the best method.

"One impression, reminiscent of this Season, was that of inferior Plant Supply. Unfortunately it ruined many earlier projects, - in those days Beech were supplied from the Northampton clay areas such as Drayton. They were mainly rootless, with severe Chafer damage and also hollowed by Ghost moth larvae. None other being available quite a proportion of these had to be used. There could thus be no pride in doing a job well. But it is only right to put on record that this was the result of hurried organisation after the last War, too long tolerated. "

Due to the poor quality of the corsican pine saplings, much of the 1930 seasons planting was of a beech/scots pine mixture. *"Introducing the S.P. into the Nursing Scheme has been both encouraging and important. It is the one species which has started into growth right from the first season, and also, - just as important in another direction - is the low relative percentage of deaths as compared with C.P. plants (altogether fair remark without stating that C.P. plants have usually been rather inferior in quality, it being a more difficult tree to produce than the S.P.). Many of our Pine Planting problems would largely disappear if Supply and planting could be organised for completion during the October period. "* During these years experiments were carried out in order to try to develop an alternative nurse crop for the beech; for this such diverse species as privet, elder, spanish broom and sea buckthorn were tried, they all failing to make the necessary growth.

In 1931, it was decided to extend westwards to above Exceat, the roadside maritime wind-belt commenced upon in 1927; again only corsican pine of a branching bushy character could be obtained; these are still in evidence. During this season greater use was made of grey alder as a nurse crop; two blocks were planted prior to the introduction of beech, one block near Friston and another through the area now containing the main forest car park alongside the Litlington road. Apart from the maritime wind-belt, all beating up (replacement of dead trees) using corsican pine was abandoned in favour of scots pine. In the summer of 1932, the notable advantage of scots pine over any other species with regard to the percentage of mortalities was reported to the highest echelons of the Commission who, disapproving of scots pine at Friston, reluctantly agreed it would probably nurse the beech at Friston. However, the following five years saw much reliance placed on grey alder; trials with spanish broom were also continued. During April 1934 permission was sought from the Eastbourne Waterworks Company to use Friston water tower as a watch tower for fire-watch prevention purposes. During 1938 an unfortunate setback occurred; it came in the guise of a three day gale of icy winds starting on the last day of May. *"Hardly a tree remained on the*

Forest area without having its leaves 'scorched off.'"

1938 saw *"the commencement of a better order of afforestation."* In Butchershole Bottom, the use of a contractor with a plough and sub-soiler together with broom and scots pine were giving encouraging results, the pines being stocky, well rooted plants. 1939 saw the strengthening of scots pines on the exposed slopes above Sheep Pen Cottages. During 1940 attention was given to *"a new type of ground"* situated around the northern end of Charlston Bottom where the valley forks. *"Primarily this area had bourne dense Gorse Coverts [used for shooting], but following very extensive fires in 1931/2 the heather gradually took the place of gorse which fire had destroyed and rabbits then prevented from recovering. Planting Mixtures:- i) In Gorse:- pure Beech and ii) in open ground - 1 row S. Pine and 2 rows of Beech. This was gradually destroyed by Military Training in 1941, 2 and 3, by tanks, B.G. [bren gun] carriers etc. who ran through the fences, which had to be removed for salvage. The rabbits completed the havoc."*

A further impasse to the Commission's work now was the handing over compartment by compartment, to the East Sussex War Agricultural Executive Committee to aid production of home grown wheat. Other areas were used by the military for small arms, artillery and tank training. During the winter of 1941-42, a total of some 214 hectares (530 acres), much of it young forestry plantation mainly in the Sheep Pen Cottages, Snap Hill and Butchershole Bottom areas, was sacrificed to the plough. The following season saw a further 140 hectares (345 acres) mainly in the area of Middle Brow, suffer the same fate. Arable farming continued to some degree upon the forest through the remainder of the 1940's and early 1950's, it being handed back at about 40 hectares (100 acres) annually.

The final paragraphs from forester Aston's article sums up the Commission's struggle to establish Friston Forest and eventually chart the course for the great post war planting operation which eventually created today's rolling forest with its maze of rides.

"At one time in the Forest's History the lack of results was the most noticeable feature. There was the same dreary round of Seasons with hope unfulfilled.

Spring, April 14th - May, with high promise in young and tender shoots.

May 1st - 14th., danger period for frost - almost inevitably the promise faded in Frosts. Recovery, in a degree, took six weeks and was terminated by the drought and heat usually coming in late June/July. Beech hung fire and reserved strength for a final attempt until having received Aug. Bk. Holiday-Week rains, they recommenced a short growth - often cut by early Frosts before hard enough to stand them.

The above is the annual history of a Moribund Beech, the reason why our Plantations take so long getting under way."

By the mid 1930's, it had become apparent to those in charge which direction the future success of the forest lay: *"By 1935/6 the District Officer and Forester were both convinced on the 'future' of S. Pine as a Nurse for Beech on any or/and every area of Friston, it having been noted that it was the only species which could start growing right from the year of planting; but it is doubtful whether its 'nursing Life' will be long enough to bring the Beech Crop to maturity it would probably have been better to use a nurse crop of mixed SP/CP and in Beating Up introduce judiciously, a few varied hardwood species of the hardier and more accommodating sorts, just as 'pay for safety measure.'"*

Resident Foresters in charge of Friston Forest have been as follows:

J. Tellfer	1927 - 1928.
Thomas Aston	1928 - 1943.
George Holter	1943 - early 1960's.
Mr. Bashall	early 1960's - ?
Mr. Hendry	? - 1974.
Chris Robinson	1974 - 1985.

Stan Fuller a native of East Dean, commenced working for the Forestry Commission in about 1938 and soon became the Warrener. In using his own nets and equipment he was permitted to keep and sell

War. Ag. Workers, left to right. Back: Jack Hall, Jack Stevens, Stan Fuller, Derek Pyle. Front: Ron Stevens, Frank Fidgett.

Forestry workers tending the forest's nursery situated near to Westdean Manor.

the rabbits he caught; pre-war, their skins fetched a higher price than the rabbit carcase, his mother selling the skins to the local rag and bone man. One Friday night during 1941 while collecting his wages from Mr. Aston, he was informed that on the following Monday morning he was to report to the War Agricultural Executive's office at Friston Place, he being transferred to help food production. Bill Couts was in charge of their operations locally at that time; many of the men employed were picked up by lorry and brought out from Eastbourne.

During harvest seasons of the 1940's, prisoners from Lewes prison together with gangs of German and Italian prisoners of war, were drafted in to swell the labour force on the forest cornfields. One year, sugar beet was grown along through Butchershole Bottom; *"children and all"* came to help with the hoeing, even an Australian cricket team who at the time had been playing in Eastbourne came and helped one day. Due to wartime food rationing rabbits were in great demand; when carrying out harvesting operations, Stan often drove a large American-made Case tractor pulling a binder operated by Wally Elliot. As they neared the centre of the field they could if lucky catch up to two dozen rabbits, they having difficulty running across stiff sharp stubble.

Arthur Haynes was first employed on the forest in 1947; in those days there were about 25 men employed by the Commission, this

Forestry gang muffled against the cold, pose during break in planting.

Some of the early thinnings being loaded on to lorry near West Dean Newbarn.

number was to increase during a slump in the building trade during 1951. Work consisted of planting during the period November to April, totalling some 1200 trees per day. A mole plough was tried which cut a 15cm (six inch) deep slot into which the trees were planted, but this method proved a failure. After this a large wheeled-plough pulled by a crawler tractor was used, the trees being planted along the tops of the ridges so formed. Upon the steeper slopes line planting was practiced using approximately six men, each with their own sighting pole in order to keep the lines of trees straight. Occasionally though, straying into the line of the next worker would occur if care was not taken! The forks used were extra long, about 46 cms. (18 inches), with metal straps running the length of the shaft; they were heavy and were referred to as 'giant killers.' Other work involved grass swapping around the young trees, and also along the entire A 259 road boundary! Nursery work took the form of weeding and planting, the nursery being situated just to the south of Westdean Manor; trees were brought in either as seed or seedlings. Later Arthur became Warrener, keeping down the rabbit and squirrel populations; during his later years the recording of birds and butterflies also formed part of his work.

CHAPTER 9

R.A.F. FRISTON - THE DOCUMENTED SCENARIO.

The first mention of aircraft flying from The Gayles in the parish of Friston, was during the summer of 1936. A small number of Hawker Audax aircraft belonging to Nos 2 and 4 Squadrons of the RAF took part in exercises, much to the consternation of the neighbouring landowner as alluded to under The Gayles in Chapter 1. (1). During 1940, an Emergency Landing Ground (ELG) was established here working in conjunction with a Lysander air-sea rescue aircraft. This arrangement was mainly for assisting RAF fighter aircraft that were in trouble or unable to return to their home bases.

With Friston being well positioned and midway along the Channel coast between existing fighter airfields, authorisation was given in 1941 for the airfield to be upgraded to a forward satellite station and was assigned to RAF Kenley, near Croydon in May. During the following winter, the airfield was closed while considerable works were carried out including strengthening of the grass runways and building of a perimeter track with sections near the buildings constructed with brick rubble, (including rubble from the demolition of Martello Tower No 63 to the east of Eastbourne). Other works included construction of fuel and ammunition storage, canteen mess and ablution buildings etc, underground air raid shelter and a sewage works. RAF Friston became operational again on May 15 1942. (1).

An article in the *Daily Telegraph* of September 8 1980, related the story of how Air Marshall Sir Gerald Gibbs, who was second in command of No 11 Fighter Wing, went sailing during the 1930's with friends off the Sussex coast. One evening, they tied up at Cuckmere Haven for the night and later had rather a lot to drink! Next morning, they went for a brisk walk along the Seven Sisters cliffs and he noticed the flat hinterland. During the early part of the war when the south east was being ravaged by lightening German Me 109 fighter attacks, the RAF decided to set up a number of smaller airfields. Gibbs recalled the area he had seen on that morning walk and supposedly, there came about the fighter station at Friston.

Two days after re-opening, the Station was visited informally by

Cabinet Minister Sir John Anderson accompanied by Lady Anderson (later Lord and Lady Waverley; some years later they resided at West Dean). (2). (In November 1938, placed Anderson in charge of the (ARP). He immediately commissioned the engineer William Patterson, to design a small and cheap bomb-proof shelter that could be erected in people's gardens – the 'n Shelter.' By September 1939 two million of these were distributed to people living in areas expected to be bombed by the . Made from six curved sheets bolted together at the top, with steel plates at either end they measured 1.95metres by 1.35metres; they could accommodate six people. These shelters were half buried in the ground with earth heaped on top, the entrance protected by a steel shield and an earthen blast wall).

Back to RAF Friston; to give some firm idea of the scale of the Station, the following statistics are taken from an official document titled 'Description of Friston Airfield' and dated December 1 1944. The north-east to south-west runway had a length of (1675 yards) and the north to south runway a length of (950 yards); these lacked any proper navigation lighting. The airfield was equipped with two 'O' type blister hangers. (These were designed to be used at dispersals, to offer protection whilst aircraft were worked on. They were small open ended hangers with a length of 45 feet and probably had canvas curtains at each end or possibly one end bricked up to provide added shelter for the ground crews. They were construction of steel cladding with a span of 65 feet). The total personnel listed on the Station were as follows: 96 officers, 175 senior NCO's, 977 other ranks; WAAF's numbered three officers, three senior NCO's and 152 other ranks, giving a total Station compliment of 1400 service men and women. (3).

OPERATIONS BOOK for RAF FRISTON.

The following information is formed of dated extracts mainly taken from the Operations Book of RAF Friston and provides an insight to life and operations on the Station during those tumultuous times. (2).

May 23 1942. The perimeter track around the airfield in a very muddy state but the operational flying surface seems to drain quite well.

June 8 1942. The flying surface still needs much work doing on it, *"all available personnel went to it!"* Airmen were being posted away quicker than arriving which only exasperated an already under-established administrative staff.

June 11 1942. Considerable difficulties were being experienced with telephone communications to the Operations Room.

June 12-13 1942. Personnel of No 253 squadron arrived by road, rail and air. Three Hurricanes arrived on the 13th from RAF Tangmere. *"Such a collection of real aircraft on the aerodrome all at once, greatly heartened the resident personnel."*

June 14 1942. GPO* engineers (*General Post Office; the telephone network was then owned and operated by the Post Office), worked throughout the night to install temporary lines to the Operations Rooms at Kenley and Tangmere.

June 16-18 1942. There was much practice flying being carried out, much to the relief of the residents of Eastbourne, who had been suffering from many recent enemy air raids.

June 20 1942. A practice beat up (attack) was carried out on RAF Ford in West Sussex, during which an aircraft flown by Australian Sgt. Pilot F.E. Murphy flew into the ground, he being killed. 7-40pm; the Sergeant Pilots marquee was completely burnt down complete with all their flying kit. The fire was thought to have been caused by a thoughtlessly discarded cigarette in the dry grass.

June 21 1942. 8-35pm; five airmen of No 32 squadron were returning from a bathe at Cuckmere Haven, when one of them trod on a land mine installed for coastal defence purposes (Map ref. 956164?). Two airmen were killed and the others slightly wounded; this area was out of bounds to all ranks.

June 25 1942. The Officer's Mess *"transferred to a requisitioned country house dispersed about 1 mile from the aerodrome."* This would have been Friston Place.

June 26 1942. No 32 squadron attacked light cargo shipping with cannon fire. The Czech Section Leader was unfortunately shot down. He was seen to be picked up by a German rescue boat off Fecamp. Another aircraft had to crash land at Friston.

June 27 1942. Marshall of the Royal Air Force, Sir John Salmond, visited Friston.

July 2 1942. 4-00pm; a Hurricane Mk.IIc being delivered to No 32 squadron from Exeter by No 1 Delivery Flight, had to make a forced landing at the edge of the minefield on the beach at Cuckmere Haven. This was due to the engine cutting out; the aircraft was severely damaged.

July 7 1942. A tank which had been brought in to demonstrate a new method of exploding a mine field, while being serviced in the vicinity of the cliffs, went out of control. It went over the 130ft. cliffs together with its Royal Tank Corps driver; he was severely injured and was rushed to the Station's sick quarters [The Ridge House?]. Both fighter squadrons left the Station today.

July 15 1942. The demonstration of exploding a minefield took place using another tank, watched by 3,000 spectators. Another demonstration took place in the afternoon watched by 5,000 spectators, using a line of derelict cars to represent a transport column. The valley was considered ideal. Finally, the spectators 'came under fire' from two Fairy Battles and four Spitfires, *"probably the first time for many, of coming under fire."* These probably took place in Limekiln Bottom; the 'spectators' were presumably military and local government personnel?

July 20 1942. No 2793 RAF Regiment took over the defence of the Station; (various RAF Regiments would take on this role, changing fairly frequently). Squadron Leader Ivo Blyton-Beesley took over from Flight Lieutenant G.V.T. Shaen-Carter as the Station's Commanding Officer.

July 24 1942. Early morning scrambles were being carried out in the dark as Kenley would not allow glim lamps to be lit in advance. They considered it dangerous, being on the cliff top and visible to German attack. It was found to be impractical to light the glim lamps less than eight minutes before flying. ('Glim lamps' were small, cylindrical cans, containing a two-volt lead-acid battery, lighting a blue or red bulb and used as temporary taxi-way or obstruction markers).

August 10 1942. The first Americans arrived on the Station, when four Spitfires of No 308 Pursuit) squadron flew in from RAF Kenley.

August 19 1942. The Station log book contains a comprehensive four page report on RAF Friston's involvement in the ill-fated Dieppe Raid by Canadian troops.

October 1 1942. Three Spitfires from No 402 squadron arrived to take part in an army manoeuvre at Cuckmere Haven, then returning directly to Kenley. Throughout this autumn, Auster aircraft arrived regularly from the Penshurst auxiliary landing ground (ALG) in Kent, possibly in connection with the Alfriston ranges?

November 15 1942. The north-south runway is described as being *"US."* Work on the eastern end of the main north-east to south-west runway was now nearing completion.

November 18 1942. No 4065 anti-aircraft squadron was formed at Friston. During the month, training took place on both Browning and light machine guns. The squadron's strength at the end of the month was one officer, one flight sergeant, one corporal and 50 airmen. (4).

November 24 1942. An American Liberator bomber landed after circling the area. Operations knew nothing of its appearance; flares were put up to assist it in finding the airfield.

1943. The year commenced with No 412 Squadron carrying out

escort flying to France.

February 9 1943. A German Dornier 217 bomber unexpectedly appeared and flew north over the airfield at about 100 feet. Fifteen minutes later, it returned from a northerly direction crossing the airfield at 10 metres (30 feet)! A single anti-aircraft gun unit to the east of the airfield opened fire, the aircraft returning fire. When the defending RAF Regiment was asked why a single shot had not been fired, the excuse given was that *"they did not recognize the machine."*

February 12 1943. A new Station Commanding Officer took charge, Squadron Leader Collier.

February 22 1943. Drainage work commenced on the eastern end of the north-east to south-west runway.

April 1 1943. Today was the 25th anniversary of the Royal Air Force. It was celebrated by a special dinner for the airmen at midday. Officers and NCO's served at table. Entertainment in the evening consisted of a dance with refreshments.

April 6 1943. The first of many films was screened at the community site on Scabs Island; *"Yank At Eton"* starring Mickey Rooney.

April 7 1943. A play was staged at the community site, Bernard Shaw's *"Arms And The Man."*

May 25 1943. Air Commodore McAvoy of Fighter Group 11 visited the Station to ascertain whether it had suitable facilities for the basing of a fighter squadron on a permanent basis.

July 16 1943. News of a crippled aircraft in the vicinity reached Friston and the flare path was lit. In the event, a Spitfire crashed into the sea just beyond the end of the runway. The Station's ambulance while going out to pick up the baled-out pilot, crashed. (This event is referred to again in the following chapter).

July 31 1943. Squadron Leader T.R. Wheatley now taken over as the Station's Commanding Officer.

August 7 1943. No 64 (Belgian) Squadron arrived from Ayr together with the No 3041 Servicing Echelon. The squadron was commanded by Squadron Leader Donnet, DFC.

August 14 1943. Friston was now very busy. There were now so many scrambles, the airfield being kept even busier by a constant flow of other aircraft landing to refuel.

November 19 1943. Two Lancasters made emergency landings.

November 30 1943. A Flying Fortress made an emergency landing.

1944. During January, no less than 68 emergency landings including two Liberators. February: RAF Friston is now a self-accounting Station as from the 15th of the month. Apart from squadron operations, 305 aircraft landed at Friston, a majority being emergency landings. This included 9 English heavies, 178 English fighters; 29 USAF heavies and 4 USAF fighters.

April 8 1944. Censorship of all the units personal mail came into force. Instructions have been received for the suspension of privilege leave for all personnel. During April, Friston and its satellite ALG Deanlands, have been very busy gathering stores in preparation for the hoped for invasion. The strength of the Station steadily increased through the month, particularly in respect of WAAF personnel.

May. Increases in the amount of stores and numbers of personnel arriving at the Station have continued. Large numbers of airmen are now billeted under canvas. The accommodation situation was becoming so acute that expectations of having to put WAAF personnel under canvas were being seriously considered.

June 6 1944. 'D' Day had arrived. There were many emergency landings. *"...the airfield began to look like a Bomber Station, when about every type of bomber and fighter could be identified."* The American mobile repair squadron present carried out excellent work and rebuilt several of the wrecked aircraft on the spot which were later flown away.

June 26 1944. The first RAF Regiment arrived for the 'Operation Diver' barrage ('diver' referring to the German's V-1 flying bomb), with also No 2835 anti-aircraft Squadron.

June 28-29 1944. Seven RAF Regiments arrived: Nos 2767, 2774, 2727, 2805 and 2824 for anti-diver duties. Anti-aircraft squadrons which also arrived were: Nos 2706, 2807 and 2792.

July 10-12 1944. The Station's Dramatic Society put on its first performance, *"George And Margaret."* It proved to be so popular that two more performances were put on. A large number of emergency landings took place during the month.

August 26 1944. Duncan Sandys MP and Chairman of a War Cabinet Committee for defence against German flying bombs and rockets, visited flying personnel involved in successful diver patrols. At about this time, the diver gun barrage was removed from the wider area administered by the Station.

September 1 1944. Postal censorship removed.

September 5 1944. Prince Bernhard of the Netherlands arrived in a Lockheed aircraft from RAF Hendon, to visit the 10th Commandos who had just returned from duty the same day.

September 8 1944. 22 Dakotas put down at Friston in the evening due to the weather.

October 23-25 1944. There were over 100 aircraft on the airfield, waiting to cross the Channel.

October 25 1944. A big dance was held at the Winter Garden in Eastbourne. During October, 310 aircraft visited the Station.

INFORMATION FROM OTHER SOURCES.

Though the infrastructure on the Station was rather basic, air and ground crew grew fond of their postings to RAF Friston (at least during the summer months) as recorded in this entry in the Log Book of 41 Squadron, dated May 31 1943. *"It is now hoped that we are able to stay at Friston for a few months as it is a delightful place, the airfield is not too good with grass runways and rather bumpy, incidentally the runway is only 950yds. in length with a sheer drop at the southern end. During fine weather the airfield and conditions are fair, but with the slightest rain the ground becomes very sticky as the surface is covered with about 6ins. of clay. The dispersals have no permanent buildings and the pilots and crew are using large marquees, but never the less the surroundings are pleasant and generally the squadron like the place. (5).*

"6th June 1943. Owing to very bad visibility with low rain clouds six enemy aircraft came in over East Dean and bombed Eastbourne without being intercepted by the squadron. All together three sections of the squadron were airborne and in trying to intercept them over the town, they were fired upon by the local A.A. A Fw 190 was damaged by fire from Brownings of RAF Reg. No.

The Swallows, a large country house at Friston which served as RAF Friston's Station Headquarters, where the Station's colours were flown.

2793 squadron. This aircraft went out over Birling Gap smoke issuing from under the fuselage and it is believed to have crashed into the sea. During the raid the station Sick Quarters was damaged by cannon shells fired by a Fw. 190 and a nearby water tower sustained slight damage." Their stay however was to last for only three weeks. (5)

During the squadron's second stay at RAF Friston: *"21st March. In the evening a party was held by 'B' flight at the Junction Hotel at Polegate. Most of 'A' flight were also present and the guests included W.R.A.F. and Y.M.C.A. workers who provide us with so much comfort on the airfield. Dance floor was put to good use, various members of the squadron providing the band, the evening was a great success."* (6).

Not all aircraft damaged or lost resulted from enemy action. On August 19 1942, a Blenheim light bomber belonging to 614 Squadron was hit by anti-aircraft fire from a British naval ship off Dieppe. It limped on to RAF Friston where its crash landing resulted in two crewmen being killed and one injured. (7).

Sadly, not all damaged aircraft actually managed to make it back to the relative safety of RAF Friston, sometimes failing by only a short distance. Lt. James Bolin's aircraft, a Flying fortress nicknamed *'Ruthless'* had on February 2 1944 been on a raid of a V-1 launch site at

Looking south-westwards today along the line of Friston's main runway, with Seaford Head in the distance; a tranquil scene of sheep grazing.

Watten in France, a day of heavy cloud and some icing. They had completed their mission and on the return flight were attacked and lost two or three engines and their instrument panel and so had to make for the nearest airfield. While establishing their identity to land at RAF Friston they had to circle back over Eastbourne. Ellin Barrow heard the approaching plane and wondered if it might be a German raider. However the engines sounded irregular and the plane was low; soon after the plane appeared, flying slowly and *"looking exhausted."* She saw an airman standing at one of the waist-gun windows and her heart went out to him; as it went by she poignantly whispered, *"Hurry home, boys."* (8).

On the lower slopes of the Downs, Audrey Armstrong was gathering sheep helped by the green-keeper of Willingdon Golf Course, when she heard the approaching sound of straining engines. Moments later, she was gazing up and could see the pilot, both realising that a crash was inevitable, the aircraft crashing into the Downs near Butts Brow and exploding. An engine tumbled down the hillside, coming to rest nearby her. After the explosions had stopped she and the green-keeper ran towards the wreck; amazingly, there were still crewmen alive. One died despite first-aid and two others died of their wounds in Princess Alice Hospital. (8).

Ground crew re-arming 349 Squadron Spitfires on a bleak, windswept airfield, winter of 1943-44. (Copyright of the Imperial War Museum)

Further to 'Operation Diver,' the code name for operations against the German Luftwaffe (referred to as 'Doodlebugs') campaign launched in 1944 against and other parts of Britain. A were deployed in several movements; initially from mid-June 1944 they were positioned from the to the Channel coast. Re-deployments were prompted by the ever-changing approach tracks of the flying bombs which were in turn influenced by the Allies' advance across Europe. Anti-aircraft gunners found that such small, fast-moving targets were difficult to hit; the average altitude of the V-1 was between 610 and 910 metres (2,000 and 3,000 feet). Static gun installations with faster traverses were more successful and were quickly built at great expense. The development of and development of the also helped counter the advantages of speed and size which the V-1 possessed. During 1944 delivery commenced just in time of an anti-aircraft based around an . (9, 10).

Fighter aircraft were also mobilised as part of the campaign; but most were too slow to catch a V-1 unless they had an advantage of height. Even when intercepted the V-1 was difficult to bring down. Machine gun bullets had little effect on the sheet steel structure and 20 mm cannon shells were explosive projectiles, which meant that if the warhead was detonated, it could also destroy the fighter. When the V-1's began appearing in mid-June of 1944, there were fewer than 30 Tempest fighter aircraft to defend against them. Few other aircraft had the low-altitude speed to be effective. Early attempts to intercept V-1's often failed but techniques were rapidly developed. These included the exacting method of using the airflow over an aircrafts wing to raise one wing of the V-1, by positioning a wingtip under the bombs wing and bringing it to within 15 cm (six inches). Correctly positioned, the airflow would tip the V-1's wing up thus overriding the bomb's gyros and sending it into an out of control dive. Another technique successfully employed was to have the 20mm cannons on fighters harmonised at 275 metres (300 yards). (9, 10).

The number of Tempest's employed was built up to over 100 aircraft by September. and -engined XIV's became involved and were tuned to make them almost fast enough. During the short summer nights the Tempests shared defensive duty with twin-engined . There was no need for at night, for the V-1's jet engine exhaust plume was like a beacon; they could also be heard from as far away as 10 miles (hence the name given them of 'Doodlebugs'). During daylight, V-1 chases were chaotic and often unsuccessful until a special fly zone between London and the coast was declared in which only the fastest fighters were permitted. Between June and mid-August 1944 the handful of Tempests shot down 638 flying bombs. Next most successful was the Mosquito (428), Spitfire Mk.XIV (303), and Mustang (232). Only seventeen per cent of all flying bombs entering the coastal gun barrage were destroyed during the first week; this rose to 74 per cent in the last week of August when on one particular day, 82 per cent were shot down. This success rate equated in an increase from one flying bomb for every 2,500 shells fired to one for every hundred. (9,10).

No 610 Squadron arrived at RAF Friston on July 4 1944; two days later they sent two V-I's harmlessly into the sea. Both pilots having exhausted their ammunition, adopted the new technique of flying alongside the bombs and tipping them into a dive. Throughout July 1944 the Squadron patrolled incessantly against flying bombs. The pilots aggregated 719 operational hours in their Spitfires and destroyed 31 'divers' bringing their total up to 43 kills. The Squadron was kept on anti-flying-bomb patrols until early September by which time the pilots had flown since June 20, a total of 2,055 hours and accounted for 50 'divers'. The squadron then moved on. (11).

No. 316 (City of Warsaw) Squadron had and active and varied career up to 1944 when, it was re-equipped with Mustang Mk.III's whilst based at Coltishall, Norfolk and assigned to bomber escort and fighter-bomber duties. During early July 1944 this Squadron also moved down to Friston for operations against the V-1 threat. The pilots of 316 Squadron proved to be particularly adept at this task and became the highest scoring Mustang Squadron with 75 flying bombs destroyed during the hectic two-month spell of the 'Doodlebug' menace. In October the Squadron moved on and became involved with several other Mustang Squadrons, providing long-range daylight bomber escort duties. (12).

On July 12, they carried out 24 anti-flying-bomb sorties with aircraft patrolling in pairs. The aircraft of Flt. Sgt. Pietrzak caught the blast while attacking one target; the pilot safely baled out but the aircraft was lost. August 15; a 'ranger' operation took place between 1815 and 2118 hours; (a 'ranger' was the interception of German aircraft flying to and from the battlefield). The route taken on this evening was Brighton, Dieppe, Beaumoux, St.Dizier, Calais, Fere, Dieppe and Brighton. While flying north of Chalom at 8,000feet, the patrol met a formation of fifteen 109e's flying at 4,000feet; in the ensuing dogfight four enemy aircraft were destroyed. (13).

August 28 1944 and four Mustang's acted as escort to a Walrus seaplane involved in the search for a dinghy off the Dutch coast eight miles west of Den Helder. Dinghy and survivors were located and picked up and the Walrus escorted back to base. The following day eight Mustang's escorted Beaufighter light bombers in attacking a convoy of four ships south-east of Helgoland. During the engagement, the second and third ships were seriously damaged by gunfire and torpedoes from the Beaufighters and left in flames. Intense flak was encountered from all ships. (13).

The following entries are taken from the Log Book of 131 (County of Kent) Squadron. 30th September [1944]. *"...12 aircraft led by Flt. Lieu. Waterhouse acted as top cover to 36 Marauders on Ramrod 1303 [ramrod- escort work] target was the bridge at Arnhem. ... Plt. Offcr. Baxter (Australian) was forced to crash land in a ploughed field between Ghent and Brussels on account of oil pressure trouble. The aircraft broke its back and Fly. Offcr. Baxter was seen to walk away from the aircraft and was soon surrounded by many Belgians."* (14).

"28th October 1944. There was improvement in the weather 12 aircraft took part in ramrod – a heavy Lancaster and Halifax attack on Cologne. No enemy aircraft were seen but there was the usual flak in the target area." (14).

A number of other incidents involving aircraft crashing during the war in the local vicinity or in connection with RAF Friston occurred, some of which are retold here. October 18 1941. An early casualty in connection with the airfield occurred 300 metres north-west of Exceat Newbarn Cottage involving a Miles Magister monoplane. PC Hyde's report is as follows: *"The monoplane took off from Friston Airfield in a strong South Westerly gale. When about 200 yards up it was seen to turn right and then nose dived to the ground. The occupants Flight/Lieut. George McClusky age 21yrs. of, 402 Squadron. R.C.A.F. Southend and Capt. Donald Robert McNabb. Age 31 yrs. of, Royal Canadian Dental Corps attached to 402 Squadron. R.C.A.F. Southend, received serious injuries and were conveyed to Princess Alice Hospital, Eastbourne, in the R.A.F. ambulance where they died the same day."* The report did not state what or why they doing there on that fateful day. (15).

May 30 1943 and PC Henry Hyde again reports, *"I have to report that- at 0650 hrs. on the 30th May 1943. I received information from the R.A.F. Station, Friston, to the effect that a plane had crashed in the valley near the airfield. At 0720 hrs. same day in company with Sergt. Hopkins, we proceeded along the Seaford Road towards the airfield when we saw about an acre of Forestry Plantation on fire. On arriving at the airfield we were informed that a plane had crashed at the spot where the fire was and that the pilot, Pilot Officer Belza (Pole) of, 303 Squadron, Heston, was safe. I summoned the Eastbourne Fire Service, we then proceeded to the spot and found the plane a total wreck having burnt out. We dealt with the fire until the arrival of the Fire Service and the R.A.F.R. [Regiment] guard. From enquiries made it would appear that the plane cut out and had to make a forced landing."* (15).

During early afternoon on July 16 1943, an occurrence reminiscent of a similar arrival on the beach at Cuckmere Haven a year earlier; a fighter crash landed on the beach some 200 metres east of the river. The aircraft was a Mustang piloted by Flt. Lieutenant S.M. Knight of No 460 RCAF Dunsford near Guildford, who had to bale out after his machine had been hit by enemy flak. The wreck was completely burnt out. (15).

February 9 1944, and an American built B-25 Mitchell bomber in service with the RAF was observed by PC Henry Hyde, flying from east to west appearing to be on fire and accompanies by two fighters. After having passed over the airfield it turned north and then south in an attempt to land there, but crashed on Crowlink Farm. Three crew members were seriously injured and one killed. Pilot Off. Struthers and Warrant Off. Exon were conveyed to the Station's sick quarter and Flt. Sergeant Browne was sent on to East Grinstead Hospital. The body of Warrant Officer Hammond was placed in the Station's mortuary. (15).

Early on the afternoon of March 4 1944, an American Fortress bomber from the 447th Bomber Group crashed and was badly damaged, about 800 metres south of the former Snap Hill Barn in

Remains of Dornier 217E carrying incendiaries brought down on Haven Brow, by anti-aircraft artillery at an unknown location, March 1944. (Copyright of the Imperial War Museum)

Friston Forest. Of the 10 crew, one was killed and one injured, the remainder were uninjured; the dead airman and the nine survivors were taken to the Station. (15).

On the evening of March 14 1944, a German Dornier 217E night-bomber loaded with incendiary bombs was hit by fire from the 3.7 inch guns of the 71st Heavy Anti-Aircraft Brigade (possibly sited at Dover?). The aircraft crashed into the ground towards the summit of Haven Brow just before midnight; due to the nature of its bomb load the wreck burned for some 24 hours; an area of stunted grass beside the South Downs Way marks the spot to this day (grid ref: TV 522978). The remains of the four crewmen were interned in Friston churchyard three days later. (15, 16).

April 29 1944. Another Spitfire crashed after engine failure on taking off and reported by police sergeant Charles Hopkins. *"This plane piloted by Flight Sergeant No. 1299851 Maureau (Belgian) of 135 Air Field, took off from Friston Aerodrome and it was noticed that the engine kept misfiring. The plane went towards the sea, made a half circle and then the engine cut out altogether, and the plane crashed at "Gate Field" Friston and caught fire. The pilot was thrown out of the plane and was drawn away from danger by Mr Maurice Haffenden of East Dean who was working close by. The fire was extinguished by The R.A.F. Fire party. The pilot was suffering from shock and lacerations to the face and was conveyed to The Sick Base, Friston."* (15).

After October 1944 the action moved further away and RAF Friston reverted to its original role as an emergency landing ground and then reduced to care and maintenance on May 25 1945, before being de-requisitioned on April 8 1946. (1). On Sunday April 22 2001, a service was held to dedicate a framed commemoration of the existence of the RAF station, at Friston parish church. (14). To look out today across that exposed, wide and slightly undulating landscape it appears simply as a green, pastoral backwater where nothing of any great consequence could ever have taken place...

SOURCES.

1) Ashworth, Christopher. 'Action Stations No 9 – Airfields of the South East.' 1985.

2) PRO AIR 10, piece 4039.

3) PRO AIR 28, piece 286.

4) PRO AIR 29, piece 883.

5) PRO AIR 27, piece 425.

6) PRO AIR 27, piece 426.

7) Warner, Graham. 'British Blenheim: A Complete History.' (2nd edition). Crecy Publishing. 2005.

8) McLachlan, Ian and Zorn, Russell J. 'Eighth Air Force Bomber Stories.' Patrick Stephens Ltd. 1991.

9) King, Benjamin; Kutta, Timothy. 'IMPACT. The History of Germany's V - Weapons in World War II.' Sarpedon Publishers. 1998.

10) Ramsay,Winston. 'The Blitz Then & Now' (Volume 3). Battle of Britain Prints International. 1990.

11) 610 County of Chester website.

12) Lancashire Aircraft Investigation Team website.

13) PRO AIR 27, piece 1705

14) PRO AIR 27, piece 942.

15) East Sussex Constabulary. Crashed aircraft reports.

16) Imperial War Museum. Photo negative H 36868.

17) The Argus. Article in April 12 2001 edition. Brighton.

CHAPTER 10.

R.A.F. FRISTON - PERSONAL RECOLLECTIONS.

Following on from the documented history of RAF Friston, we can elaborate on those official archives by painting in the personal recollections of men and women who served at or had memories of action associated with Friston and, including wartime experiences within the 'study area,' during those sometimes sombre but often exhilarating days. Concerning the airfield only the earliest account is from 1941, the period when Friston was no more than an emergency landing ground; other accounts originate from the Station's heyday, with the final accounts from its twilight phase in 1945 and its legacy.

During 1935 Lillian 'Dot' Nash and her husband Fred moved from West Dean to Friston, for he had recently accepted employment with the Eastbourne Waterworks Company who required him to live at one of their cottages adjacent to Friston water tower. During the Second World War they shared their cottage with a family of Belgian refugees, the husband of which being employed in the pay office at RAF Friston; Nash's made do with living on the ground floor. To spread the demands upon the shared kitchen, one family would cook during the morning while the other had its use in the evening. All available space had to be used to its utmost; sometimes they would put up airmen who were convalescing, who otherwise would have been billeted under canvas. At another period during the war they had three land army girls billeted with them; Dot did not approve of the concept of these girls driving tractors on the steep downland slopes. Fred could remember German bombers returning from air raids so low that their crews would wave to people on the ground! After their return to Belgian the two families remained close friends for the remainder of their lives.

Percy Budd (b. 1876), lived at Friston and had fought in both the Boer War and First World War and was keen to play his part in the current war effort. He was appointed Head Air Raid Warden for the rural area bounded by East Dean, Exceat, Alciston and Jevington. The following are extracts taken from the diary he kept of his ARP duties: October 11 1940. The first recorded bomb falling in the 'study area,' when *"Friston Place bombed, 3 craters found; damage to Cottages, doors blown in, windows broken and tiles off. Barn demolished and glasshouses wrecked. (On the following day, 4 more craters found; later, evidence found of unexploded bomb. Cottages evacuated and notices placed. Next day (Sunday), Hailsham Control wanted to know the distance between this and the Pumping Station)."*

August 9 1942. *"Air raid 22.50 to 23.10 over Friston Air Force Ground and Downs towards West Dean, one H/E [high explosive bomb] on Air Force Ground, numerous Incendiaries on Afforestation, no damage reported."*

January 20 1943. *"12.45 Enemy attacking convoy off Seven Sisters, also further attempted Raids on London."*

January 21 1944. *"At 20.33 Alert sounded and soon after large numbers of Raiders passed over who sent down many H/E's and Flares with I/B [incendiary bombs] in direction of Seaford, Alfriston, Hailsham, Willingdon and Eastbourne. Saw 2 Planes coming down in flames one at Firle and the other at Alfriston. All clear at 22.00."*

June 13 1944. *"First P.A.C. passed over."* [pilotless aircraft – V-1 flying bomb].

June 19 1944. *"Flying Bomb brought down in sea off Friston damaging ceiling Transept in Friston Church."*

Clem Berry was a bus driver during the Second World War for Southdown Motor Services Ltd. and recalled the first occasion he saw the diversionary lights which would have resembled Newhaven when viewed from a night-time flying aircraft. He only witnessed this on two or three occasions during the early period of the war. On the first occasion he was driving a bus up Exceat Hill towards Eastbourne; Seaford had already been blacked-out as an air raid was expected. Suddenly, thousands of small lights were switched on resembling house lights; they were situated in and on either side of the valley. Neither he nor his colleagues could recall seeing men working on their installation.

Miriam Monico was in her twenties during the war years. When called upon for war service, she was rejected on account of her invalid mother with whom she lived in Friston. After being turned down she commenced voluntary work for the Eastbourne branch of the Y.M.C.A., administered by one of the town's general practitioners, Dr. John Bodkin Adams (who during the 1950's stood trial on suspicion of murdering one of his wealthy, elderly lady patients). To begin with she toured the gun positions within the Eastbourne town area selling tea and chocolate etc. In 1941 she and another woman were put in charge of the Y.M.C.A. facility at RAF Friston; this comprised of a nissan hut situated on the west side of the airfield entrance, opposite the airfields first aid post. Ultimately they were assisted by a band numbering some 30 volunteers.

In those early days on the airfield Miriam cycled to and fro to work but subsequently, she was allowed the use of a car in view of the fact that each night, she had to take the day's takings home. Typically, the day commenced at seven o'clock with the cleaning out and lighting of a large coke-fired range affectionately referred to as 'Ermintrude,' which served to boil water for the tea urn, cooking and for heat; during times of emergency it might be called upon for heating of water for the first aid post. Miriam usually reached home often towards midnight, seven days of the week, this routine lasting until the winding down of Friston. The chore of keeping Ermintrude stoked often fell to her; for this she would don dungarees and a turban and when ever a new squadron leader arrived at the airfield and came to introduce himself, she would say that Miss. Monico would be in later and then quickly go and have a change of clothes!

During the Station's heyday, the facility got through about 30 loaves of bread a day for making sandwiches, all made using margarine. These were filled with cheese, 'Spam' and when there were Americans present on the airfield, peanut butter. A brisk trade took place in baked potatoes as did 'wads' - large scones containing a jam filling. Tea had to be taken to the fighter pilots at the dispersal area towards The Gayles itself. In the event of a possible air raid a hooter was sounded and all non-essential personnel were supposed to make for the air raid bunkers, but they were seldom used except by rats! For a toilet she and her volunteers had nearby, a small corrugated iron hut complete with bucket and seat; for much of the period it was roofless due to a low flying aircraft! While mentioning low-flying aircraft, on another occasion an aircraft making its final approach from the north, lost power and glided down onto the end of the runway. The first knowledge that the Y.M.C.A. staff had of this was when the chimney of the range was demolished, smothering hundreds of freshly-cut sandwiches with soot! Early in 1941, a Mosquito bomber flown by an Australian crew landed from a southerly direction with two metres missing from one of its wings and no brakes. As it neared the northern end of the runway, with the Y.M.C.A. and first aid buildings looming up fast, the pilot veered the aircraft sharply right, across the airfields entrance road, and so avoiding Miriam and her girls! A visiting Air Marshall was once heard to remark that from the air, RAF Friston resembled *"a sloping postage stamp"* and considered its use risky in an airworthy let alone a damaged aircraft!

One WAAF who served at Friston for some considerable time from

1941, was Ruth Williams who served in the motor transport section and who later during the 1950's was to become a household name when she married an african student, Seretse Khama, who later became Botswana's first President, she becoming Lady Ruth. She recalls: *"I remember Friston more than any other station I served on, partly I suppose because I stayed there longer than anywhere else and because it was different. We were very small in numbers, most of the time not more than 100 people [women]. It was an emergency landing ground, and did not really even qualify at the beginning to be called anything more. There were a couple of spits that would only take off when given permission to do so from RAF Kenley. It was most frustrating for us all but more so the pilots, who were chewing at the bit to get away and challenge the enemy. We were at times sitting ducks. However, fortunately that all changed.... One of our responsibilities was to look for aircraft that had come down and we would be given a five mile radius. As you know there were no road signs so we had to ask if any-one had seen or heard a plane. We always found them and very often in some-ones cottage having been taken for tea and refreshments by the villagers. A lot of these planes also crashed on the emergency airfield. It was always very shattering to witness these incidents and when a plane, badly crippled, managed to land without anyone being hurt, there was great jubilations. The WAAF's did not have a mess of their own but there was one mess on the station for all N.C.O.'s. The Gayles was another experience. The beautiful house on the station, which was haunted. We were billeted there until it mysteriously burnt down. The fire started in a room which was always locked. No one had a key. It was an invisible ghost but very noisy. We all every-one of us heard it. It used to climb the stairs and at the top stop. At other times we were doing ambulance duty from dawn to dusk for a week at a time. It was exhausting particularly in the British success. It was the station I enjoyed the most serving on."*

Bill Clarke was in the Signals Wing attached to RAF Friston from late 1941 until early 1942. The Station had a strength of approximately 40 men; the officers were billeted at The Gayles with the other ranks in nearby nissen huts. On several occasions the Station was cut off by snow which necessitated walking from Eastbourne railway station when returning from leave. Sometimes they would receive a 'red signal' from the authorities at Hailsham, which indicated the possibility of an enemy landing by possibly paratroopers and meant going to bed with their rifles! During its early days, RAF Friston was a backwater in relation to World War Two; life on the airfield being fairly relaxed, they often spending time snaring rabbits. The main task of the airfield was air-sea rescue work; this was carried out by a Lysander aircraft flown by Flt. Sgt. Hurst and involved dropping dinghies to ditched airmen prior to rescue by the RAF air-sea rescue launch based at Newhaven.

Following the upgrading of facilities at RAF Friston, A.R. Costin who was involved in airfield control, was posted to Friston from RAF Kenley in June 1942. He recalled that the 'control tower' consisted of a *"large nissen hut with a built-on upper attic with all round view and windows. Radio and direction finder with several telephones for Controller. 'Darky Watch' manned by 2 WAAF's all 24 hours. Normally day flying only but electric cable for lights laid on one side of long runway every day after flying ceased. Air field party laid electric lights and plugged into cable; also 'goose necks' (paraffin flares used in fog) and a couple of approach indicators with Chance Light (flood light)."* One notable day occurred sometime during the period autumn 1943 or early 1944; he recalled that Flying Fortress' taking part in a large raid encountered strong headwinds over France and were running low on fuel. Many had to make crash landings wherever they could, some in the Channel, some on mined beaches, several at Deanlands near Chiddingly (Friston's auxiliary landing ground and stores) and two at Friston. Southdown buses were requisitioned to pick up and ferry the aircrew to various collection points.

The airfield was responsible for at least one lasting relationship, that of former WAAF Jean Morey who came from the Isle of Wight and Canadian airman Jack Ivamy. She was a driver at Friston for about a year from August or September 1942; they met when she was despatched to Eastbourne station to collect an airman, Jack! WAAF's were only allowed to drive vehicles of two tonnes or less officially; in practice due to a shortage of airman they often drove the large crash ambulance which exceeded this weight. An incident occurred in July 1943, when an aircraft was reported to have crashed in the vicinity of the Seven Sisters cliffs; the crash ambulance was at once scrambled, crewed by WAAF driver Cynthia Reade accompanied by a medical orderly. While negotiating one of the steep slopes near to the cliffs, the vehicle rolled over on to its side; fortunately the vehicle and its two occupants escaped unscathed. Her officer Flight Sergeant Grindley, was dreadfully worried that he would be *"for the high jump,"* but the incident was hushed up. Ironically the pilot was picked up near Seaford by a civilian. While in Bexhill one day collecting provisions for the airfield, she promptly had to dive beneath her van when German fighters suddenly strafed the town. Similar trips involved driving to Eastbourne; bread was collected from a bakery in Old Town, loaves being passed by human chain - WAAF driver, mess sergeant, an airman and bakery staff and loaded on to the swept floor of the van. The other trip was the weekly collection of the Station's beer ration from the Star

Brewery in Old Town! Once a week, mail was collected from Shoreham; returning at 6pm they would pick up any airman returning from leave at The Ship Inn in Brighton. On one occasion while taking pilots of Squadron 412 (Canadian) back to their quarters at Friston Place, they were passing an unattended coal lorry along the Jevington road. Ordering her to suddenly stop, they promptly transferred half of the coal into the back of her vehicle!

During the evenings, a three tonne lorry would take Station personnel into Eastbourne, often to the Winter Garden where dances were regularly held, it returning to RAF Friston at about 11-30pm; late stragglers either had to walk, or wait for the van which toured the cinemas distributing the films, this would pass the airfield entrance gate at about 1pm. Christmas Day 1942 saw action of a different kind; Jean had the task of driving the Medical Officer and a couple of colleagues around the hotel bars of Eastbourne; immediately upon arriving back at the Station she crashed out upon her bed!

Jack Ivamy was attached to RAF Friston for a six week spell during April and May of 1943, he being a member of a team of four radio telephone operators working from a forward-relay VHF radio van. They operated independently of the airfield; their task was to relay orders received via land line, to aircraft often far away over France and logging all transmissions received. This facility was manned 24 hours a day; during his night shifts, Jean would sometimes keep company with Jack, aided by mugs of cocoa. Once while standing in the airfield control tower, within the space of three minutes he watched seven German Me 109 fighter aircraft swoop in low from the sea, Jack actually looking down upon them! Having flown low up through Crowlink Bottom they would circle overland and then strafe or bomb Eastbourne as they returned over the coast.

The next account is vividly retold by ex-sergeant Frank Royle: *"In 1943 I was posted to Friston to be I.C. Officers Mess cook (chef). The C.O. being Flt. Lt. Shaen-Carter. We had taken over Mr. Leslie Hore-Belisha's lovely house and grounds near Beachy Head. [Friston Place; not actually his house though he often had visited there. His name was given to the pedestrian road crossing beacons.] Also there was a WAAF and Airmens Unit and a contingent of the East Surrey Regiment. The least said about them the better. Also we had 1 of the earliest Lysander open cockpits operational. I remember well the flights I was given me by Sgt. Pilot Bob; I never knew his last name. We flew as near to the coast of France as we dare me sitting in the rear cockpit on a revolving stool gripping the handles of a Lewis gun, hairy to say the least. Now for quite a while we in Officers Mess lived off the products of the gardens it being a glorious summer. Fresh figs in abundance, asparagus, raspberries, strawberries, currants and all kinds of Veg. under intense cultivation. Milk, fresh daily was supplied to us by two lovely local landgirls one of whom I shall call Ginger, more of her later. Airmens rations were drawn alternately from Bexhill and Hove. I being in the "Trade" often managed to extract a whole fillet of beef for special dinners.... On one occasion the NAAFI was burgled and a couple of weeks later again. Result, the East Surrey Regiment posted to where I do not know. However no more burglaries occurred. Back now to Ginger, who lived just over the hill opposite the camp and who owned an old Austin 10. Once a week she would take one or two chaps to the Cinema in Eastbourne and back and very enjoyable too. I was also invited to her house for coffee and biscuits! and to meet her parents a lovely retired couple. All airmen as I remember were billeted in a vacated holiday camp in a hollow a ? of a mile from the camp proper* [the former Holiday Fellowship facility at North Barn, Crowlink].... *One afternoon I was preparing dinner and the kitchen was just below ground level with an open window on the side, when suddenly a pair of legs slid through followed by a body, the owner being none other than Grp. Capt. Douglas Bader, tin legs and all. He then said to me where is your Boss? So I took him to Flt. Lt. Shaen-Carter who was the C.O. and who was a grounded Spitfire pilot, also he was Irish and a lovely soft spoken Gentleman.... On the whole life at Friston was fairly humdrum.... Now more memories of this time, a village called East Dean where we as troops were warmly welcomed by its inhabitants. Also we were invited to dances in the Village Hall and "Ginger" on hand to try and teach me to dance with two left feet. She never achieved it. All good fun."*

The next account details an unusual use to which RAF Friston was put for a short period during the latter part of 1943; the story is related by Group Captain John Wray, DFC: *"In 1943 I commanded what I think was the first fighter/bomber squadron in this country to be equipped with the 3 inch rocket and 40mm 'S' gun as alternative armament. We were at Manston [Kent] at the time. Although we settled for the rockets as our main offensive weapon because of their devastating power at that time, we kept about six aircraft armed with the 40mm gun to use on low level attacks against soft targets in France and Belgium, particularly against trains. This was because at that time we were not permitted to carry our rockets over enemy territory and could only use them against coastal shipping.*

The 40mm gun had to be fired to harmonise it and, moreover, it had to be fired over its effective range of 600 yards. This meant that it had to be fired only on an airfield that was right on the coast. We used Friston for this purpose. We would fly in to Friston, and a large canvas square was set up at the far end of the airfield with a three foot circle on it. The Hurricane was anchored down in it's flying position at 220 MPH. i.e. one degree nose down, six hundred yards from the canvas target and the two guns were then sighted on the target with the aid of a breech periscope which allowed one to look down the barrels.

When the guns were 'sighted' single shots would be fired from one of them. To harmonise the guns correctly, three successive shots had to penetrate the three foot circle; adjustments being made in between shots to achieve this. The same procedure then followed with the other gun. So, shot the size of that used in Bofors guns would whistle across Friston, out to sea, until the guns were harmonised. This practice did not last long, because we carried out the very first attack against a land target with the three inch rockets and from then on we dumped the 40mm gun and used only the rockets. However, for a short time in the latter part of 1943 we used Friston for this fairly unique operation."

Harry Keeley was a member of No.2751 squadron of the RAF Regiment which was stationed at Friston for about one year from late 1943. The gun position that he was attached to was on the site where now stands Dean Lodge on the edge of West Dean and consisted of a 40mm Bofors gun, twin Browning machine guns in case of low flying enemy aircraft and four tents; enemy aircraft on route to London were too high for their guns. In charge of the site was Sergeant Potts; at night they worked in conjunction with a searchlight positioned opposite West Dean Newbarn Cottage. These two positions were linked by telephone and it was during the laying of this cable that Harry was to meet his future wife Ruth, from the village. There was another AA gun positioned on top of the hill between West Dean and Exceat. They made use of the communal facilities situated at Scabs Island, including the NAAFI where the all important tobacco could be purchased! Pay and cooked food was brought down to them from Scabs Island; by the time food reached them it was not very pleasant!

Freddie Bicks was for many years, well known in East Dean for his involvement in the staging of village theatre productions; in fact, this particular pursuit stretched back to the war years. During 1943-44, Freddie was the Dental Surgeon and Entertainments Officer for RAF Friston; his surgery was situated in the requisitioned, capacious house The Swallows. Responsibility rested on him for arranging visits by ENSA (Entertainment's National Services Association) groups, which included several well-known theatrical personalities. One particular play which was popular at that time which he recalled staging was *'George and Margaret.'* At the time, there was a theatre-carpenter serving on the Station with whom Freddie had arranged to construct a stage and two stage sets within the airmen's mess near The Gayles. This airman was subsequently demoted to the lowest rank for all his hard work, for many of the wooden mess-room tables were inexplicably spirited away!

The Station Commander at this time was one Squadron Leader Wheedle. Freddie recalled that the Station's Medical Officer was based at another large requisitioned house, known as Friston House, to which were attached the Station's sick quarters. At one stage, a detachment of naval personnel were stationed on the airfield; on pay days they would march from the airfield to their headquarters situated in the house Gala at Friston and would march time while awaiting their turn to be paid.

D.E. Dean served with the RAF Regiment, being part of No.2803 squadron comprising of some 200 men and was stationed at Friston during the period February through to June, 1944. In his account he states the following: *"Gun position - situated on the brow of one of the Seven Sisters [Brass Point?], extremely close to the cliff edge. Approximately 10 yards north of the gun site was a domestic site. Also close to the gun site was a glass fronted observation hut manned by the Canadians, and used to observe shipping when the Canadian artillery range, situated in the area of the Birling Gap was being used for test firing. I have no knowledge of the position of the other gun sites. The RAF Regiment bofor squadron comprised twelve 40/mm. Bofor guns and at that time were still operating under predictor control. The C.O. was Squadron Leader Bouton, M.C. The most spectacular crash occurred when a Fortress came in from the east very low and narrowly missed the radio mast [in the vicinity of Flagstaff Brow], two engines had been knocked out, and extensive damage was observed on the wings and tail. The aircraft crashed on the airfield and within minutes burst into flame. I understand that the crew members escaped.*

The only local residents I remember was an extremely pleasant middle aged lady, who lived in the cottages. She regularly visited the site driving a mobile canteen and offered us the facility of using her bathroom for a weekly bath, which was accepted with gratitude. The lady had one draw back, she repeatedly told us that the gun site was much too close to the cliff face as each year, part of the cliff erode away. I can assure you that standing on guard at night and listening to the waves pounding against the cliffs didn't exactly give one a pleasant feeling. One other person, although not a local was certainly a character. The Royal Marine Commandos regularly used the area for battle training. Their point of attack being the demobilised house [coastguard cottages?]. The Officer in charge was a one armed man called the "mad major." As the exercises were carried out with live ammunition an occasional ricochet would whistle over us and on the arrival of the marine unit would mean getting our heads down until they departed. On one occasion a bullet struck the glass in the Canadian observation hut and narrowly missed the occupants. He quite naturally complained to his H.Q. Within a short while an extremely angry one armed marine officer stormed into the gun site and despite our protestations that we were not responsible for complaining, accused us of being the biggest cowards that walked the earth. Obviously his language was much more colourful!"

During 1988, the author was involved in negotiating with a film location company for the making of the TV series '*A Piece Of Cake,*' (a story of a Battle of Britain squadron which received a great deal of criticism in the national press), for which, part of the former RAF Friston runway required reinstating. Initially they had approached Shoreham airport but the airport management were not interested. During discussions however, it was suggested that the author ought to speak to the airports manager, Alexander 'Ben' Gunn. A jaunty Scotsman, Ben brought back vividly something of those intense, exhilarating days of Fighter Command during World War Two.

At that time, Ben was serving with No.501 Squadron commanded by Squadron Leader Barnet, and consisting of around 18 Mk.Vb Spitfires and two Mk.IX's. They were based at Friston during 1944 from April 30 till July 2 and were initially involved in pre-dawn and after dusk sweeps together with other missions during the day. The squadron was of an 'international' flavour with 4 English, 2 Scots, an Australian, 4/5 Canadian including 'Smudger' Smith - a black gentleman, a Dane, 5/6 French, and 4 New Zealanders. When asked if those days were memorable or otherwise, Ben replied that life was exhilarating, *"the best days of their lives!"* Fighter pilots *"lived for a day at a time,"* with a high degree of comradeship and they took the philosophical view that if anything happened, *"it was all over very quickly!"* To release some of the psychological stress which they built up as fighter pilots they were rather given to performing pranks. One such clownish episode involved the deep well close by their imposing quarters at Friston Place. The well was reputedly haunted by the ghost of a woman who had once fallen down it. One of their number Pilot Officer Davis, decided he would take history in his own hands and put to rest this fable once and for all! The well shaft was fitted with two pairs of hinged hatches, one pair at the top and the second pair halfway down. He began by throwing down the potentially explosive mixture of grease and oxygen in the form of an oxygen bottle from a Spitfire. Having no success he then proceeded to pour petrol down the shaft, still with no desired result. Finally, with a small crowd of cowering colleagues watching from a safe distance, he then introduced a lighted twist of straw and hastily shut the top hatch lids... Immediately, there was an almighty explosion, the closed hatches flew open, the small building which housed the well violently shook causing tiles to cascade from off the roof! On hearing this explosive report, their Commanding Officer came running to the scene demanding what on earth had happened!

The following incidents Ben recalled from out of his pilots log book: May 22 1944; beating up in preparation for the Normandy landings had commenced; trains which had until now been 'used' for various purposes by the French Resistance, were now fair game. During one of these sorties on this particular Sunday morning, 'Smudger' Smith and Ben were attacking a train near Le Havre, both aircraft suffering slight damage from return fire. The standard defence of a goods train by the enemy, was to have three flak trucks - gun platforms along the length of the train, one behind the locomotive, one midway and one at the rear of the train. To attack these it was usual practice to come in from behind, it being far easier then to strafe the entire length of the train. Their particular Fighter Group lost quite a number of aircraft on this particular morning.

June 6 1944 'D-Day.' Ben's squadron was first over the beach-heads 40 minutes before first light, the last sortie one hour after dusk. Ben flew a total of 2hrs. 15mins. upon that memorable day. While carrying out these sweeps above the beach-heads the squadron experienced a lot of turbulence; they were later to learn that this was caused by the slipstream from the two tonne shells emanating from the naval bombardment out at sea!

June 14 1944, and during a sortie over French territory Flight Officer 'Lulu' DeLeuze, one of the Frenchman in the squadron was observed to land. Later during the day he returned to Friston and upon landing, was found to have packed around him in the cockpit, a large quantity of Camembert cheese! During the succeeding month this particular aircraft bore the odour of cheese! June 15 1944 and Ben was involved in escorting a force of American Mitchell bombers upon a raid of the German Panzer headquarters to the south of Cannes. The following day he was vectored on to his first V-1 flying bomb but failed to locate it.

June 30 1944, and a number of the squadron ran low on fuel, but fortunately managed to locate and put down at a French landing strip operated by the Americans near the village of St.Mere Eglaise. While they were being driven around the neighbourhood, he first became aware that the Allied forces were not always welcome with open arms. He put this down to the fact that under the German occupation if they kept their nose clean, life was bearable; after the Allied landings, many of the villages and farms were laid waste and life greatly disrupted. While this 'tour' was being undertaken, news of their circumstances had not been reported back to Friston, where near panic had set in at the prospect of a majority of the squadron's aircraft having gone missing! In desperation their Commanding Officer set off with the eight remaining aircraft in an attempt to locate them; however, the two sections of the squadron met up over the Channel, this being followed by an inquest on their return! After a grilling, the pilots were given the rest of the day off and they drove their cars down to Seaford complete with German helmets and grenades, where they descended upon the Pelham Club in Dane Road (which now houses a café opposite Morrison's supermarket), where they caused a near riot! Flying crew incidentally, were the only personnel allowed to obtain petrol within 30 miles of the coast. After the war, Ben rose to become Chief Test Pilot for the aircraft manufacturer Boulton & Paul.

The two following accounts are from airmen who both served in the same squadron, No.350 (Belgian) which was stationed at Friston at the same time as Ben Gunn's No. 501 squadron. First, we will look at the account of ground crew member, 'Mac' Greener: *"I was an 18 year old ex Halton 'brat' serving with 350 (Belgian) Sqdn. who operated from Friston from 26th April 1944 until 3rd July 1944. The squadron was flying Spitfire V b's with clipped wings and the 45 M/55 M Merlins (cropped blowers for low altitude). The C.O. was S/Ldr. (Baron) Michael Donnet (later C. in C. Belgian Air Force); the sister squadron was 501 and the wing was lead by W/Cdr. Don Kingaby (The 109 King).*

The squadron was engaged mainly on sweeps and bottom cover escort work and in the period immediately after D Day it carried out first and last light patrols over the Normandy beachhead. A few days after D Day the weather clamped down but the squadron still put in an appearance at some cost. The weather prevented a home landing and they put down where they could, one as far north as Cranfield. At least one pilot was killed as a result and several aircraft damaged.

I was a Fitter IIA on the servicing echelon [unit] and recall long, but interesting hours with 24 hours off per week which the younger element usually spent in Brighton. On the evening of Monday June 4th anyone not working was rounded up to paint black and white stripes on the aircraft and all expected D Day next day. D Day was comparatively quiet. The main event that I can recall was a damaged B26 Marauder of USAAF making a tricky one engine landing (and perhaps under carriage trouble - but that could have been another occasion). I assisted the crew and one member told me it was his third sortie of the day (but, in the fashion of the time we all reckoned that Americans exaggerated).

....The Halifax [British bomber] arrived during the night, damaged and, on landing, its damaged under carriage caused it to slew off the main track, just missing an AA gun and demolishing one of the gun crews tents -fortunately the empty one of the duty crew.... 350 Sqdn. was having a rough patch and an ATC lad wandered into the blister hanger and informed us that two of our Spits had collided and gone into the sea - one pilot lost and the other rescued by the

air sea rescue.

Friston's position made it a "first sight" for damaged aircraft, particularly with wounded aboard and many damaged kites came in. So many of these were American that there was a permanent American ambulance on hand and an area of the field was a repair area for US kites and mobile repair workshops for the American ground crews. On nights when we finished early, the Yanks would run the workshops down to some pub, chock a block with British, Belgian and US airmen.

One night a German dropped 2(?) bombs on the main grass track (many of us never even woke up), but the only damage was to the tail plane of one of 350's Spits. I changed it next day and the damaged one was repaired later. I think this occurred on the evening of a 'refuelling' day, when petrol arrived by lorry, from the rail at Seaford, in packs of 2x4 gallon cans and was manually poured into the installation. I can't recall if this was the usual way for fuel to arrive.

The ground crews lived in 1914-18 bell tents (date stamped on them) and these were multi-hued as we doped on patch after patch in a futile attempt at proofing. There was one amusing set of events connected with the tents - when people went outside to watch the AA blazing off at enemy aircraft, they all put tin hats on but took them off when back under the sheltering canvas! On lying down they placed the tin hats over a lower region. The sewage plant would shut down for days at a time and it was very obvious when this occurred. ....Certainly, I could find no trace of the airfield location when I visited the area in 1980 - a sad reflection on the thought given to the people who fought for them - perhaps even a plaque or notice board could be erected."

For those servicemen forced to flee their homelands, the expectation of liberating Europe after four or five long years of occupation and tyranny, created great exhilaration as shown in the account from Belgian, Eddie 'Tiny' Viaene: *"We were stationed at RAF Friston with 350 (Belgian) Fighter Squadron and 6350 Echelon. I will always remember it because it was around 'D' Day we had come from West Hampnett [West Sussex] and we then moved on to Hawkhinge [Kent] to tackle the Flying Bombs.*

My recollections of Friston were happy ones. I was in charge of Equipment for the Squadron and had my office in one of the blister hangers along the east side of the drome. I recall it was the only station on which we had to sleep under canvas and we were in a field right over the left hand side beside the main road and hill [Scabs Island] going down towards the valley and Seaford. It was from inside this tent that I heard my first flying bomb. It was late at night and we all thought inside the tent it was a motor bike struggling up the hill, until one of my colleagues near the tent entrance said look at this plane on fire, it flew over towards Seaford and Newhaven from where we could see tracer fire going up

What must have been the billet with the greatest view of all! Situated above Crowlink, this is the sole remaining wartime building of RAF Friston.

The Tiger at East Dean was a popular watering-hole for the Station's personnel when off duty.

towards it.

I can recollect we had Station cycles, having to go right past the northern side of the drome towards Friston to the Canteen. I also remember quite a few Flying Fortress's just making it back to the coast, often having been damaged on the other side. We used to laugh at the number of men the U.S.A.F. used to send to patch up a plane, in comparison to the number of mechanics, riggers and armourers etc. we used.

Being a Belgian Squadron you can imagine the excitement when we issued the white paint to have the lines painted on our Spits. We all realised the big day was near. I can remember our disappointment when the original day was called off. But the jubilation on 'D' day will always stay in my memory. Some of these Belgians had not seen their families since Dunkirk and they knew they were now on the way back. It was sortie after sortie.

I can also remember an amusing outing to Eastbourne. We had quite a night out and missed the last bus. We got a lift on a lorry and can remember I felt very bad being shaken up at the back, so bad I asked to be let off. I believe it was called East Dean, not realising the climb and long walk I had left myself back to our tent. I remember too cycle rides on our evenings off down to that lovely village of Alfriston."

John Player, who went on to live in New South Wales, had one very convenient posting during the hostilities *"I was born in Newhaven in 1924 and was called up and served in the Fleet Air Arm, and after training with the R.A.F. they decided to give us some first hand experience on the airfields in Sussex. When my name was called to go to Friston, at first I couldn't place it, I knew Alfriston of course, so when we got off the train in Eastbourne, and then got on a number 12 Bus, I knew my luck was in. We were living in Saltdean at that time, so it didn't take me long to get home. At Friston we lived in tents in a field at the back of the house, there was a large pit there with the septic tanks there, and we had a long rope at the top of one tree and could swing from one side to the other.*

There was two spitfire squadrons and I was lucky to be put on one for a while. We took over the R & R section - rearm and re-fuel, we didn't get a lot of action but had a few laugh's.... Our P.O. [Petty Officer] had a real old gypsy caravan by the nissen hut, what it was doing there I don't really know but he spent most of his time in it, and if he was in a bad mood which was quite often, so we used to ask him to do a show for us; before the war he used to do an act round the halls, so he would come out of his caravan, dressed in an immaculate cowboy outfit and do a few cabaret tricks and dances, then put a postage stamp on your nose, and take it off with a 20ft. stock whip, that always settled him down. We were there during V.1 times, it was certainly an amazing sight to see them streaming over the cliffs and our planes trying to catch them. Our time came in the end on invasion day, I had been home for the night, and when I got back in the morning there was every one painting black and white stripes on the planes, and from then on we had plenty to do with fighters dropping in all day, mainly rocket firing Typhoons and Tempests."

The following account is recounted by Esme Larkin and Lill Thompson of Seaford, who witnessed the following incident (with additional information from researcher Andy Saunders); neither woman was in the services or at RAF Friston. Esme was walking along Firle Road in the Blatchington area of Seaford when she witnessed a fighter aircraft attacking a V-1 flying bomb just to the south of Blatchington reservoir. Her delight was quickly dashed when upon destroying the flying bomb, the aircraft and/or its pilot were fatally damaged by the blast of the exploding bomb. The aircraft continued but on an erratic course, all the time losing height disappearing out of her sight towards Newhaven. After her initial delight, Esme was deeply upset. Lill and another girl had recently been taken on after leaving school at Wheatley's scrapyard situated along The Drove at Newhaven. She and her colleagues were on July 7 1944, disturbed by the sound of a large explosion; upon rushing out on to The Drove, they witnessed a Spitfire crashed into the meadows several hundred yards south of where they were gathered. A number of men employed at the scrapyard ran towards the aircraft which began to burn furiously; however due to the intense heat the would-be rescuers were unable to

Fleet Air Arm armourers seconded to duties at RAF Friston standing in front of Lockheed Lightning.

approach the wreckage due to exploding ammunition. Lill's mother and a woman from Denton later made a collection on behalf of the pilots relatives; this they took to RAF Friston, where an officer refused to accept the collection except on behalf of the airmen's benevolent fund. It transpired that the aircraft was a Griffon-engined Mk.XII Spitfire of No.41 squadron based at Friston, flown by Flight Officer G.M. McKinley.

A local man who spent part of his military service at RAF Friston was Freddie Tarrant; he served with No.2803 Squadron of the RAF Regiment, which was equipped with bofors guns which provided anti-aircraft cover for the airfield. He vividly remembered his six months at Friston in 1944 from July to December, in fact on the 31st he recalling they left one cold and icy night for West Sussex, the AA guns sliding about on the icy roads. During the squadrons first week of duty at Friston, their headquarters was at the requisitioned house Treetops; after this the squadrons headquarters was at The Gayles. The gun site to which he was attached was situated on the south side of the A 259 midway between the airfield and the village of Friston, the site today marked by a small thicket. Other gun sites he could recall were at the western end of Scabs Island, and at the southern end of the north-south runway; there were also several gun sites positioned down through Crowlink Bottom, the concrete billet for these still standing. More outlying sites were positioned within Friston Forest equipped with tents and Valor stoves. The gatehouse at The Gayles acted as a billet for naval personnel, drafted in to assist with re-fuelling and re-arming of aircraft. If extra billeting was required due to a fresh influx of airmen Freddie would offer to sleep at his parent's house in Eastbourne.

On the ground, airfield security consisted of rolls of barb wire and sentries, with RAF police on duty at airfield entry points. Along the cliffs a minefield had been laid. The cook with the gun crew positioned at the end of the runway Henry, had a habit of shooting at these mines or lifting them and throwing them over the cliff edge. One morning he was not to be found and it was assumed that he had slipped into Seaford to meet his girlfriend; later his body was found in the minefield. A number of the imposing residences upon the Downland Estate at Friston were requisitioned by the authorities; Freddie recalled that The Swallows served as the Station Headquarters where the colours were issued; on the south side of the village, The Flints became the pay account office. The sergeant's mess was housed in the property known as Little Friston at the start of the Jevington road.

The perimeter trackway which provided all-weather access to both runways continued west from near the airfield entrance, to serve the communal site situated in the vicinity of the present day entrance to Exceat Newbarn. Here was to be found the ablution blocks, small sewage works, airmen's and WAAF's mess canteens and stores. Up until the late 1960's some of these buildings served as a piggery for Exceat Farm. Freddie recalled that during the period July to September 1944, bombing raids were being carried out on V-1 flying bomb launch sites by Lancaster bombers, which if having sustained damage, would sometimes make for Friston where they were either repaired, or dismantled and taken away by road on large lorries referred to as 'Queen Mary's.' At the same time, daylight raids were being carried out by USAF Flying Fortress and Liberator bombers and also Marauder fighter/bombers; these would also make for Friston if unable for some reason to safely reach their home bases. Also during this period, Dakota transport aircraft were being used to tow gliders to France; some mornings there would be as many as 30 of these parked around the airfield after returning from night missions. On one occasion, in the region of 50 Auster and Walrus ambulance planes were grounded by fog further on along their planned flight path; authorisation was given that some of the Station's ground crew could be given joy rides!

On one occasion, Freddie witnessed three Spitfires/Mustangs pursue a V-1 flying bomb over the vicinity of Exceat. There was a huge explosion which appeared to engulf the three aircraft; however, they all returned safely. The tailpipe from the V-1 lay for many years just northeast of West Dean village. Just prior to Christmas 1944, Freddie was out strolling with some of his colleagues when a Mustang fighter began circling over the airfield; eventually but with some difficulty, the pilot managed to land. The reason the pilot had experienced difficulties was because the aircraft was very light, it having been stripped of all armament and non-essential equipment. This was in order so that it could return to France with a payload of beer and whisky, which was duly collected from the Star Brewery at Eastbourne! That Christmas, the Station put on a party in the WAAF's mess for children from the villages of West Dean, Friston, East Dean and Jevington. Station personnel had saved their chocolate rations and this was given out to the children; Father Christmas duly 'arrived' via an Auster aircraft, and a Christmas tree was 'obtained' from the forest. Freddie was able to attend with his children.

Reg Walker was a Leading Aircraftsman Fitter and served at Friston from early December 1944 until mid June 1945 and as the gradual rundown of the airfield took place, was detailed to carry out general ground crew work. One of his tasks was the driving of a tractor used for hauling a 450 gallon fuel bowser and attached motorised pump for the fuelling of aircraft with 100 octane petrol. The Station's motor transport section was by this time based in a little repair garage on the hill down into East Dean village; he vividly recalled that once while returning down the steep hill to East Dean, the brakes failed on the bowser, pushing the tractor down the road zig-zag fashion aided by the high octane fuel! This bowser proved very inadequate when it came to refuelling large aircraft; one occasion he recalled was when they were ordered to refuel a Halifax bomber that had arrived. Their small bowser with its little pump and short hoses proved very inadequate for the fuel tanks high up on the wings of a Halifax. Two other incidents that occurred whilst Reg was at Friston involved large aircraft. A Lancaster crash-landed still with a bomb aboard; on being defused Reg had to tow the bomb away from the stricken aircraft with a tractor. The other incident involved a Flying Fortress which came into land with its brakes inoperative, the pilot's only just managing to bring the aircraft to a halt before running out of runway. He also remembered the Austers because they being light, had to be roped down to prevent them flipping over, the ropes requiring to be altered if the wind changed direction.

Robert Fry was one of three cadets from No.172 (Mid Sussex) Rural Air Training Corps squadron who volunteered for service during the cold January of 1945. The three *"....proceeded down there in Jan. 1945 arriving just after they experienced a 90mph gale and a snowstorm. The sight that greeted us was a number of USAF A.O.P. [Austers?] aircraft with wing tips hanging down and even one flat on its back where the gale had done damage. The airfield was covered in snow and one of our first tasks was to sweep and shovel strips of grass clear of snow either side of the runway and markers, nearly all the spare station personnel seemed to be engaged on this work.*

We were billeted in a requisitioned private house in E. Dean village which was also the billet for several NCO's from the RAF Regiment. For heat in the billet the very hard service coke was supplied and on our way home to the billet each evening we took it in turns to collect pieces of a discarded wattle fence to get our fire going, this was a difficult and time consuming job but after an hour or two we would have a fire going in the open hearth which would provide some heat and comfort to go to bed by. Anyone awakening at night was able to keep it stoked up. I valued a hot breakfast and used to get up in time to walk up to the cookhouse, just off the main public road to have good breakfast before reporting for work. Sweeping the strips by the runway, freeing the windsock from its pole, and a bit of visual watch-keeping in flying control were jobs I recall."

The last account concerns another Halifax bomber; these were similar to their more illustrious cousin, the Lancaster. This particular machine a MkIII, powered by four Bristol Hercules MkXVI 14 cylinder, 38 litre radial engines was part of No.347 (French) squadron. This account is taken from translated notes and diary extracts of two of its crew members, navigator and captain, Commandant M. Noirot and rear gunner Sergeant Roger Burel. The squadron had left its home base at RAF Elvington, Yorkshire during late afternoon, forming part of a 700 aircraft bombing raid on Chemnitz in southern Germany on the night of March 5 1945, *"very dark night with foul weather"* with lightning and heavy rain. They were ordered after the raid to divert to southern England as there was no chance of reaching their base due to the weather. Navigator Noirot was slightly injured during the raid and his navigation aids had ceased working and so he navigated *"by the feel"* westwards spotting Dieppe and then the light of the Beachy Head lighthouse, *"...we start to breathe again, because we are in the air for well over eight and a half hours..."* and were feeling *"deadly tired."* Being very low on fuel and now with the radio having failed they fired off their emergency flares. A response was immediately made at RAF Friston where the landing lights on the north- south runway are switched on in *"sandra position."* [Three 'Sandra' searchlights were used to 'cone' the overhead position of some airfields.]

"At first sight the airstrip seems to be a short one and we are the more uneasy as it is positioned towards the South, the seaside, where the glimmer of the "sandras" show the foam fringed cliffs, just at the field limit. Definitely the landing should not be missed otherwise we'll dip into the pond... We have not enough fuel to go and try our luck elsewhere and we have to land at any price. So SANTI [the pilot] starts his descent but he cannot possibly land, because even before the wheels touch the strip we have reached already the end of the runway, marked at the southern limit by red lights, which approach in an alarming way. He starts all over again: once, twice but it's every time the same story: the damned red wall [earthen bank with red lights placed along it] runs into us even before we have landed. We made already two overshoots and a third one is excluded as we have only fuel left for some minutes; the crew is calm, my men are silent, but I feel their uneasiness , as they witness the fruitless efforts of the pilot and they hear what we say over the interphone; the mechanician announces a zero-level of our fuel tanks and we can expect any moment the final deadline that will mean a complete disaster as we'll be unable to regain altitude to parachute. So we'll have to crash at any price and I decide to make a belly-landing, with the landing-carriage drawn in, to limit the damage; every one resumes the position we were taught, theoretically, as we never practiced (the case); the pilot sticks to his steering stick and the others retire to the emergency

posts with two axes of the board equipment, to destruct the fuselage if need be. SANTI manages perfectly, just as if he had only practiced crashes in his career as a pilot; his approach and landing are flawless; he kills the engines, some tenth of seconds before landing and... he waits, hanging on to the steering stick to parry the shock, which will be rude, as he knows by intuition. And here comes a perfect crash. The shock was, so to speak, hardly perceptible and we glided only some tens of meters before we penetrated into the soil; as a matter of fact the covering of the landing strip is very soft, quite contradictory to our expectations and thanks to our speed is next to zero when we hit the red wall, where our plane falls apart, without any personal damage whatsoever; we proceed to leave the plane using the emergency exits, even without the necessity to use our axes.

It is slightly past one o'clock in the morning and our nineteenth mission has been accomplished, not quite in the way we had imagined when we started, but better than we had feared just a few minutes ago. Almost at once a car of the fire-brigade and a four-wheel drive ambulance arrive, but their presence is superfluous, but for transport to the Control Tower, from which we contact Elvington... We have been very well received and the good care towards us even doubled when we mentioned our nationality; we felt that both here and in France the presence of Frenchman in the R.A.F. failed appreciation... The next day, or rather: the same day, as the night was well on its way, when our adventure was over, we returned to the airstrip to fetch our belongings and to render the last honours to our plane...

At the end of the morning, after the regular breakfast, we took the train to York, via London; our warrior's appearance, dirty and muddy, with a two days' beard, as well as our bulky luggage, not suitable for the railway carriages, made us feel a bit ashamed, but very soon our fellow-travellers put us at ease; they outdid each other to please us, notably when they learned that we were French: everybody offered us whiskey and sweets, that English people always carry around on their travel, as well as cigarettes and cigars, but we could not make everyone happy to accept all these gifts and we thanked them, in our way, to tell them our adventures, especially the last one, which explained our presence today."

As a postscript to these two chapters about RAF Friston, during two periods in 1987 men from the 33 Explosive Ordnance Devices Regiment, ('EOD'), systematically re-searched most of the former airfield for ordnance, these operations being observed by the author. The airfields original clearance certificate was dated February 1946. Heavy equipment used included a 'JCB-type' digger and a 360°tracked excavator that was remotely operable from inside a Saracen armoured personnel carrier. When the strengthened grass runways were laid, they had placed beneath them, 'pipe mines.' These consisted of up to 40 metre lengths of 10cm diameter steel piping which were

The secluded Friston Place whiched served as the Officer's Mess; standing in front is the well-house containing an ancient donkey wheel and where Pilot Officer Davis attempted to eliminate a ghost.

hydraulically pushed into the ground at an angle to about 2 metres; these were then packed with polar blasting gelignite (PBG). Three previously undetected complete mines were found in 1987, one of which, its shallow end being scrapped over during routine ploughing each autumn! These mines were remotely unearthed, cut into sections and the sticks of gelignite carefully removed, charges then being placed on the explosive and bang! Over the long intervening period this explosive had become somewhat broken down and chemically unstable. The pipes were then flushed with water to ensure removal of all explosive.

CHAPTER 11

COUNTRY LIVING IN THE EARLY TWENTIETH CENTURY.

Through the years of persistent investigation which eventually lead to the putting together of this book, I count myself fortunate in that during these investigations, I met and corresponded with many respected and some often colourful characters. Some of these reminiscences I have already used in the forgoing chapters, but many of these tales however remained closed away in my files. To partially rectify that situation, this chapter goes on to relate some of those tales of life during the earlier years of the 20th century and hopefully help 'fill in some of the gaps' within the preceding chapters.

EXCEAT. The first account was related by Wilton Kemp: his father Walter William Kemp, carried on the ancient craft of wheelwright during the period when the mass-produced automobile began to topple horse power from its place of prominence in everyday life. Walter William was born at Brightling (to the north of Hastings) during the early 1890's; he came to live at Exceat when his father Walter Thomas Kemp, also a wheelwright took on a sub-lease of Exceat House in or about 1899. Before becoming apprenticed, Walter William was told by his father that in order to know what an item of equipment had to withstand, he should become a carters boy. So, for a period in excess of one year he served under 'Ned' Reed, the carter then based at Exceat itself, something that young Walter was not too happy with!

When going on a shopping expedition to Eastbourne, his parents Walter Thomas and Annie would use a horse and trap, they walking up the steepest gradients; Mrs. Kemp was conspicuous locally for the large, flamboyant hats she was fond of wearing. On the Sabbath the family would worship by singing and playing hymns, working their way through their hymn book starting where they had finished the previous Sunday. Walter Thomas would play piano, with Walter and his brother Weston accompanying on violin, and their sister on mandolin. On Boxing Days, a duck shoot would be arranged to which were invited a number of their friends. For these occasions, Mrs. Kemp

Walter Kemp the wheelwright at Exceat employed a blacksmith, seen here shoeing a draught horse.

would arrange for the making of a large steak and kidney pudding. Having been secured within a cloth early in the morning, it was placed in the copper and slowly cooked. While on the subject of food, a favourite dessert with the Kemp household at Exceat was 'butter pond pudding,' a steamed pudding with a centre consisting of butter and demerara sugar.

Incidentally, the Kemp's rented rooms to a newly married couple during an 18-month period in 1904-5; these were Ina and Inglis Sheldon-Williams, they having met at the Slade School of Art in London during 1897-8. He had then travelled and painted extensively: across Canada; in 1899 he recorded the Boer War; travelled to India to record the Coronation Durbar of 1902-3; also in 1903 he covering King Edward's visit to Lisbon; depicted the Russian-Japanese War travelling via Cape Horn and travelled back across the United States in 1904. During their honeymoon they spent their time sketching and painting life on Exceat Farm and the surrounding area. Later during the First World War in 1916, he decided to send Ina to Canada for safety; her ship was torpedoed from which she survived; their crated Exceat paintings however, were washed up in the Outer Hebrides! He was commissioned as an official Canadian war artist. Inglis was fascinated by the draught horses while Ina was likewise with the oxen, she writing in the 1930's, *"These black oxen belong to the past history of the Downs and are the one's bred by Mr. Gorringe near Seaford... I knew them all by name and used sometimes to hold the plough behind eight [six?] of them, to watch their movements."*

One of the oldest characters whom I was privileged to have met, was one Arthur Mewett born at Polegate in 1897. For his age, Arthur possessed an outstanding recall of those years long ago in the Cuckmere valley. His father took employment as a shepherd, he previously being a looker - a roving stockman on the Pevensey Marsh; the family moved to Foxhole when Arthur was only six weeks of age. His mother Lydia though, was not happy living in such an outlying hamlet as Foxhole; they moved frequently: Seaford, Exceat Bridge Cottage and lastly, returning to Foxhole where they lived in No.3. Finally while Arthur was aged 13, his mother abandoned her family and home; shortly after this blow he and his father moved to Black Robin Farm near Beachy Head. The unpopularity of living at Foxhole with women-folk before the age of relatively affordable motoring, has been borne out by a number of persons that I have interviewed. While living here, Arthur attended the village school at West Dean but was sometimes sent home because he suffered from nosebleeds; on these occasions he would be accompanied by the Stace daughters, Mary and Carrie; (George Stace at this time being the farm foreman at Exceat).

Occasionally on Good Fridays, the local boys would go up to the vicinity of the Seven Sisters adder hunting, they receiving two old pence for each snake killed, the same rate as for the killing of rats in Foxhole Barn. His father would mow the lawn at Exceat House for the Kemps using a hand-push mower, Arthur following behind pulling off any remaining stalks. Bread was delivered to the Pullen's who lived at Exceat Cottages, it falling to Arthur to go and collect the families bread; sometimes he would make a halfpenny in the change with which to treat himself to some chocolate.

Arthur was first employed at the age of eight as a shepherd-boy taking over from Alf Holter. Occasionally, after perhaps a day on the hill overlooking Cuckmere Haven, he would go down to the pools which then formed behind the shingle beach, to catch fish trapped by the receding tide; sometimes he would take home as many as he could carry. He recalled that occasionally the pond at Foxhole would dry up, forcing the eels that formally inhabited it into the surrounding grass and dying; the sheep dogs would then roll upon them and stink! At other times he would be called upon to fill in for Ray Moore, the ox-boy.

If asked to name the person who had probably lived on Exceat for the longest duration the distinction would have to go to William Holter, born in 1881 at the former Peakdean Farm in East Dean and the oldest of seven children. His father Thomas Holter, took a carters position on Exceat Farm for Edward Gorringe, the family moving into Newbarn Cottages in or about 1897. Gorringe was in particular seized by the fact that Thomas and his wife Marian had seven sons! Sadly 'Old Will' died a few months after I first met him, he having lived continuously on Exceat for some 78 years. Fortunately a few years previously, John Gascoigne together with the former Radio Brighton, had interviewed him at some length. Much of what follows is taken from a copy of that recording.

Starting a tale, he would often begin with *"My dear man"* or referring to John or one of his former employers as *"Master;"* he spoke with a very broad Sussex dialect. Will had but little schooling and began helping his father with his four horse team ploughing at the age of 10. On their arrival at Exceat, Will then being aged 16, he was initially employed as teg shepherd, ('tegs' term for sheep aged between six months and their first shearing). After a short period he was made up to carter, so following in his father's footsteps and earning a shilling (five pence) per day. In those days, the foreman paid the men before midday on Fridays; groceries were delivered once a week on that day, the grocery van pulled by a white horse, would be met at Exceat Bridge. At Newbarn they had no access to fresh milk, Will using tinned milk all his life, the proverbial 'cow in the cupboard.'

Thomas Holter with his team in 1910. Thatching of a rick taking place in background.

Gorringe's would buy coal, several full rail trucks at a time, of both domestic and steam coal (for the ploughing and thrashing engines). Farm employees could then purchase three or four tonnes at a time, this arrangement eventually ceasing after two men proved to be bad payers. After this Will collected his coal as a return load from Eastbourne at 15 shillings per tonne. To eke out their income, Will would 'wire' or snare rabbits, there being masses of them in Limekiln Bottom. At one time, Will owned a shotgun with which he would poach duck; on his first trip via a call at the Plough & Harrow pub at Litlington, he hit three birds with his first pull. On this occasion, he led a *"cat and mouse chase"* with the local constable who happened to be in the vicinity and had heard the shots! On Friday nights, the men from Exceat and West Dean would meet up and walk to the Plough & Harrow or The Tiger at East Dean for a couple of pints and a game of rings, dominoes or shove-ha'penny. Sometimes on a Saturday night they would walk into Seaford for a drink.

Will recalled that there were three flocks of sheep run on Exceat, all Southdowns and were intensively folded. After the harvest, there would be up to 48 ricks of corn at Newbarn alone as well as the barns at Newbarn and Exceat full, plus thrashed grain in the granary. Beef cattle were yarded at Newbarn through the winter and then driven down to *"Pev'sey"* in the spring to be fattened on the lush pastures. At Newbarn around the turn of the century three teams of six oxen were kept. The backbone of the farm's workforce in those days were a working foreman, three shepherds, three carters and the oxen drivers. While driving his team on the open road, the first motor car he encountered was towards Jevington carrying two ladies. Will pulled over to allow them plenty of room to pass, however the driver managed to get herself jammed on one of the rear wheels of Will's wagon causing some damage to the car. When groomed and dressed up for agricultural or county shows, Will considered *"the horses were as proud as a woman with a good frock on."*

Next to the Holters at Newbarn lived the Popes. Charles 'Curly' Pope holds the distinction of being the last person in England employed to break-in and drive oxen solely for a living. The following reminiscences are related by his son William 'Bill' Pope, born in January 1914 while his father was away with the oxen in Manchester, promoting Camp Coffee. His father also assisted with thatching of the corn ricks at Newbarn. Sometimes Bill would go and play at Crowlink, it still then being possible to scramble down the cliff to the foreshore. Probably an unpleasant experience for young Bill was when the Comtessa de Flandre ran ashore; he was given some liquorice from her and told, *"eat plenty, it's good for you!"* 'Neddy' Patching of Crowlink and shepherd Charlie Picknell who lodged with Dick Fowler at Foxhole, both used to earn beer money by making and selling prawning nets.

Holter's used to keep a pig in their garden and when the fateful day came, Curly would assist with the slaughtering and in return for his assistance receive some of the offal.

Nellie Burton was born into the world in 1912 at Sheep Pen Cottages, which lay just to the north of West Dean village. Her father Albert worked on West Dean Farm and then for the Forestry Commission for a total of some 30 years. He carried on the duties of church verger while her mother was responsible for polishing of the church silver. Nellie attended the village school in West Dean, this being housed in the extension on today's School Cottage. The Reverend Lawrence had difficulty attracting qualified teachers, so schooling of the village children would fall to Fanny Pullen (later Streeter), or sometimes one of the other women in the village. Nellie was taught the art of needlework capably, she also recalling that they sang a lot. While she was aged eight years of age the small village school closed with all the pupils having then to go to Seaford. Due to their previous elementary schooling, the village children were considered educationally backward for their ages in subjects such as history and geography. On reaching the age of fourteen, Nellie left school and entered into service for the Schweirs at Exceat House; after a year had passed Schweir had to terminate his tenancy of Exceat Farm and Nellie was offered the chance to go with them. However her father would not hear of this as Schweir was possibly of German extraction!

During the summer holidays of the years 1920-4, Jack Harris would be sent by his widowed mother to stay with his aunt and uncle, Elizabeth and George Stace at Exceat Cottages. Elizabeth was also tall with her grey hair pulled back into a bun. George was a tall figure of a man with a grey beard and well into his sixties. As was quite common in those days, Jack's aunt carried on a sideline in the form of selling to passers-by, cups of tea, various sweets and *Stones* ginger beer which came in earthenware bottles. When she required further stock items, she would give a written order to the conductor of a passing bus who would take it round to a wholesaler in Eastbourne. When the order had been made up, it was dispatched upon a particular bus for collection at Exceat; incidentally the westbound bus stop in those days was between the two sharp corners at the bottom of Exceat Hill. Water, from the well in front of the cottages would be stored in a large earthenware container. Jack had a novel way of earning a little pocket money; he would spend time waiting towards the top of Exceat Hill with a container of water. Many of the early motor cars such as the 'model T' Fords had a gravity feed petrol supply, which on steep hills necessitated the car reversing up the hill; on having climbed the steepest part of the hill, the engines were often over heating and their radiators requiring more water, hence Jack's little earner. During the harvest period Jack would often act as the 'stand hard kid,' moving on and stopping the ox team as the sheaths of corn were stacked on the great farm wagons.

Grace Fowler was the adopted daughter of Dick Fowler, who we discussed in the chapter on agriculture; Fowlers moved to 2, Foxhole Cottages after Gorringe relinquished their lease on Crowlink Farm in 1922. With the family lodged Charlie Picknell, he having lost his wife in childbirth and acted as under-shepherd to Dick. A Mr. Pitcher delivered groceries and provisions on a weekly basis as was the delivery of post brought by 'Postman Green' on his bicycle which had a sign-written box on the front of it.

During the early 1930's, Burtons moved to Exceat Newbarn Cottages, her father having taken the offer of work from Colonel Watson after a disagreement with the Head Forester, Mr. Aston; her mother cried at the prospect of leaving the village and her friends. At Newbarn, mains water only extended as far as the farm buildings some 250 yards away, her father having to fetch water with the aid of a yoke and buckets. Later during the early 1950's her parents moved to No.3, Foxhole Cottages. Once, Arthur Pattenden asked her father to look after some geese; these would each day troop in a long procession down to the river, returning in the evening. The family was heartbroken one day, when as Christmas approached, the geese were slaughtered! In future they agreed to only look after duck upon Foxhole pond.

For many people today, the chance to stay in the camping site or barn at Foxhole gives them the opportunity to savour this downland backwater. This is no recent phenomena as people were camping in this vicinity many years before now. Kay Ketcher warmly recalled her days with the Chertsey Girl Guides Company from Surrey which totalled some 24 members. They stayed two years running (possibly 1931-2), with use being made of the flint barn during wet weather. Water and milk was obtained from Exceat and the *"firewood party"* scavenged for wood with which the porridge was cooked during the evening, this then being placed within a *"hay box"* to keep warm in readiness for breakfast the following morning. The Company attended church at Friston and also took part in a church fete at West Dean, in which they were told not to keep winning all the events but to let the local children have a chance!

Mention of the Guides camping at Foxhole brings us to the recollections of Barbara Cooper, a retired school teacher from Surrey.

During her formative years she attended a boarding school at Bexhill; during the July of 1932, a party of girls from the school including her camped at Foxhole. They travelled from Bexhill to Exceat by coach where upon arrival, their equipment was loaded on to a farm cart and ferried down to Foxhole. It seemed that Colonel Watson, who incidently was considered *"quite good looking,"* showed concern at these groups of young girls camping unattended. At the beginning of each day he would ride over from Exceat upon his chestnut horse, dressed if the weather was inclement in gabardine riding coat, cap and spurs, to check on the well-being of the dozen tents and their occupants. They also were glad to make use of Foxhole barn if unsettled weather conditions prevailed.

Now, we shall return to the memoirs of Bert Miller who we came across earlier in the chapter on agriculture. It seems that Col. Watson kept quite a number of chickens behind the walled gardens at Exceat (where today the access drive is to the cycle hire business). One day Bert was asked by his father to feed these chickens, the feed already having been made up by his father; unsuspectingly Bert grabbed the bucket and proceeded to feed the chickens. Awhile later, Col. Watson came rushing up to Arthur Miller full of concern for his chickens, for they were all falling over and dropping eggs everywhere. It transpired that Bert's father was fond of making wheat wine which contained grain, raisins, yeast and sugar and that young Bert had taken the wrong bucket! On realising what had happened the two men had a good laugh!

Ian Hillary recalled that he knocked on the front door of Exceat House one day during the 1930's, to enquire about any possibility of camping. A male servant came to the door and stated that Col. Watson saw nobody without an appointment. At that moment, a well-spoken voice called out, *"What do they want,"* and came to the door. Ian explained again that he wished to camp, Watson then asking if he had a sporting gun, to which Ian replied yes. He was then informed that he could come and camp as often as he liked, providing that he shot as many rabbits as possible as they ate the sheep's grass.

Jim Palmer lived with his family at No.1 Foxhole Cottages, they residing there from the mid-1930's till about 1940. His father William was the last full-time shepherd to be employed on Exceat and had in his care a flock of the native Southdown sheep; he was a Wiltshire man who had married an Eastbourne girl. Lambing was carried out in and about Foxhole Barn and during these weeks, Jim's father would seldom come home he living in an old touring caravan adjacent to the lambing yard. The shepherd's caravan would stay up in the fields where the flock grazed at other times. The Colonel was looked upon as a kindly, considerate employer. Bath time for the family was carried out using the proverbial tin bath; the original toilets were situated where now stands the asbestos barn; new brick toilets or 'privies' were built within the cottage gardens during the Palmer's time when the cottages were modernised. It was while walking to the outside loo during one cold spell that Jim's mother slipped and broke her ankle; she had to be conveyed to Newbarn from where an ambulance had been arranged to pick her up, presumably because of the icy condition of Exceat Hill.

Jim attended the National School in Steyne Road, Seaford. Often on the way home he would borrow one of the small railway trucks from the beach wharf and having given it a good hearty push, it would coast down to opposite Foxhole ferrying Jim. Newspapers were delivered to the Exceat, the Palmer's reading them the following day before passing them on to Will Holter, who would have his step-daughter read them to him. Jim and his brothers would sometimes go up to beyond Foxhole Barn where the Girl Guides held their summer camps, releasing the guy ropes on their tents and letting them down! This brings us to one of Jim's fathers other duties during the summer period, that of collecting camping money from the caravans to the south of Foxhole. Colonel Watson kept a large brown painted caravan at Foxhole, while at Cliff End his wife had a chalet complete with verandah. The Palmer's moved from Exceat to Black Robin Farm near Beachy Head probably in 1940 after Colonel Watson sold virtually all his sheep, mainly due to military requisition and operations.

During the 1930's, Brian Cornelius used to come down regularly with his parents from London to stay in an old showmans-type caravan sited permanently in the small chalk pit immediately to the south of Exceat Newbarn. They also had a touring caravan which they would tow behind their Citroen car and which would be positioned on Scabs Island close to the A 259. During 1936, his family decided to move down to Eastbourne thus reinforcing their connection with Exceat and Colonel Watson. In 1939, an opportunity arose when many young farm workers who were also members of the Territorial Army, were called up due to the impending hostilities with Germany. Brian in effect became an unpaid 'apprentice' carter working under the directions of Bill Holter, who taught him the ways of the countryside: cartering, farming operations, guns and ferreting. He left Exceat when his family started farming part of the Eastbourne Downland estate during the early 1940's.

Brian recalled that Will's wife Marian May who was rather petite, would always address Will as *"William"* or *"Willy."* She would always be asking him to do this and do that, to which he would reply *"Yes my dear,"* or *"No my dear,"* it being rather like water off a ducks back until he could take no more and would then calmly say as he walked out the door, *"I do hope it do keep fine for ye."* Brian likened her to a *"terrier round an elephant!"* She would sometimes request him to get a rabbit for the pot and off he would go with his shotgun around the bushes. She would listen out and if she heard two shots would upon his return comment wryly, *"Willy, that were a dear rabbit!"* for rabbits were worth about six old pence each and cartridges cost about 2? pence each. Brian recalled that due to Will's broad dialect, that after perhaps a chance conversation between his mother and Will, Brian would have to partially translate it to her. Later during the war, Will's dialect showed quite a marked change for during this period Will conversed with the RAF 'ack-ack' gunners who came from differing parts of the country. Will's mother lived at West Dean Newbarn Cottage and was keen on producing various wines which were kept in bottles upon a high shelf where they were allowed to mature; once Brian was given a small glass and being young and unused to alcohol found it rather strong, it going straight to his head!

During this period, Will's team consisted of six year old Suffolk Punch's. The horses that Brian and Jim drove were Shires and Suffolks, all well into their twenties; these were all stabled at Newbarn. The Shire horses were ponderous and slow, 2mph as opposed to the 7?mph working speed of the Suffolks. It used to be said that *"a Sussex wagon with its larger front wheels, harnessed to a team of Shires needed two acres to turn!"* He recalled that on one occasion, a lady parked her small Morris 'drop-head' car just inside The Ladders field near the entrance to The Gayles, in which there were four unbroken Suffolk colts. Within about twenty minutes they had virtually destroyed it! Instead of at once shooing them away, she stood back and watched in horror as they first ripped off the canvas hood and then proceeded to kick the car repeatedly! During the winter the muck in the yards at Newbarn would accumulate to a depth of some four feet aided by muck thrown out from the stables. After sheep folding, the soil was ploughed to depth of only four inches, using on the lighter chalk soils a two furrow plough pulled by three horses. During the late 1930's, the well water at Foxhole Cottages was condemned; one of the women who then lived there, considered this well water far superior for making tea and used the water brought down once week by churn, for washing purposes!

Brian recollected that William Palmer was as most shepherds

would have been, a solitary figure with whom he worked relatively little; they would perhaps pass the time of day, if their paths crossed, Brian addressing him *"Good morning Shepherd."* It was general folklore on Exceat as elsewhere, that the weather could be forecast by the stance of the shepherd as he stood up on the hill, there being *"various permutations."* Sometimes Brian would be given the order by Colonel Watson to go and shift shepherds fold hurdles to another field or some other task involving the use of a horse team. Everyone helped out with washing of the sheep (which Brian thought ceased during the mid 1930's); dipping was carried out using a sulphur-based or other compound in a dipping trough near the meanders, where nowadays the car park area is. If they were still hay making at the end of the day, shepherd would perhaps help to toss the last of the hay on to the elevator, perhaps as a goodwill gesture towards the help that he would receive throughout the year.

Colonel Watson was referred to as *"the Boss."* He often would wear canvas cavalry leggings known as *"pipe clay leggings,"* thus doing away with the necessity of wearing riding boots. Other characters Brian could recall on the farm were: Alf Smart who drove the team of horses at Exceat itself and carried out general and dairying duties and also a cowman. He could also vaguely recall two keen Land Army girls starting on the farm. After the outbreak of war, Brian could recall lying on his back and watching calmly in a *"rather detached"* frame of mind, aircraft embroiled in dog-fights high above. As a Local Defence Volunteer, Brian used to patrol with just a shotgun and an armband, this being before the setting up of the Home Guard. He considers himself *"the original Pike of TV's Dad's Army!"* As his period at Exceat came to a close he recalled that machinery had commenced grading the land for the airfield runways of RAF Friston.

Vera Wilson (formally Pattenden) recalled that shortly after their arrival at Exceat Farm, they were invited to a party held on the communal site of RAF Friston. The minefield laid within the valley at the start of the war was being, or had just been cleared; however, there was still no access allowed and the beach which was still fortified with barb wire. Electricity was not laid on to Exceat until probably 1946? Until then Exceat House was lit by candles and acetylene gas. Foxhole Cottages were derelict.

After the former RAF Friston ceased to exist flying recommenced in a different guise with the formation of the Southdown Glider Club. Ray Brigman was one of the founder members of the club, the following account being recalled by him. The first flight was made from the site on August 24 1946. At this early stage all equipment had

Farmer Col. Watson visiting the girl guides camp site at Foxhole in 1932.

West Dean Homeguard posing on School Hill above Exceat; the corporal is George Holter.

to be brought on to the airfield each weekend whenever flying was to take place. For launching purposes, a petrol-driven winch attached to an old farm trailer purchased from Arthur Pattenden was used; this in turn was anchored to one of the two concrete block houses situated towards Haven Brow and Rough Brow. These were later blown up by a RAF demolition team using he understood, 500lb. bombs. When the Rough Brow block house was dealt with, debris fell on their hanger situated in a chalk pit on the eastern slopes of Limekiln Bottom, causing damage to both the building and gliders stored within it! Later on, their machines were stored firstly in a RAF blister hanger until its removal and then a large shed near to The Gayles itself. Finally in 1948, their own hanger arrived from Portslade; this building served the club with mixed blessings, for it blew down twice until concrete stanchions were built, coupled to steel cables which served to brace it. During the first collapse the aircraft were badly damaged, club members having to use car jacks to lift the heavy steel roof trusses off their aircraft.

During these early years, a nissen hut within Rough Bottom was used as a club house and for occasional overnight sleeping in. The club owned one two-seater and four single-seater gliders; later on there were a number of privately owned machines. The site was good for novice pilots but being coastal it generally lacked strong thermals, one thousand feet being the order of height generally reached, with occasionally two thousand feet being attained over the slopes of Haven Brow and Beachy Head. Because their main runway crossed the boundary of the two farms a lift-out section of fencing had to be removed on flying days. On one occasion a glider taking off in a northerly direction on the shorter north-south runway failed to gain sufficient height to clear the A 259 coast road; an obliging woman motorist stopped to allow the passing glider negotiate the road! During 1947 there was a flying fatality.

Arthur Pattenden was never too pleased to have the gliding club using part of his farm, the last straw being when he learnt that one of the leading lights of the club had entered into negotiations with the Church Commissioners, to purchase his part of the airfield. Following this the President of the gliding club Sir John Salmond, Marshall of the Royal Air Force, and brother-in-law to the then Lord Gage, arranged for the club to lease an area at Bo Peep near Alciston on the Gage's Firle Estate thus ending their use of land near the Seven Sisters.

Vic Keith worked for Pattenden's from the mid-1960's, his main responsibility being the string of racehorses kept upon the farm but also helping out with other tasks on the farm. One day he recalled the

Mick Balkham and Tony Parsons with racehorse outside stable at Exceat (today's loos).

following drama. While mucking out the bull pen then situated in the corner of the cattle yard adjacent to the A 259 road, he had secured the bull in the milking parlour using a cow chain. The chain in turn was linked through a large ring secured into the wall. Suddenly there was a terrific commotion; the bull which was usually very placid, had heard a cow bellowing south of the road. The bull accompanied by the cow chain, the iron ring still secured to a large block of masonry, tossed the yard gate aside and trotted across the road smashing down the field gate opposite and very shortly was with the cows - still with the piece of masonry! Farmer Pattenden on hearing the commotion from the house hurried around to Vic to enquire what on earth was going on. Vic replied, *"You bloody well tell me!"* Awhile later the bull still complete with piece of masonry, was led peacefully back into his pen!

During much of the 1960's, Gerry Holton was employed on Exceat Farm by Arthur Pattenden. Later he was employed by Gayles Farm as their stockman when they grazed the Country Park during the 1970's and early 1980's. For much of this time Gerry lived at Foxhole and was a natural when it came to the telling of a good yarn. After fellow ranger Richard Mash and the author came to live at Exceat, we would periodically be treated to these little cameos, perhaps while we were carrying out fencing or some other task... Steadily, the air would fill with the drone of the 'little Furgie' (a Massey-Furguson 35 tractor with no cab) its tall exhaust belching black smoke and Gerry sitting astride. If the weather was cold or inclement, he would be wrapped up in an ex-army great coat. Upon reaching us, the engine stop button would be pulled and silence would temporarily return, apart perhaps from the wind playing it's never ending symphony with grass, fence wire or bushes, accompanied by a chorus of larks, gulls or lapwings.

During deliberations over the latest happenings, weather or how the farming year was progressing he would in his Sussex dialect, recall some experience or other from his working life or childhood. As stated earlier, Gerry was a gifted teller of yarns and after awhile Richard and I would be straining our sides as the tale unfolded! During his youth, Gerry had enjoyed working with draught horses but this affection did not extend to Pattenden's race horses. One of the stallions had a disagreeable habit of holding on to a person's ear if the unwary stood outside his loose-box. The first time this happened to Gerry, he froze until the brute decided to let go! While on the subject of the male gender, the farm once owned a very docile Hereford bull; it would lay down in the milking parlour at Exceat during milking time with the consequence that in bad light, people would sometimes trip over his legs, the bull never flinching!

Duncan Hunter the herdsman, while working in the cattle yard which then existed adjacent to the buildings at Exceat opposite the telephone call box, heard a cow out on the meadows bellowing while calving. As he began to cross the road, a MG sports car sped around the corner from the direction of Seaford and bowled poor Duncan over. On seeing what had happened Gerry rushed down the road to his aid and to halt any oncoming traffic. The unfortunate herdsman thankfully only received superficial injuries to his scalp; as a precaution an ambulance was called to take him complete with trousers impregnated with the essence of sour milk to hospital! After a week or so had passed, Duncan asked Gerry if he would mind removing the stitches which he had received; Gerry declined. Shortly afterwards Duncan travelled to Brighton and while there visited a barbers shop; while cutting his hair the barber commented on the fine set of stitches in his scalp. Not missing the opportunity, Duncan persuaded the barber to remove them!

The next two tales involve what is today the Park Centre. Gerry having just finished stacking some bales, was standing in the large south-facing wagon doorway from where he observed a Bedford lorry loaded with grass turf descending Exceat Hill. At the same time, the farm's dairy herd of some 100 cows were commencing their slow procession across the road into the cattle yard prior to milking. The driver alarmed by what he saw at the bottom of the hill, applied his brakes but with the weight of the turf behind him and the slow progress of the herd across his path looming ever closer, the driver took the only evasive action he could, steering the lorry into the farm driveway which then led to the barn. Gerry having watched the unfolding drama, dashed across the barn away from the doorway! Moments later, Gerry nervously called out through the thick cloud of dust to the driver, who much to Gerry's relief answered, emerging from his cab suffering only from shock and scratches.

On another occasion, a fellow who had a quarrel with his wife or girl-friend deliberately crashed his motorcycle into the above barn, hitting one of the flint buttresses. Upon hearing the crash, Arthur Pattenden rushed out to the scene to investigate; on arrival he found the rider sprawled on the ground bleeding profusely from a head wound. Arthur's first reaction was to reassure the forlorn rider and went to wipe the blood away from his forehead; as he did so, the riders scalp slipped backwards, he was wearing a hair piece! The well-meaning comforter was so startled his heart missed a beat.

WEST DEAN. We have already read about life for Lillian Nash at Friston during the Second World War; Lillian however spent much of her early life living in West Dean. Her father was H.A. Burgess, a well-known housing developer in Seaford; he had bought a lease upon the then abandoned forge and had converted it into a second home. She recalled how she often drove their horse and trap to and from Seaford; often while on Chyngton Hill she would get whistled at by soldiers from the South Camp on marching exercises. During a cold spell of weather during the First World War she could remember people skating on the river meanders, the ladies muffled from the cold in their long dresses and as the winter daylight faded and dusk advanced, people bearing lanterns.

Shortly after her marriage to Fred Nash their financial situation necessitated them moving into the family's Forge Cottage. In the adjoining cottage lived Fanny and Harry Streeter (the former Mrs. Pullen and school teacher); Streeter's had use of the piece of land on which now stand West Dean Cottages. On one occasion a swarm of bees settled upon the bough of a nearby tree; Harry a keen bee-keeper produced a ladder and proceeded to climb up in pursuit, having asked Fred to stand on the bottom of the ladder and not to flee should any bees fall. Harry then proceeded to saw off the section of bough supporting the swarm, the tremors of which caused more and more bees to fall around and on the apprehensive Fred who finally abandoned his position and ran off, hotly pursued by a cluster of angry bees!

Other neighbours of theirs were the Williams, who lived in Pond Cottage and ran one of several smallholdings in the village. Maurice

Williams was formally the bailiff of West Dean Farm prior to afforestation, they formally living at West Dean Manor. One day the Nash's were puzzled by the labours of Maurice's wife Kit; she was busily employed in cutting a gap through the garden hedge that faced on to the road. Following this action a number of tables and chairs then appeared within their garden. It transpired that Kit had decided to open up a small tea garden; during its life trade modestly flourished, Kit being a very able cook, she being assisted by fellow villager Alice Holter. With the outbreak of war and talk of imminent invasion and the fact that Maurice had suffered from shell-shock, the Williams' moved away to stay with relations at Oxford. Their smallholding was taken over by Jack Dunfee; he had been connected with the theatrical business and with only a limited knowledge of agriculture, proved a source of amusement to the other villagers.

Ilene Chant (neé Pullen) was born just after the First World War at Chyngton Cottages, the red brick terrace at the top of Chyngton Hill. Her grandparents were Fanny and Harry Streeter (who we read about a moment ago) and with whom she spent much of her childhood during the 1920's early 1930's. In the field behind their cottage Harry kept chickens, bees and a pony with which to pull their trap when requiring to journey into Seaford. Fanny although very religious was a keen wine maker; as well as formally being the village school teacher she also doubled as village midwife. During church services she would take up her seat beneath the Heringod monument

Maurice Williams and family; photo probably taken at Pond Cottage 1930's.

so as to keep an eye on the choir boys. A salesman from an Eastbourne firm of outfitters would regularly visit the village armed with two large suitcases for the purpose of plying his wares. Occasionally the villagers would hold a rook shoot; in due course a rook pie would be delivered to her parent's at Chyngton. Every year a village party was held by the villagers in Streeter's field. She recalled that a gypsy family by the name of Baker, used to set up camp during the summer on the rough grazing of Ewe Down. They used to carry out various tasks locally such as setting up the stooks of corn. By the road on Chyngton Hill there used to be many glow-worms along the roadside.

Now on to the recollections of the Hall family... 1929 saw Jack Hall move from his position as chauffeur to the Davis-Gilbert's at Birling Manor, to taking up employment with the Forestry Commission and staying there including a spell with the War Agricultural Committee till 1946. They resided in School Cottages in West Dean; to begin with he earnt a weekly wage of twenty six shillings (£1.30), the hours being from 7am till 5am; during the winter period while carrying out tree planting he was paid at a piece-work rate. The Hall's also had use of half the barn to the west of their cottage, the remaining half being used by Maurice Williams who also grazed the land that went with their cottage. Before starting his full-time work each morning, Jack would help with the milking of the Williams' ten cows. Maurice Williams also kept a number of caravans on the hillside overlooking the village pond together with a few pitches for touring caravans. After completion of hay making, Boy Scouts from London were allowed to camp on Little Wish meadow to the west of the pond. The Hall's neighbour at School Cottages was Albert Pickett who had the use of the building behind their cottages and the adjacent land as a smallholding; in Kelly's Directory he is listed as a tobacconist; yet another small 'shop'.

Harry Hall together with the other youngsters in the village must have enjoyed something of an idyllic childhood. Probably the most colourful character at that time in his and sister Ruth's life, would have been their uncle, Charlie 'Brassy' Hall who when not at a local hostelry, resided at one of the Coastguard Cottages overlooking the Haven. For a living Brassy carried out building repairs for amongst others, Colonel Watson. On Sunday afternoons while on his way home by cycle from the Plough and Harrow at Litlington, he would often call in at West Dean. Harry remembers that he always produced from his pocket, a bag of enormous humbugs which his mother would have to break with a flat-iron. Harry was friends with Jim Palmer at Foxhole and on one occasion clearly recalls going over to him to collect a ferret. Other personalities he was acquainted with were Harry Hyde the village policeman from East Dean and Mr. Smith the coastguard from Seaford who patrolled along the coast to Birling Gap. At The Glebe lived William Adkin, as of the Adkins Tobacco Company renowned for their *"Nut Brown"* tobacco. Mrs. Adkin acted as chorister and organist in the village church; on one occasion she abruptly terminated a routine choir practice after one of the boys fired a toy gun! Annually, a service would be held upon the site of Exceat's former church with the choir in attendance. The bus stop serving the village was situated at the top of Exceat Hill and was reached via the Postman's Path as it is was known (which is still there).

With the outbreak of hostilities Harry was soon required to cease his schooling, so at the age of 13? he began his first employment as gardener for Mrs. Clarabut at Westdean Manor; she also employed a butler and maid. Following working at the Manor he worked for Jack Dunfee on his smallholding; one of his tasks was to take the milk up to Frowd's Dairy in Seaford by pony and trap; on the return journey he would stop to pick up the Keeper of the lights. These were laid out across the valley meadows so as to resemble Newhaven and so draw German bombers away from Newhaven and thus, off target for London. At one period early in the war, a detachment of the Royal Sussex Regiment was billeted with the Hall's; they took over one of the barns in the village and used the Hall's living room as their mess room.

CHARLSTON. In 1915 when he was just three months old, Albert Reed's family moved into one of the two cottages into which Charlston Manor was then divided. His father Frederick had moved from Chyngton Farm to take up employment as a teamster (or carter) for Richard Canning Brown. Brown owned and farmed a large swathe of land in and around Litlington including Church, Charleston and Clapham Farms extending eastward to the Jevington parish boundary, much of which now forms part of Friston Forest. Corn from the southern areas was drawn to Snap Hill Barn, a typical Sussex flint barn but with a slate roof; there were also a number of bullock yards situated there. An early type of tractor was used to haul Brown's thrashing tackle there from Litlington. Nearby, Hill Barn was just a ruin even in those days as is Snap Hill Barn today. One of Albert's earliest recollections of work involved the bullocks yarded at Snap Hill; when forage was running low the stock were allowed to graze in the valley to the south of the barn, it falling to Albert to herd them within this valley.

Substantial areas of what has now been afforested were used for rough shooting, Brown being a keen shot, with partridge in the morning while in the afternoon a pack of beagles were taken out to flush rabbits. Corn was put down for the partridge to encourage a good population. His owned a few racehorses and in addition to others from a racing stables situated in Alfriston, were trained on gallops within Charlston Bottom, this still in evidence today as a broad forest ride. During the winter period two men, Tom Eldrington and Tom Bond, both 'Yorkies' who came down south with the previous farmer John Bray, were employed by Brown to ferret rabbits from across this extensive, wild area. Sheep were watered either at one of a number of dewponds or driven via Adder Bank to the ditch bordering the road and Shin Brook. Adder Bank is today the heavily wooded slope bordering the lane south of Litlington village.

Mushrooms were very plentiful, Brown selling them in large wicker baskets; anyone else caught helping themselves had their haul confiscated. In view of this, his workers would go out during the hours of darkness to pick their share of this fungal bonus! After a break in employment with farmer Brown, Albert returned during 1936-37 as cowman to the Clapham dairy herd, working seven days a week for what was then a good wage, often carrying out milking in the fields using a bail (a portable milking stall on wheels). During the wartime period Brown sold his dairy herd and Albert went to work for the "War Ag" as a stockman, looking after the five bullock yards constructed from straw bales and scaffolding in the centre of West Dean village.

CHYNGTON. Florence 'Minnie' Hutchinson vividly recollected life down at Cuckmere Haven during the inter-war period after the coastguards had relinquished the station, its five cottages having been bought by a Mr. Smelt. During 1930 Florence a Newhaven girl, married George Hutchinson they moving into No.1, the western-most of the cottages. Her brother-in-law Bill who it seems was quite a character, lived next door; at No.3 was Charlie 'Brassy' Hall and finally at No.4 lived Mrs. Wittiers adjacent to where the outside toilets were. George earnt his living boulder picking on the beach for Wilson's of Newhaven; these were conveyed by punt up to Wilson's wharf near Exceat Bridge. Bill was employed as a gardener by the Hardy's at Chyngton House until they moved away to Devon during 1939. Florence and George were allowed the use of Mr. Smelt's garden at No.5 for the growing of vegetables; in their own garden they kept approximately sixty duck. Another little earner for them was putting walkers up for bed and breakfast and brother Bill would ferry people across the river for 1? pennies (about a ? pence). While rowing their boat along the river one day George came upon an unarmed bomb or torpedo which had been dropped by an RAF aircraft, it poking vertically up from the river bed. For reporting his find to the authorities, George received a reward of ten pounds.

While out together one day poaching rabbits, the two brothers fell foul of the law, they being caught by farmer Daniel Paul and subsequently charged. When the day of judgement arrived the two brothers cycled to the Magistrates court at Hailsham where they were each fined one pound. However, for having his say Bill was fined an additional one pound! During the ensuing days, they promptly went out and poached as many rabbits as they could in order to pay their fines! Rabbits then fetched 9d (approximately 3.75 pence), plus 3d (a little over one pence) for the skins which were sold to the rag-and-bone man. On another occasion Bill was stopped by Seaford police sergeant's Ford and White; they demanding to know what was contained in the sack slung over Bill's shoulder. He would not co-operate and challenged them, that they were too frightened to put their hands into examine the moving contents! The contents transpired to be ferrets so they were unable to accuse him of any crime.

The last account in this chapter deals with the fight that the local authorities put up in order to protect the South Downs from rampant development which was then threatening large tracts of Downland during the years leading up to the Second World War. I was fortunate one day to meet in the Park Centre, Lawrence Kitching MBE, who had been largely responsible for the detailed work for the preservation of the Downs and to whom together with the then County Planning Officer of East Sussex County Council, we owe a great debt to this day. His account is as follows:

"In 1937 I was a senior Engineering Assistant to the County Surveyor (H.E. Lunn) dealing largely with the control of building development under the Restriction of Ribbon Development Act 1935. During the period 1936-7 there had been an attempt by the E.S.C.C. to secure the preservation of the Downs by an Act of Parliament, but was frustrated by opposition from the then County Borough of Brighton who owned considerable areas of downland & wished to be able to develop them as they wished.

Meanwhile W.O. Humphery, who was then Engineer & Surveyor to the Hailsham R.D.C. had begun to negotiate Private Open Space Agreements under the Town & Country Planning Act 1932 with owners of Downland in that District. These were negotiated under Section 34 of that Act which provided for land within areas likely to be threatened by building development to be the subject of legal agreements limiting or preventing such development, with or without the payment of compensation. In this case the agreements were made by the County Council with the agreement of the District Councils. My recollection is that the Act provided for this to be done in advance of the preparation of town planning schemes by the D.C.'s but required such agreements to be scheduled to the schemes on completion.

The C.C. decided to adopt this approach and appointed W.O. Humphery as County Planning Officer. At the time I was working on proposals for a by-pass to Lewes (part of which has since been built). I had qualifications and experience as a Planner and was known to be very concerned about the Downland. Hence I was appointed Deputy C.P.O. & a small department was formed, (four in all).

My first job was to survey the area to establish boundaries of the area to be preserved. The one inch plan was the result. The C.C.'s original decision had been to secure all the Downland above the 300ft. contour. In practice I brought it down to ownership boundaries or strong visual lines generally lower down. I also made an impassioned appeal for the addition of Cuckmere Haven & the whole Cuckmere Valley less Alfriston village, which impressed Lord Gage (Planning Cttee. Chairman) & this was subsequently added. The Falmer Valley had been included in the original resolution.

Many owners did not ask for compensation but there were some difficult areas. One was the valley from East Dean down to and including Birling Gap. Here, because of the then growing East Dean Downlands Estate, there was said to be building value. I was instructed to prepare a detailed estate layout for the whole area showing the roads, open spaces, provision for main sewerage, surface water drainage & other services. This was then priced & a total cost arrived at. I then estimated how long development would take - based on the then current rate of development of the East Dean Downlands Estate. [This plan is now deposited with the ESRO at Lewes].

Any areas not likely to develop within 21 years were considered to have no current value. Humphery (the Valuer) then worked out a current value of the remainder based upon the period of deferment before development was likely to occur, and the cost of that development as above. My recollection was that it worked out to about £6 (six pounds) per acre and I think settlement was reached on about that basis. Humphery did most of the negotiations because I became very involved with advisory work for the District Councils in preparing their Town Planning Schemes under the 1932 Act.

By the time war broke out in 1939 (when Planning closed down for the duration) agreements had been signed to preserve 28,000 acres of downland at a cost of £80,000 - or about £3 per acre. Such agreements were for the purchase of the building right - the agricultural rights were left with the owners. In certain cases we also acquired the right to prevent afforestation. All these agreements were formally prepared by the Clerk of the C.C.'s Department and entered in the Land Charges Register - where they should still be available for inspection..."

SUGGESTED FURTHER READING.

BECKETT, Arthur. The Spirit Of The Downs. (5th. Edition)
Methuen. (1930).

BRANDON, Peter, ed. by. The South Saxons. Phillimore. (1978).

BRUNSDEN, GARDNER, GOUDIE, JONES. Landscapes. David &
Charles. (1988).

CREASEY, WARD. The Countryside Between The Wars, 1918-1940.
Batsford. (1984).

DELVE, K. The Military Airfields Of Britain – Southern England.
The Crowood Press Ltd. (2005).

DREWETT, Peter. The Archaeology Of Bullock Down, Eastbourne,
East Sussex: The Development Of A Landscape. Sussex
Archaeological Society. (1982).

FLETCHER, Anthony. Sussex 1600-1660 - A County Community In
Peace And War. Phillimore. (1980).

HOSKINS, W.G. The Making Of the English Landscape. Penguin.
(1970).

HUGHES, Graham. Barns Of Rural Britain. The Herbert Press.
(1985).

McGOWAN, Alan. The Ship, The Century Before Steam. HMSO.
(1980).

NIXON, David. Walk Soft In The Fold. Chatto & Windus. (1977).

PAYNE & PAILTHORPE, ed. by. Barclay Wills' The Downland
Shepherds. Alan Sutton Publishing. (1989).

PORTER, Valerie. The Southdown Sheep. Weald & Downland Museum. (1991).

RENNO, D. Beachy Head Shipwrecks Of The 19th Century. Amhurst Publishing Ltd. (2004).

RICHARDS, Bertram. Smuggling In Sussex 100 Years Ago. Sussex County Magazine. (1938 volume).

SEDDON, Quentin. The Silent Revolution. BBC. (1989).

SMART, G. & BRANDON, P. The Future Of The South Downs. Packard Publishing Ltd. (2007).

SPECTRE & LARKIN. Wooden Ship. Houghton Mifflin Co., Boston, Mass. (1991).

SUSSEX ARCHAEOLOGICAL SOCIETY. Tenement Analysis Part 2, Litlington, Lullington, West Dean. (1995).

SUSSEX DOWNS CONSERVATION BOARD. The Landscape Of The Sussex Downs. (1996).

WAUGH, Mary. Smuggling In Kent & Sussex 1700-1840. Countryside Books. (1985).

WOOLDRIDGE, GOLDRING. The Weald. Collins, 5th. Impression. (1972).

YOUNG, Arthur. General View Of The Agriculture Of The County Of Sussex (1813). David & Charles Reprints, (1970).

INDEX.